THE LOCATIONS OF COMPOSITION

The Locations of Composition

Edited by
Christopher J. Keller
and
Christian R. Weisser

STATE UNIVERSITY OF NEW YORK PRESS

Published by
State University of New York Press, Albany

Printed in the United States of America

For information, contact State University of New York Press, Albany, NY
www.sunypress.edu

Production by Diane Ganeles
Marketing by Anne M. Valentine

Library of Congress Cataloging in Publication Data

The locations of composition / edited by Christopher J. Keller, Christian R. Weisser.

p. cm.

Includes bibliographical references and index.

ISBN-13: 978-0-7914-7145-6 (alk. paper)

ISBN-13: 978-0-7914-7146-3 (pbk. : alk. paper)

1. English language—Rhetoric. 2. English language—Rhetoric—Study and teaching. 3. Report writing—Study and teaching (Higher) I. Keller, Christopher J., 1972– II. Weisser, Christian R., 1970–

PE1403.L63 2007
808'.0420711—dc22

2006025044

10 9 8 7 6 5 4 3 2 1

For Cole, Carson, and William

Contents

ACKNOWLEDGMENTS

We owe debts of gratitude to many people in locations far and near, starting with those scholars who contributed chapters to this collection. We want to thank them for the time and energy they spent producing such high-quality work, and we are grateful for the friendships and professional relationships that grew out of their participation in this project. Reading their work has not only been intellectually stimulating but downright fun as well. We would also like to thank the anonymous peer reviewers whose insightful comments and suggestions made us rethink many of the ideas and assumptions that drove *The Locations of Composition* from beginning to end. Their feedback was not only helpful but crucial as this project evolved over the last few years. Additionally, we express thanks and gratitude to our many colleagues at the University of Texas-Pan American and Florida Atlantic University, whose conversations with us about space, place, location, and composition studies helped improve this collection in significant ways.

We also want to thank the editors and staff at State University of New York Press for their confidence in this project and their many suggestions along the way. In particular, we would like to thank Priscilla Ross, James Peltz, Larin McLaughlin, Diane Ganeles, and Wyatt Benner for their efforts in bringing this book together.

Finally, we thank those closest to us for their love and support, and their encouragement and patience that makes our work possible—especially Cindy, William, and Chloe Keller and Traci, Cole, and Carson Weisser.

INTRODUCTION

CHRISTOPHER J. KELLER AND
CHRISTIAN R. WEISSER

> It goes back to the second Day of Creation when "God . . . divided the waters which were under the Firmament, from the waters which were above the Firmament," thus the first boundary line. All else after that, in all History, is but sub-division.
>
> —Thomas Pynchon, *Mason & Dixon*

Nearly all of the conversations in composition studies involve place, space, and location, in one way or another. The field's conversations focus upon the ways that places both "include" and "exclude" people based upon the particularities of their various subject positions, the tensions between composition's roles "inside" and "outside" of the classroom in particular and the academy in general, the problematics of "real" and "imagined" places in the formation of disciplinary theory and practice, and a host of other issues that address, to some degree, *where* composition resides. There is no way to easily characterize or codify these various scholarly conversations and activities, in part because of the multitude of differing ways these terms are defined and employed in the scholarship of composition studies. Because of this, or perhaps in spite of it, some scholars have turned toward a more critical scrutiny of how we define and are defined by our understandings of space, place, and location. This collection brings together some of those scholars in an attempt to further our understandings of how place, space, and location enmesh, problematize, and shape the field's work.

The purpose of this collection is not to simply define terms like "place," "space," and "location" in any permanent sense. These terms mean and do different things in different contexts—attempting to define and stabilize them across and beyond contexts is to strip them of their power, to take away their ability to enrich the discipline in its diverse manifestations, and to disregard the fascinating and valuable history of these terms as they can and should contribute to the work of composition studies. With that said, however, there is some need to discuss how these terms—particularly "place," "space," and "location"—are used and understood as the basis of this collection. This is not to finalize how these terms can and should be used, but rather to provide readers with a context about how and why this collection came to be, how and why it is structured the way it is, and how and why the collection impacts the field in important and timely ways.

One significant aspect of this collection is the breadth of ideas involving location and composition that is covered here. Contributors write about many different places that are important to the field of composition studies: classrooms, campuses, cities, workplaces, community centers, public spheres, MOOs (Multiuser Domains, Object-Oriented), and blogs, among others. Even books and others kinds of texts themselves are considered as places, not just documents or material objects, though they are these things, too. Importantly, this brief list of places that find their way into this collection marks a *range* of places, those that are seemingly real and material as well as those that appear metaphorical and immaterial. Naming a classroom or campus a "place," that is, seems like a much more literal designation than, say, suggesting a public sphere, a textbook, or a blog is a "place." The collection does not privilege either the materiality or immateriality of a place, however; one major premise underlying *The Locations of Composition* is that all places—material and metaphorical—are equally *real.* The "reality" of places and their ability to influence the discipline, in other words, is not determined solely by whether they are material and physical or immaterial and imagined. Composition is structured by various kinds of places physical and imagined, neither of which should be privileged, both of which should be investigated, because places are imagined, arranged, represented, and distributed in discourse and texts. However, it should not be forgotten that physical places themselves contribute to these activities of imagining, arranging, representing, and distributing. Physical places can be imagined and reimagined; imagined places can be made physical and materialized. Strict dichotomies between material/immaterial and real/unreal break down easily. How these places enrich or diminish the discipline is the important question.

Yet to understand how a place enriches or diminishes composition studies is to understand how it is *located.* The terms "place" and "location" are often used synonymously, though doing so is in some ways a misinterpretation that elides their differences. The collection starts from and builds upon the general theoretical position that places are *bounded areas endowed with human meaning.* To clarify, Robert Sack suggests that place

> refers to the countless areas of space that we have bounded and controlled. These humanly constructed and maintained places—or places-as-territories, many of which can be virtually identical in their look and function and found repeatedly over the landscape—range in scale from a room to a continent and support innumerable projects we undertake: a kitchen, as a delimited area of space, is supported by rules about what may or may not take place that help make possible food preparation; and a very large area of space, such as Antarctica, because it is bounded and thus partly constructed by international treaties, helps maintain and even restore what we think of as elements of nature. (2001, 232)

Sack contends that places are "tools" that provide the means for humans to undertake their "projects." He suggests that "places add to the nature of the projects. That is, projects not only require place in the sense that they need a place to occur, but the place becomes an active agent in the project and thereby affects it" (232). This includes writing projects, as many of the chapters in this collection suggest. However, we want to extend this understanding of place a bit further by noting that places are located and relational. Evaluating, studying, or defining a place is an activity that must consider the place's position in relation to others. As Leibniz writes (in seventeenth-century gender-exclusive language), "Men fancy places, traces, and spaces, though these things consist only in the truth of relations and not at all in any absolute reality" (qtd. in Casey 1997, 162). To be located, in other words, is to be positioned—either physically or metaphorically. One may be physically located or positioned east or west of a place, above or below it, or inside or outside it, for instance. One may also be metaphorically located or positioned inside or outside a place, behind or in front of it, floating on it or sinking in it, for or against it, beside it, far from it, moving toward or away from it, or even between it and another place. Therefore, by naming this collection *The Locations of Composition* instead of, say, *The Places of Composition,* we mean to suggest that studies in composition are made up of various different places—both physical and imagined, though all real—but coming to terms with these places derives from working to see how they are located relationally, as well as by recognizing our own locations on, in, under, against, between, away from, and/or among these places.

"Space" is another term often entwined in studies of place and location; it is a multifaceted term that also does not lend itself to easy definition or appropriation, a term privileged above place and location in many theoretical and philosophical inquiries. It is common, for example, to understand space as the prior condition of place, as Robert Sack does, or, to look at it the other way around, place is often seen as a modification of space; space is devoid of meaning, while place is endowed with meaning by humans; space seems open-ended and undelimited, while place is bounded and structured. Yi-Fu Tuan, for instance, in "Space and Place: Humanistic Perspective," writes that place "has a history and meaning. Place incarnates the experiences and aspirations of a people. Place is not only a fact to be explained in the broader frame of space, but it is also the reality to be clarified and understood from the perspectives of the people who have given it meaning" (1974, 236). Places no doubt have histories and meanings, yet we instead contend that space is not prior to place, not a preexisting condition of it. Rather, space is the outcome or product of place.

A simple analogy: when we travel by airline we are assigned a seat in most cases. The airlines, that is, usually assign us a *place* to sit—12B, 17F, or, if we're lucky or privileged, 1A. These places are *located* relationally to each other. We find 12B or 17F based upon where these seats are in *relation* to the other seats, rows, and aisles. It is usually not until we find our place, however, that the issue of *space* comes about. How much space will there be between me and the people in my row and how much space will be available in the overhead compartment or under the seat in front of me? In such cases, space is a *product* of the place—the inside of the airplane in general and one's seat in particular. Importantly, however, one must recognize that these spaces are not empty containers or voids—small ones at that—that exist underneath the seat in front of us or in the compartments above us. If they were nothing more than containers under the seat or in the overhead compartment, they might simply be understood as additional places—those simply located in relation to other places. Rather, we can recognize the space under the seat and the space in the overhead compartment as such when we understand them not only as products of place but also as products of human activity: the activity of *making room*. On the airplane, to continue this analogy, we have to *make room* in this place—adjust and contort our bodies, condense and scrunch bags, cram and jam suitcases together as closely as possible. The inside of an airplane is a bounded place endowed with a great deal of human meaning. Yet from this place, spaces are activated by how humans make room for themselves and their belongings. Space and making room are outcomes of human activity in the place itself. Making room, furthermore, *adjusts* locations. I may wish to make room for my body by reclining the seat back as much as possible; however, doing so also adjusts the relationship between my seat and the seat behind me, therein reworking the relationship—the location—between them. Thus, place, space, and location are separate but interrelated. To understand one, in some sense, it is important to understand them all.

This analogy may be a crude one, but it can be extended to the workings of composition studies generally and this collection specifically. By emphasizing locations, then, we hope to emphasize places and their meanings for the discipline, with particular emphasis upon how those places lead to new spaces, new activities, and new instances of making room in the discipline. This is also to emphasize how those places and activities constantly shift and move in relation to one another. Thus, to emphasize locations is to focus on the positions, activities, changes, and motions of and within composition. Locations tell us about relationships, but they also imply adjustment and modification. Composition studies may be a discipline that includes places such as classrooms, writing centers, public spheres, and rhetorical topoi, for example, but studying these places—understanding their benefits and weaknesses, recognizing how they can and cannot enrich the discipline—is a matter of studying how these places are located: how they relate to other places inside and outside the discipline, how our activities carve out new spaces from these places, and how these places allow us to alter, change, position, reposition, and move through our scholarly work and practices.

Therefore, this collection is not an attempt to *map* the discipline of composition, to provide a layout of all the important and not-so-important places on a current chart of composition studies. Creating a map is to stabilize places, to show how they look at a moment frozen in time. Mapping is reducing possibility to simplicity; mapping is to fix the ground rather than to show how the ground is made to seem fixed; it is to chart grounds already made rather than to explore how the grounds are made in the first place, how the grounds are remade, and how the grounds could have been made differently. As editors of this collection, we like to think that such a map of composition studies is an impossible document, one that could not exist because the field is always on the move. Rather, we are more interested in the relationships between places, the spaces they create, the locations that alter and (re)orient, and the ways the work of composition studies contributes to all of these activities. To ask, in other words, *where* composition *is* can be problematic, because that is to ask where composition is standing and stable, where its places have been solidified and made permanent: this is to deny its movement, its amorphous qualities, its contingent and multifaceted, yet impermanent and transitory, structures. The purpose of *The Locations of Composition*, then, is not to introduce brand-new places of inquiry in composition studies (readers will likely already be familiar in one way or another with the different places covered in these chapters), though we admit that part of making room—the activities of using spaces brought forth by places—is to bring new places into view for the discipline.

Furthermore, we do not mean to suggest that all contributors to *The Locations of Composition* agree with the ways we have defined and problematized the terms "place," "space," and "location." Our vision for the collection as a whole may certainly—and productively—differ from the ideas presented in individual chapters. Such tension should be viewed as an asset to these conversations instead of a liability. Terms such as "place," "space," and "location" are open-ended terms whose meanings are contextual and specific to individual arguments. The larger argument we hope this collection makes can differ from the specific arguments proposed by authors of individual chapters. As readers will discover, additionally, the chapters in this collection present a broad range of places to be considered. As we hope is obvious, it was never our goal to develop a collection dedicated entirely to one kind of place, such as public spheres, workplaces, classrooms, cyberspace, or cities, for example. Including chapters that discuss such a broad range of places, instead, allows the collection, first of all, to function in some ways as an introduction to the different places of composition and how they can and do relate to each other, though most compositionists should still find a great deal of interesting material in these chapters. Furthermore, the broad range of places written about in this collection affords readers the opportunity to make their own connections among the various chapters, to recognize their own locations in relation to these various places, and to *make room* in their scholarly work for a greater range of places that structure composition.

The collection is comprised of three sections of five chapters each: "Across the Field," "Inside the Classroom and Beyond," and "Among the Institutions." The first section of *The Locations of Composition* includes chapters that examine different notions of place and location as they affect of the field of composition studies in a broad sense. Sid Dobrin's chapter "The Occupation of Composition" provides specific definitions of place and space based upon the writings of philosophers and critics such as Edward Soja, Georges Perec, and Henri Lefebvre. Dobrin theorizes these terms and what they can mean for composition studies and explores in particular the ways that composition as a discipline has come to "occupy" certain places as well as the ways it has (and has not) conquered space in academic territories as a means to find safe places. In this sense he is very much interested in the way composition as a field has positioned itself and is located.

Elizabeth Ervin's chapter "Composition and the Gentrification of 'Public Literacy'" argues that, recently, compositionists have been turning away from the composition classroom as a topic of scholarly discussion and focusing instead on the implications of public discourse. This trend may be fueled by self-interest on the part of compositionists—the desire for subject novelty and a need to enhance professional and material status by establishing a more relevant identity for the public. The danger in this trend is that composition studies may sacrifice academic literacy for the sake of exploring public discourse; the responsibility of teaching students the basic conventions of writing will fall to faculty who do not specialize in the study of composition. This conflict suggests that compositionists must consider the following actions: self-reflection on the subject of academic engagement with public literacy, the goals of composition for the university itself, and challenging the traditional understanding of academic success and its rewards.

In "In Visible Texts: Memory, MOOs, and Momentum," Cynthia Haynes writes that MOOs, in an educational situation, provide opportunities for multiple-users to interact with each other (using text) in real time and supply an environment for learning in an adaptable virtual world. Haynes claims that our understanding and memory of words are resistant to a change in velocity—words that are in motion tend to stay in motion—and that the visual representation of moving words calms viewers into learning and retaining what they have learned in memory.

Thomas Rickert, in "Invention in the Wild: On Locating *Kairos* in Space-Time," argues for the necessity of connecting *kairos* to a rich, material sense of place, for a view of *kairos* that is "implaced." Without place, Rickert suggests, *kairos* is an empty concept. His version of *kairos* is a way toward "developing a richer understanding of environment and our inventive relationship within it" and provides the means to understand invention as an ambient activity rather than a subjective one; invention, that is, "itself is an emergent process extending far beyond the bounds of an autonomous, willing subject." Thus, these notions of *kairos* and invention must be understood in terms of "posthuman subjectivity," rather than in terms of traditional subjectivity that views the subject as "autonomous" and "willing." This suggests invention "less attuned to advantage or success *over* an audience than working with what an audience in a material situation brings forth." On first glance, a chapter about *kairos* and invention would appear best suited for the section of *The Locations of Composition* that deals more with classroom and pedagogical concerns; however, Rickert's essay focuses specifically on a profound issue in contemporary rhetorical thought, reviewing and challenging key texts in the discipline written by authorities in the field. Thus, he is not simply rethinking how *kairos* can be used in the classroom, or what we can do with *kairos*; rather, Rickert is reconsidering what *kairos* does to us.

Peter Vandenberg and Jennifer Clary-Lemon's chapter, "Looking for Location Where It Can't Be Found: Possibilities for Graduate Pedagogy in Rhetoric and Composition," looks at graduate work in composition studies that concentrates on how theory-based scholarly writing limits the effectiveness of future writing teachers in interacting with location—such research is "placeless" in that it operates solely in generalizations. Implicit expectations of graduate work can control students' research to the point that "success" is defined by abstractions rather than interpretation of and applications for local places. By encouraging community-based graduate research, graduate students will be able to go beyond the "objective" perspective by engaging with a place beyond the university and by putting themselves in relation to that place and its inhabitants. It will also allow them to examine the ethical implications of interpreting the "other" by looking at the issue through the eyes of people outside of the academy.

The second section of *The Locations of Composition,* "Inside the Classroom and Beyond," mainly examines issues of place and location as they relate to student writers and praxis in the classroom and elsewhere. John Ackerman's chapter, "Teaching the Capital City," examines the relationships between writing instruction and social geography. Ackerman sets forth a georhetorical methodology as a means to help not student writers but students as writers "replot the coordinates" of their metaphysical centers and to practice composition in such a way that it garners a distinct authority derived from "residences." Ackerman highlights the concepts of "adjacency" and "substitutability" as means to help students "discern the center and periphery of daily living at a complex institution [the university] that is premised on hypothetical and deliberative worlds of majors, disciplines, and future employers in imagined constructs such as a workforce or national economy." Ackerman's essay not only provides a variety of rich theoretical insights but also allows readers to draw such insights into the realm of their teaching endeavors.

Robert Brooke and Jason McIntosh contribute to this collection "Deep Maps: Teaching Rhetorical Engagement through Place-Conscious Education." This chapter argues that students need to see themselves in place—that is, need to be aware of the ways places surround them and structure their responsibilities, choices, views, and conflicts. "Deep maps" is a term coined by William Least Heat-Moon. Deep maps are used as invention exercises in composition classrooms, as developed at the University of Nebraska-Lincoln and the Summer Institute for the Nebraska Writing Project. Deep maps, they argue, "aren't road maps like state highway maps, but are drawings of psychological locations (both literal and abstract) created by writers to represent their relationship to place." Deep maps serve as invention exercises as well as creative experimentation and the beginnings of place-conscious education. They are meant, in part, not only to provide students with intellectual exercises to foster writing but also to encourage their civic participation—to write not only about places but for them.

In "Between Perception and Articulation: Imageword and a Compassionate Place," Kristie Fleckenstein writes about the need to create compassionate classrooms where students "experience connection rather than alienation," a project of utmost importance especially for teachers who engage in critical writing pedagogy and teaching about conflicts. Creating a compassionate classroom comes about by altering the traditional Western notion of places as static and unchanging. Fleckenstein argues that doing so can happen through the lens of "imageword," "a way of knowing comprised of image-making and word-making," whereby place can be understood as a product of perception and articulation—that is, a "a sensuous, coproduced, and dynamic reality." Importantly, Fleckenstein suggests that imageword helps develop compassionate classrooms, but these are not places that cure all social ills and problems. Rather, they serve as the beginning of ways students can connect with one another on affective and intellectual levels.

Johndan Johnson-Eilola and Stuart Selber's "The Locations of Usability" creates a "landscape of usability" that provides teachers and theorists of composition with new ways to envision usability outside the usual contexts of technical communication theory and practice. Their "landscape of usability," in particular, includes the following "locations": metaphorical, rhetorical, methodological, and pedagogical. Each of these locations is interestingly described and theorized as well as applied to composition scholarship and teaching practices. "Mapping locations of usability against locations of composition (as both text and activity)," they write, "provides one way of enriching our changing notions of what it means to write and read in the world."

Tim Lindgren and Derek Owens contribute "From Site to Screen, From Screen to Site: Merging Place-Based Pedagogy with Web-Based Technology," a chapter that explores the relationships between place-based pedagogies and new media in writing classrooms. In particular, they explore how various metaphors structure our understanding of and relationship to places as well as the ways that "locative media" technologies connect information and people with places, create knowledges of place, and impact places and communities. Additionally, Lindgren and Owens detail two of their own online pedagogical projects—WhereProject and 21st Century Neighborhoods—that "ultimately seek to foster online communities of interest that in some ways transcend the limits of geography but where the rhetorical goal is to encourage the cultivation of local knowledge." These projects, importantly, provide spaces to explore the complex relationships between writing, place, and technology.

"Among the Institutions," the third section of *The Locations of Composition*, uses the term "institutions" in more than one way. While we in the academy often understand institutions as universities, this section also explores different aspects of composition studies as "institutions" and their relationships to other, more traditionally defined, institutions such as universities and workplaces. Amy Devitt, in her chapter "Transferability and Genres," suggests that first-year composition classes are not, and are not intended to be, lessons on how to write papers throughout an undergraduate's education nor a substitute for learning to write all genres within the university or the larger context of professional writing. Locations, in the both the sense of literal environment and the metaphorical cultural and institutional environment, are significant components of written work and help define its standards. Providing students with a critical awareness of genres would enable them to understand not only how genre shapes written work, but also how to adapt the genres (and associated rhetorical forms) they know to new situations and locations. Having an awareness of antecedent genres will prepare students to assess the applicability of known genres to new genres and anticipate possible shortcomings and adjustments necessary to adapt to new writing situations.

Nancy Myers, in "Relocating Knowledge: The Textual Authority of *Classical Rhetoric for the Modern Student*," alters our perspectives on institutions somewhat by examining how "a textbook [Corbett's *Classical Rhetoric for the Modern Student*] acquires institutional and disciplinary authority," as well as how, implicitly, the textbook itself has become a kind of institution in and of itself in composition and rhetoric studies. Myers argues, furthermore, that the textbook forms its own multifaceted location, where it is situated in time and space. As a type of location, it serves as "a nexus point where academic contexts and cultures, systems of texts, and ways of reading intersect to produce textual authority." Analyzing the textual authority of *Classical Rhetoric for the Modern Student* in this sense allows us to understand how knowledge—disciplinary, institutional, and social—is located and relocated, stabilized and reproduced.

Nedra Reynolds's chapter, "Cultural Geography and Images of Place," argues that cultural geography shapes writing and must be taken into consideration when situating composition within the context of the university or nonacademic communities. Because the field of composition increasingly communicates through visual media, it is important to consider how images can represent—and misrepresent—the reality and effect of time and place on student writing. The Harvard University video *Shaped by Writing: The Undergraduate Experience* assumes a placelessness to writing instruction that is not an accurate representation of the cultural (or physical) landscape that students must negotiate on other campuses—the classic academic writing that is appropriate at Harvard may not be appropriate at other colleges that focus on professional or electronic writing. The limited view presented by this video indicates that visual representations of the study of composition should be guided by the relationship between local spaces, identities, and culture.

Christopher Schroeder's "Notes toward a Dynamic Theory of Literacy" examines student locations and spaces that constitute and surround Northeastern Illinois University, a Hispanic Serving Institution (HSI). Schroeder notes how difficult it is to account for the various locations that students inhabit and move through: physical, ideological, linguistic, and experiential locations, among others. And he critiques composition's dominant models of literacy by studying these various student locations and by showing the difficulty of simply applying disciplinary concepts such as language, discourse, and identity on top of them. He uses these critiques to begin developing a "dynamic theory of literacy" that helps fulfill composition's ideas of social justice so prevalent in the field and "permits those of us who are concerned about social justice to come closer to fulfilling the rhetoric that surrounds our work, if only because it affords an opportunity for other practices to be admitted as legitimate means of intellectual work."

Tom Deans's chapter, "Shifting Locations, Genres, and Motives: An Activity Theory Analysis of Service-Learning Writing Pedagogies," argues that teachers and scholars interested in service learning should recognize the locations in which service learning happens less as places and more as activity systems, which asks that we rethink our notions of discourse communities that are typically associated with these distinct locations. In this chapter Deans explores the relationships between and among the university and the community-partner organization as activity systems that overlap with the service-learning classroom. In doing so he discusses why some service-learning programs succeed and why some fail; he also offers pedagogical advice for those implementing service-learning programs, and he lays out new directions for service-learning research in composition studies.

The activity of putting together a book like this, as Mason from Pynchon's *Mason & Dixon* reminds us in the epigraph beginning this introduction, is an activity of dividing and subdividing from beginning to end. We realize that these chapters have been artificially joined with and divided from one another—they have been located in particular ways in this collection by us the editors. Contributors did not compose their chapters with these divisions in mind, nor did they compose them knowing the titles of these divisions. But readers, we hope, will continue to redivide, reconnect, and relocate these chapters and do so from their own ever-changing locations.

Works Cited

Casey, Edward. 1997. *The Fate of Place: A Philosophical History.* Berkeley and Los Angeles: University of California Press.

Sack, Robert. 2001. "Place, Power, and the Good." In *Textures of Place: Exploring Humanist Geographies,* ed. Paul Adams, Steven Hoelscher, and Karen Till, 232–45. Minneapolis: University of Minnesota Press.

Tuan, Yi-Fu. 1974. "Space and Place: Humanistic Perspective." *Progress in Geography* 6: 36–52.

Part I

Across the Field

1

The Occupation of Composition

SIDNEY I. DOBRIN

I write: I inhabit my sheet of paper. I invest it, I travel across it. I incite blanks, spaces (jumps in the meaning, discontinuities, transitions, changes of key).

—Georges Perec, *Species of Spaces*

Space is a doubt: I have constantly to mark it, to designate it. It's never mine, never given to me, I have to conquer it.

—Georges Perec, *Species of Spaces*

When we say that a thing is in a given place, all we mean is that it occupies such a position relative to other things.

—René Descartes, *Principles of Philosophy*

When we evoke "space," we must immediately indicate what occupies that space and how it does so.

—Henri Lefebvre, *The Production of Space*

The Idea of Space

Places, the geographer Yi-Fu Tuan tells us, offer security; space, he says, is freedom. Spaces are marked and defended; places have "felt value": they have been given identity (1977, 3–4). Places are spaces to which meaning and organization have been attached because, as Tuan explains, "'space' is more abstract than 'place.'" Spaces become places as those spaces are endowed with values, for spaces and places depend upon one another for definition (6). Furthermore, Tuan writes: "The ideas of 'space' and 'place' require each other for definition. From the security and stability of place we are aware of the openness, freedom, and threat of space, and vice versa. Furthermore, if we think of space as that which allows movement, then place is pause; each pause in movement makes it possible for location to be transformed into place" (6). This essay is about that pause, about that transformation, about how composition moves from space to place and the dangers in doing so. This essay is about how composition has (seemingly) become complacent in the safety of the places it has acquired in the American university without acknowledging the possibilities held in its spatial freedoms. More specifically, this essay is about the occupation of composition studies, the places it occupies, and the methods and manners in which it has attempted (and likely failed) to conquer space in American academic territory to find a safe place. Beginning with the understanding that spaces are made up of infinite places, this essay works toward an understanding of place and space from the perspective of composition. As this collection and other recent work in spatial theory in composition studies bear witness, the spatial dimension of composition studies is of crucial importance. As spatial theorist Edward J. Soja notes, "[T]he spatial dimension of our lives has never been of greater practical and political relevance than it is today" (1996, 1), and this is also true for the "life" of composition.[1] In the space allotted to me in the following pages, I address the spatial and "placial" positioning of composition studies not in an attempt to codify that space—and certainly not in an attempt to make it safe—but instead to examine the idea of space as it pertains to composition studies.

Tuan distinguishes between places and spaces, identifying the safety of places and the freedom of spaces. Distinguishing between spaces and places may seem confusing and contradictory, yet seeing the two as distinct yet enmeshed is crucial to understanding the role of places and spaces in the occupation(s) of composition. Like Tuan, other theorists work to distinguish space and place. For Michel de Certeau, place is the "order (of whatever kind) in accord with which elements are distributed in relationships of coexistence" (1984, 117). It is this ordering of places that makes them familiar, and accountable. De Certeau's ordering of place echoes Tuan's concept of place as "safe" in that the places that can be ordered and secured in that order. The security of order elicits safety. Like nearly all who write about space, de Certeau cannot escape the relationship between the spatial and the temporal, and as compositionists, we must also acknowledge that there is an equivalent relationship between the spatial and the rhetorical. For de Certeau, when two objects are in the same place at the same time, they are, in fact, adjacent to each other in different places, and unable to occupy the same space at the same time; they are "*beside* one another, each situated in its own 'proper' and distinct location, a location it defines" (117; italics in original). He writes: "A place is thus an instantaneous configuration of positions" (117). What is most important about this understanding of place is that for de Certeau, places are produced by those "things" which occupy those places, and that occupation of places is limited. Locations/places are occupy-able and dependent upon those occupations for their definitions. Strikingly, too, de Certeau is clear that the configuration of places by their occupying elements "implies an indication of stability" (117). This moment of stability is a moment of meaning, a moment of rhetorical understanding. Of course, that order is relative, is rhetorical. Order is imposed through power, and though one body orders a space to a particular end, that order is not necessarily recognized or obeyed by all who enter that space. Yet, stability, order, and safety are all inscribed upon the pause of place in writing the meaning of that place. Give a place meaning and you give it safety; you make it a place.

Space, on the other hand, is not stable; it lacks meaning. "Space," de Certeau writes, "is composed of intersections of mobile elements. It is in a sense actuated by the ensemble of movements deployed within it. Space occurs as the effect produced by the operations that orient it, situate it, temporalize it, and make it function in a polyvalent unity of conflictual programs or contractual proximities" (117). For de Certeau, then, space is ambiguous; it is not given location by context, by meaning. It is undefined. Space stands in distinction to place specifically because of its lack of stability, its lack of meaning. According to de Certeau, spaces are produced by practices of particular places, by inscribing meaning onto and through places; spaces can be read by the places within them. Like place, the very idea of space is dependent upon the "things"—in this case the practices, the meanings—that occupy the places of those spaces. What is central to de Certeau's definition of space is that it is *produced.*

Space, then, is ambiguous in that it is freedom; it may be bordered or identified by means of places within its borders, but space is unstable and uncertain because of the possibilities it contains for occupation. Space is yet to be written. It is potential; it is imagination; it is the possibility and means of every discourse to disrupt every discourse, to disrupt its own discourse. Space is yet to be written because space has not (yet) been given meaning; it awaits occupation. Space itself does not then occupy a different location than place, but the same locations, only as locations yet to be written, yet to be produced. Place is a (temporal) moment when space is defined—defined through and by its occupiers and occupations. Place is the temporal instance of observation of a site of ideological struggle and is written by whomever is winning the struggle at that moment. The production of space, the writing of place, is the inscription of power onto the freedom of space in order to embed the safety of an order onto/into a place. There is, after all, security in definition. Space is where hegemony is trying to happen, but where counterhegemonies still have footholds. Space is the ever-present trace of possibility that the meaning of a location—whose interests are represented by the social as natural, as right, as in the best interest—might be changed. Place is where consent has been achieved.

Like de Certeau, Henri Lefebvre identifies space as the result of production. "To speak of 'producing space' sounds bizarre," Lefebvre writes, "so great is the sway still held by the idea that empty space is prior to whatever ends up filling it" (1991, 15). For Lefebvre, the concept of production of space is inseparable from power, and his spatial theories grow from his critique of representations of power. As Soja explains, Lefebvre links difference and otherness with spatial theory by "insisting that difference be contextualized in social and political practices that are linked to *spatio-analyse*, the analysis, or better, the knowledge (*connaissance*) of the (social) production of (social) space" (Soja 1996, 34–35). For Lefebvre, the concept of the social, of the dialectic, is no longer bound to temporality, but to space and spatiality (Lefebvre 1976, 17).

For Lefebvre, space can no longer be considered merely "a preexisting void, endowed with formal properties alone," or as "a container waiting to be filled by a content—i.e., matter, or bodies" (1991, 170). Rather, space is produced socially, dialectically, just as place is produced socially, dialectically. Following Lefebvre, then, we can say that space is that which, within every discourse, has the potential to disrupt that discourse; place is the discourse. Space is the site of ideological struggle; place is the result of that struggle. Space is where bodies struggle to make meaning, and in doing so, make place, produce the location of hegemony. Space is social space, or as Lefebvre writes it "(social) space" (73). Everywhere that place can be identified, space can be identified in the same manner (and for the same reasons), just as, according to Foucault, everywhere that discourse is found, so too is the means to dismantle that discourse. The relationship between space and place is never linear, never progressive. It is always fluid, always overlapping, always simultaneous. Space and place are not either/or. Space and place coexist and coconstitute. Place is space given temporal meaning through social practice and hegemony by the ideological position that has gained an upper hand in the struggle for meaning (at the given moment when the place is identified). Thus, to speak of place is also to invoke the temporal, as there can be no place out of time. For composition to speak then of space, it must do so in an acknowledgment that composition itself is a place and time of hegemony.

The Idea of Occupation

> Ideally, the book would begin by giving the sense of a space occupied by my presence, because all around me there are only inert objects, including the telephone, a space that apparently cannot contain anything but me, isolated in my interior time, and then there is the interruption of the continuity of time, the space is no longer what it was before because it is occupied by the ring, and my presence is no longer what it was before because it is conditioned by the will of this object that is calling. The book would have to begin by conveying all this not merely immediately, but as a diffusion through space and time of these rings that lacerate the continuity of space and time and will.
>
> —Italo Calvino, *If on a Winter's Night a Traveler*

> The observer stands perplexed before the beauty of a seashell, a village or a cathedral, even though what confronts him consists perhaps merely in the material modalities of an active "occupation"—specifically, the occupation of space.
>
> —Henri Lefebvre, *The Production of Space*

> Istanbul was Constantinople
> Now it's Istanbul, not Constantinople
> Been a long time gone, Constantinople
> Now it's Turkish delight on a moonlit night
>
> —Jimmy Kennedy and Nat Simon, "Istanbul"

> I wouldn't be happy if I were occupied, either.
>
> —President George W. Bush, April 13, 2004

To address any notion of space requires that we also address the idea of occupation. As the Lefebvre epigraph in this chapter suggests, when we speak of space, we necessarily speak of what and how that space is occupied, for as Lefebvre indicates, "space considered in isolation is an empty abstraction" (1991, 12). The simple follow-up to this would be to say that spaces are defined by their occupation and that the identities of those occupiers/occupations—here I am speaking both in terms of subjectivity and physical occupation—are defined by the spaces they occupy. However, such a simplistic formulation fails to fully examine the role of occupation in/of space and traps/limits/misunderstands definitions of space; it fails to distinguish between definition of space by occupation and the production of space by occupation.

To begin to examine the idea of occupation, it is necessary to understand the very idea of occupation from four inseparable, yet distinct, positions.[2] First, *occupation* refers to the act of occupying or being occupied, the taking possession of a space. Conceptually, "taking possession" means social and political practice; it means imbuing space with meaning, producing a place. More often than not, this use of occupation refers to an action, an active taking—often a kind of violence and often a military action—in which a space is gained by force: liberation, invasion, intrusion, intervention, transfer, relocation. In this way occupation is militant; vying for space is combative. Because vying for meaning is combative, and since occupying space creates its meaning (and our own, which together make place), occupation, then, is clearly a struggle of power, an ideological struggle to inscribe meaning. This notion of occupation may also carry a temporal meaning: the length of time in which a space is occupied. Here we see the metonym, "the occupation," referring to both the act of the violent takeover of a space and the duration of that occupation. This metonym is never innocent or apolitical; it secures its own political/ideological/spatial occupation, as its speaker invokes a sense of invasion, of unjust violence *against* the speaker's position; for instance, "the occupation" might be uttered by an opponent of Israel's presence in the West Bank, the Gaza Strip, and East Jerusalem. Even such a position occupies varied ideological space—say, the difference between the PLO's use of "ending the Occupation" as leading to an "end of Israel" versus, say, the "US Campaign to End the Israeli Occupation." While it is easy to see the violence attributed to occupations of geopolitical spaces, this understanding of occupation occurs in all notions of space. All occupations are political; all considerations of the spatial must account for the political. All occupations are discursive, rhetorical, hegemonic. Through its occupations, space is not merely social, it is political. It is precisely the political occupation of a space that imbues that spaces with its placeness. Conflict for control over naming a place, for controlling the power to say what can and cannot occupy a space, is often a fight to change the way that place has been named by other occupiers who held power in different temporal moments. Occupations may change over time, but inscribed meanings may not be erased for all who know a place. A place may be Palestine to one subject and Israel to another, no matter who names that place in any specific moment.

The second understanding of occupation derives from the first and refers to the state of being subject to the action of occupation. In this instance, we think of occupation not in the active/invasive sense as the previous definition, but as the result of that action, as the direct object of that verb form. Example: New cultural apparatus (the ban of one kind of literacy and the promotion of another) enforced the occupation.

Third, occupation refers to the taking up or filling up of space. In the previous understandings of occupation the term carries not only spatial meanings, but temporal ones as well in referring to the length of time a space is occupied. Place, we recall, is the temporal occupation of space. This instance of occupation refers to the act of holding a position within a space, to the hegemonic writing of a place. This definition emanates from Archimedes' principle of displacement: any object, wholly or partly immersed in a fluid, is buoyed up by a force equal to the weight of the fluid displaced by the object—the definition de Certeau relies upon. Archimedes maintains that an object displaces a volume of liquid equivalent to the volume occupied by the object that displaces the liquid. Derived from this is a basic principle of physics: no two objects can occupy the same space at the same time. Again, the temporal becomes critical in understanding the spatial. From this we derive that things occupy spaces, not only physical things, but all objects, events, ideas, phenomena, and utterances. De Certeau clarifies, however, that objects occupy adjacent places, not the same place.

The fourth degree of occupation is more problematic in its transcendence of the spatial into the realm of the temporal. This understanding of occupation refers to the manner in which individuals occupy their time through engagement or the pursuit of an activity. This may refer to employment/work (those terms distinctly different), a profession, or a calling. Certainly, here the idea of the temporal comes into play as occupation refers to how one fills one's time; however, occupations should be seen as primarily spatial in that they distinguish particular *positions* in time held by individuals; often, in fact, occupations are referred to as such.

From the rhetorical tradition, we understand that the idea of occupation is derived from *occupatio.* For Cicero, *occupatio* meant both the acquisition and ownership of property by taking possession of—that is, by occupying—that which had no previous owner (*De officiis* 1.7).This notion of ownership and property leads to concepts of *res nullius*: physical things that do not have or never have had owners. A thing that is *res nullius* may be physical, but it cannot have an owner; it cannot be property. For example, light is *res nullius,* but a rock found by a river or an object captured in battle is not. Such concepts became crucial to concepts of Roman law, and this early understanding of *occupatio* distinguished between things lost or abandoned out of necessity. Cargo abandoned by a sinking ship could not be repossessed by a new owner because it was abandoned out of necessity. However, a thing abandoned not out of necessity could be possessed; it was understood as *res derelictae,* property abandoned by an owner. For Justinian, *occupatio* became the method for acquiring property that was to be accepted by nearly all people as *adquisitiones naturales.*

For Kant, space is an inseparable condition of the objects that occupy it (85). Space, Kant explains in "Principles of Pure Understanding," cannot be perceived by itself. Objects—or using Kant's term, *materials*—that occupy spaces give representation to those spaces (80). Without occupation, space is a nonentity. This same notion can be found in a number of philosophers' concepts of space, most notably that of Gottfried Wilhelm Leibniz, who argued that space is necessarily occupied in order for it to be identified. What occupies space, then, are bodies, specific bodies that mark and identify the space they occupy. According to Lefebvre, that occupation provides orientation to the space; space without orientation has no identifying characteristics (1991, 169–70). Space requires content. Bodies occupy places within spaces, giving spaces orientation and discernible boundaries. Spaces are infinite; bodies are finite. Only through such occupations can spaces be demarcated. Spaces—infinite, indiscernible—defy the grasp of identity through the movement of perpetual transformation. Only the pause of place, the moment of orientation and of identity, permits the momentary identity of a space's boundaries. This can be seen in the (not so) simple production of maps: the actual terra firma we stand on and measure exists spatially and temporally. It is only the identity of country, of state, that becomes place. So, Istanbul's not Constantinople, and as the song says, "No, you can't go back to Constantinople / Been a long time gone, Constantinople," because places on maps appear only when a discourse emerges, however briefly, victorious for long enough to inscribe meaning to Istanbul or Constantinople; that is the moment of orientation and identity in which the land can be named a place, and given identifiable boundaries. The map will change as new occupiers, new occupations, and new practices create new meaning, new identity, new places. It is that instability of space—the possibility for changing meaning—that exists in countersignature with place. This is why Lefebvre's claim that space is infinite is so important. Recognizing/

imagining space is critical and is the first step toward counterhegemony, toward creating new meanings through occupation, to producing new places through occupation. Identifying the use of space in any given moment—the *occupation* of space in any given moment—provides the opportunity to reveal contrasting, contradictory uses of space, to identify the ideological struggles that look to inscribe meaning.

This does not, however, translate into the simple formula that bodies define the spaces they occupy. Lefebvre explains:

> Can the body, with its capacity for action, and its various energies, be said to create space? Assuredly, but not in the sense that occupation might be said to "manufacture" spatiality; rather, there is an immediate relationship between the body and its space, between the body's deployment in space and its occupation of space. Before *producing* effects in the material realm (tools and object), before *producing itself* by drawing nourishment from that realm, and before *reproducing itself* by generating other bodies, each living body is space and has its space: it produces itself in space and also produces that space. (1991, 170; italics in original)

Deleuze and Guattari say about the body, "[W]e know nothing about a body until we know what it can do, in other words, what its affects are" (1987, 13). It is specifically the affect of occupation by/of the body that becomes central in thinking about spatial occupation. For Foucault, as he explains in *The Archaeology of Knowledge*, subjects take up positions in space, that is, occupy space. Granted, Foucault does not address what space is in the way that Lefebvre does, but his attention to occupation can be seen in much of his work.

Once given orientation through the occupation of places, all spaces have particular functions. Those functions—as well as those spaces—are dictated by social convention, by inscribing meaning. What spaces we may occupy and in what manner we may occupy them is socially dictated. Perec, in his discussion of the function of rooms, identifies (offhandedly) the manner in which functions are defined by the occupations of those rooms: "A bedroom is a room in which there is a bed; a dining room is a room in which there are a table and chairs, and often a sideboard . . ." (1999, 27).[3] The architect of spaces—and by architect, here I do not mean the occupation (job) of being an architect, but the very power structures which design, delineate, and produce what spaces may be—produces spaces with a focus on how the places of that space will be occupied. For instance, when preserves/

parks/habitats are set aside by governing bodies (bodies that occupy authority), there is an underlying idea of how that space will be occupied that drives how it is constructed, just as there is the distinction between a classroom space and, say, a writing "lab" space. While these are concrete (pun intended), easily defined/defended examples—the architect of an office building thinks first about how it will be occupied in order to design its use-function—the same holds true with all spaces, abstract or concrete: spaces on a page, spaces in culture, imagined spaces, thirdspaces. That is, whether considering firstspaces or secondspaces, the occupation of those spaces produces those spaces. Gregory Ulmer's notion of apparatus becomes crucial in understanding the idea of occupation. For Ulmer, apparatus refers to "the matrix of a language machine" composed partly of the technological and partly of the social that functions in any give time—though, I would argue, in any given space as well—to make meaning. Apparatus is not merely the technology of language—a pencil, ink, a typewriter, the alphabet—but the institution and that institution's methods and practices that evolve with the technology, what Jody Berland refers to as "cultural technologies." Apparatuses are the ways in which knowledge is named. Through Ulmer's "apparatus," we come to see occupation, then, not as a mere case of functionality, of the function-ability of how a space may be *used.* *Use* suggests the occupation of space produces space only through its usability, through how the occupation of space uses that space. When and how that space is occupied extends beyond use to the apparatus of that space: its technological and social practice. How that space is made through its technological and social functions defines how, when, and by whom that spacc can bc occupied.

Can there be spaces, then, without use, that are unusable, that are without occupation? The very move to set spaces as usable or without use, as occupied or unoccupiable, is itself a use-function, an attempt to identify that unusable space as used for the unusable—basic Derridean otherness. Unused space can be seen as "other than the used," and, therefore, serve the use of being unused. Perec, too, lets us consider unused space by identifying that language does not allow us to articulate the unused space as space. Perec, in trying to convey what the unused space might be, writes: "A space without a function. Not 'without any precise function' but precisely without any function; not plurifunctional (everyone knows how to do that), but a-functional. It wouldn't obviously be a space intended solely to 'release' the others (lumber-room, cupboard, hanging space, storage space, etc.) but a space, I repeat, that would serve no purpose at all" (1999, 33).

There are unusable spaces and spaces that are not used, but not a space without use—not even imagined spaces. There are spaces that are unoccupiable and spaces that are unoccupied, but not spaces that cannot be occupied. The use-function of a space is bound up with how a space is occupied, even in its unoccupation. This echoes Lefebvre's concept of spatial orientation and unoccupied spaces. Space requires occupation. However, constructing unused space as Other space affords the dominant occupier of space, those who write meaning in place, the opportunity to make the Other the same, to turn the unused into the used.

Occupation imposes partition (this is Perec's phrase); partitions/borders/boundaries become/are political, are rhetorical, are discursive. Without demarcated partitions, there is no space, no space to occupy, no formation of place. The space is defined by the boundaries imposed by its occupiers. To make the partitions/borders/boundaries appear natural—appear nonexistent, if possible—and to appear nonpolitical is the ultimate goal of use: to identify occupation as appropriate, as natural, as correct. This is my space; it always has been. This is the manufacture of consent; this is hegemony. This is how this space is used; this is how it has always been used. Then the space can be seen as a factor in constructing the occupier's identity, not the opposite—though, of course, this is an illusion. The relationship becomes eventually reciprocal in that those who come to occupy a space—say the space of the university—must mold their identities to fit the space as defined by previous occupiers/occupations. This is also Soja—via Lefebvre—asking us to not only think about how occupation demarcates spaces, but the manner in which those spaces demarcate the occupiers.

For Perec, partitions, from the political perspective of dividing geopolitical regions, give name/identity to the idea of country, which are marked by divisions of frontiers—unnamed, unoccupied spaces that mark boundaries between spaces. Perec, in an interesting maneuver, says that some spaces are uninhabitable, but when listing what uninhabitable spaces might be, Perec does not mean to suggest that uninhabitable spaces are uninhabited (for instance, he identifies shantytowns, towns that smell bad, the out-of-bounds, the corridors of the metro, and so on), only that they should not be inhabited. Though he does not do so explicitly, Perec moves to a distinction between habitable and occupy-able. For Perec there are spaces that have been occupied in such a fashion that it renders them no longer habitable. This is specifically the moment in which the primary occupier of space can shift the nonuse, the uninhabitability of a space into a used space, a habitable space. The primary occupier of a space can construct the uninhabitable shantytown as used space, as place, positioning the occupants of that place in the ranks of the hegemony that defines the place. In such a case of Other space, of unused space made used, there is little difficulty in seeing how a dominant discourse imposes occupation, imposes order to maintain its own safety. Remember, places may be safe, but they are only safe for those who make them. For composition, this is crucial.

The ordering of occupation can also be seen as an economics of storage, of how spaces are occupied. Occupation itself is a spatial storage: places to put things, to occupy, to be occupied, to keep occupied, as well as places to save, to be saved, places to cage, to be caged. Occupying a field and guarding its borders keeps the invaders out, but it keeps the (e)state in (power) by writing those borders as containing what can safely be contained and what can be excluded safely. As Barthes notes, "[W]hat can be separated can also be filled" (1977, 120); this is what Lefebvre refers to as the "logic of container *versus* contents" (1991, 3; italics in original).

To invoke language, to name a thing, to consider knowledge (that is by thinking/talking about anything) is to deploy all of these into a space, thus naming that space by its occupying force. Perec asks, "What does taking possession of a place mean? As from when does somewhere become truly yours?" (1999, 24). These are questions of identity, of a place's identity, and ultimately of the occupier's identity. Identity is the attempt to mark a container (both as a container and in terms of its use) by naming its contents. Unoccupied containers are unmarked spaces. I am thinking here of the kind of unmarked spaces to which Italo Calvino refers in "A Sign in Space" in *Cosmicomics*. Space, Calvino notes, is not definable until that space is occupied by sign: "[S]pace, without a sign, was once again a chasm, the void, without beginning or end, nauseating, in which everything—including me—was lost" (1965, 35). What Calvino is getting at are points of reference, the ability to identify what is occupied, to demarcate, to mark:

> In the universe now there was no longer a container and a thing contained, but only a general thickness of signs superimposed and coagulated, occupying the whole volume of space; it was constantly being dotted, minutely, a network of lines and scratches and reliefs and engravings; the universe was scrawled over on all sides, along all its dimensions. There was no longer any way to establish a point of reference: the galaxy went on turning but I could no longer count the revolutions,

> any point could be the point of departure, any sign heaped up with the others could be mine, but discovering it would have served no purpose, because it was clear that, independent of signs, space didn't exist and perhaps had never existed. (39)

To make a sign in space is to give signification. To signify is to assign meaning, to produce a place, to occupy that place. To occupy a place is to produce that place; to produce a place is too occupy it, to write it in the script of hegemony, to make it safe in a glimpse of time.

The Occupation of Composition

> Passing again beneath the ginkgo, I said to Mr. Okeda that in the contemplation of the shower of leaves the fundamental thing was not so much the perception of each of the leaves as of the distance between one leaf and another, the empty air that separated them. What I seemed to have understood was this: an absence of sensations over a broad part of the perceptive field is the condition necessary for our sensitivity to concentrate locally and temporally, just as in music a basic silence is necessary so that the notes will stand out against it.
>
> —Italo Calvino, *If on a Winter's Night a Traveler*

> Once composition could be named a field, a concept reflecting absolute space, then it could wield power.
>
> —Nedra Reynolds, *Geographies of Writing*

> The present epoch will perhaps be above all the epoch of space. We are in the epoch of simultaneity; we are in the epoch of juxtaposition, the epoch of the near and far, the side-by-side, of the dispersed. We are at a moment, I believe, when our experience of the world is less that of a long life developing through time than that of a network that connects points and intersects with its own skein.
>
> —Michel Foucault, "Of Other Spaces"

Out of a need for vocabulary, composition has (reluctantly) adopted spatial metaphors—classrooms, writing environments, sites of conflict, and so on. Nedra Reynolds maintains that "[s]patial metaphors have long dominated our written discourse in this field ('field' being one of the first spatial references we can name) because, first, writing itself is spatial, or we cannot very well conceive of writing other than spatial" (1998, 14) and that "[s]pace is usually described or represented by making comparisons with familiar objects or ideas—like an academic discipline being called a field (giving it the boundaries of absolute space)" (2004, 13). But, unlike Reynolds, who has undoubtedly given much thought to the role of spatial theory in/and composition, most in composition only embrace such metaphors halfheartedly—and often are inattentive to the implications of the spatial dimensions of those metaphors—as an easy way to talk about composition, and generally just composition pedagogy.

Much more so than its embrace of the spatial, composition has entrenched itself in concepts of the temporal. Composition (as a field) is obsessed with its own history, with its own identity, and how that identity is manifest historically. Talking about what composition is/does is so much a prevalent part of what composition does/is that having such conversations *is* what composition does. Asking about composition's identity is (part of) composition's identity. Despite its relatively recent inception (1963), composition spends an immense amount of time attempting to place itself historically.[4] Much like what Soja says of historians and sociologists, compositionists have privileged historical placements in culture and, for the most part, have rendered spatial determination and occupation nearly insignificant. Of course, the want to claim history is an attempt at validation; things with histories must be (or at least must have been). An ever-accumulating past signifies a solidity of present and the potential for future. Even the recent passing of first-generation compositionists (Berlin, Corder, Corbett, Kinneavey, Bishop, Connors, France, Sledd, Hairston) helps confirm composition's place temporally as it accumulates historical figures; their deaths allow composition to identify its own pantheon, to claim a canon. History will likely not rob those who died as compositionists of their composition identity, securing for composition historical markers. Context for composition is historical, is temporal. As Romy Clark and Roz Ivanic mention, "[T]he past is revered as cultural heritage, as if it somehow confers glory on the whole [field]" (1997, 39–40).

To see composition's attachment to the temporal, one need not look further than some of what have been heralded as the most important works in/of composition: Steven North's *The Making of Knowledge in Composition*, Susan Miller's *Rescuing the Subject* or her essay "The Feminization of Composition," Jim Berlin's "Contemporary Composition: The Major Pedagogical Theories," and Richard Fulkerson's "Four Philosophies of Composition." These are attempts to tell the (his)story of composition. More recent histories such as Robert J. Connors's *Composition-Rhetoric*, Joe Harris's *A Teaching Subject*, Thomas P. Miller's *The Formation of College English*, Lynn Z. Bloom, Donald A. Daiker, and

Edward M. White's *Composition in the Twenty-first Century*, John C. Brereton's *The Origins of Composition Studies in the American College, 1875–1925*, and Sharon Crowley's *Composition in the University* are all works of temporal placement—though I might argue that Crowley's (perhaps one of the most important books in composition of recent years) is actually a book of spatial dimensions despite the fact that she does not approach her argument as such.[5] Composition, it seems, is determined to find a foothold in temporal placement in history.

What composition has failed to do, though, even its minimal attention to spatial metaphors, is attempt to understand its spatial occupation. Failure to locate a space of composition, and instead finding tenuous comfort in delicate places of composition, has created an anxiety of composition, a lack of safety in those pauses of place, because within those pauses, composition lacks the freedom of space. What composition must recognize is that its attempt to find even temporal ground is dependent upon not its histories but upon its occupations and its abilities to continually produce counterhegemonies that question composition's places. Composition must become attuned not to spatial metaphors as a method for speaking *about* its work, but rather to the very dynamics of the production and occupation of spaces in order to elucidate the complexity of composition's (ever-shifting) position(s): historically, institutionally, territorially. Composition's identities and histories can "no longer be sought (as they once were) simply in the abstract realms of 'ideology' or 'discourse', but very precisely in the grounded and interanimating practices of the . . . bodies whose organized everyday life reproduces the spaces in question" (Murphet 1999, 204). That is, composition must become attuned to its own occupations. Or, to borrow from Foucault, I believe that the anxiety of the composition era has "to do fundamentally with space, no doubt a great deal more than with time" (1986, 23).

In his landmark book *The Poetics of Space*, Gaston Bachelard explains that we do not live in empty space, in homogenous space. Space, he claims is filled by quantities, with occupations (though for Bachelard, these occupations may be phantasmic). Composition is a social space, a cultural space, an occupied space. Its bodies and boundaries are produced by the occupiers of that space and the occupations the defining forces of those spaces. Understanding the spatiality of composition then allows for not only productions of new places and of new ways to occupy the places of field, and a new opportunity to define more than places and boundaries, territories and fields, but also the very politics of those places and boundaries, recognizing the hegemonies that mark those territories and the counterhegemonies that necessarily must question and resist those hegemonies. Composition has become complacent in the safety of the pause, in the safety of the place of composition. That complacency has left composition defending the illusions of borders, not of spaces, but of places. Compositions must become attuned to its contingent frontiers, contingencies which may be adverse to the "field," frontiers that can be riddled with the possibility of disorder and violence to the stability of the field. Frontiers, we discern from Hegel, always involve violence. Occupation is often violent; occupation is a maneuver toward new frontiers.

Composition's simulacra and safety of place rests on its want to claim disciplinary status, its want to be seen as field. But fields are demarcated by boundaries, generally discernible, claimable boundaries. As composition has witnessed in its "history," its field is often penetrated by occupying forces (think Minnesota, think Florida, think Brodkey).[6] Fields with defendable borders are also exclusionary, both in terms of territoriality and in terms of identity. Hegemonic discourses maneuver (within) borders to protect their places, to protect their rights to construct those places, to protect their own safety. In composition the safety of the home field risks becoming exclusionary, guarded against incompatibility with ideologies and (perhaps incursive) missions of other field boundaries, guarded against counterhegemonies, guarded against space. And, yes, as difficult as it is to admit, composition is hegemonic. Despite its self-congratulatory discourse of openness and diversity, of freedom and emancipation, composition is adamant about its fields, about its places. Composition guards its places by presenting a discourse of inclusiveness, by making that discourse seem a natural part of the field's discourse. But that diversity, that openness to dissent, must share occupation within composition's places. No two objects can occupy the same place at the same time; they may only occupy adjacent places. Composition and countercomposition cannot occupy the places of composition at the same time; they cannot be of/in the same place.

To move beyond the safety of composition's place requires first an acknowledgment of composition's heterotopic space. "Heterotopias," Foucault pronounces, "always presuppose a system of opening and closing that both isolates them and makes them penetrable. In general, the heterotopic space is not freely accessible like a public space. Either entry is compulsory . . . or else the individual has to submit to rites and purification. . . . To get in, one must have permission and make certain gestures" (1986, 26). Heterotopias, too, Foucault explains, may "seem to be pure and simple openings, but that generally hide curious exclusions. Everyone can enter into these heterotopic sites, but in fact that is only an illusion: we think we enter where we are, but by the very fact that we enter, excluded" (26). This is the power of occupation.

"The political synthesis of social space," Michael Hardt and Antonio Negri tell us, "is fixed in the space of communication" (2001, 33). From this we understand that it is the very language of composition's occupation—the manner in which that space is occupied—that protects composition's places in safety, protects composition in its places, not casting more than a glance beyond its places to the frontiers of its spaces, to the territorial occupations, accepting its exclusions and its being excluded. This is why the very metaphors of "conversation" as well as the increased role of heterotopic conversations (think WPA-L) are powerful producers of composition's space, of defining and defending composition's occupation. Communicative entities are able not only to impose controlling structure over the composition place, but also give credence and validation to that occupation. As Hardt and Negri put it, "Power, as it produces, organizes; as it organizes, it speaks and expresses itself as authority. Language, as it communicates, produces commodities but moreover creates subjectivities, puts them in relation, and orders them" (33). For composition, a central question of its spatial inquiry must be a question of the powers that produce and organize the (social) spaces of composition, that organize the relative safety of composition's places. Composition's places can no longer afford to rest in the safety of recirculated conversations of temporal/historical identity, of imposed subjectivities, of self-validation. Composition must move to occupy other places that can—à la Bhabha—move beyond its simulacra safety, its artificial safety, to explore its contingent frontiers in order to produce its own counterhegemonies, in order to not accept the natural boundaries of composition's field. The occupation of composition is not merely an occupation of the fourth order—that of a task to occupy time. It is an occupation that requires critical attention to the very spaces it occupies, its occupation of those places, because it is in those occupations that we see composition's places as rhetorical demarcations, as dependent upon the meaning inscribed on those places. Composition is an occupied territory, and in its occupation risks creating a homogeneous composition space, a naturalized place. And as Baudrillard explains, "[H]omogenous space, without meditation, brings together men and things—a space of direct manipulation. But who manipulates whom?" (1994, 76). Composition is in need of spatial disruption.

Ultimately, composition must acknowledge its spatial positioning, but in doing so must also initiate a move to counterspaces. Counterspaces, as Lefebvre defines them, are "spaces of resistance to the dominant order arising precisely from their subordinate, peripheral or marginalized positioning" (1991, 68). Composition must deterritorialize, must give up the safety of its places—places that claim occupational/disciplinary authority, yet constrict the domain of that authority to limit situations such as "the teaching of writing." Composition needs Baudrillard's polyvalent space, spaces of mass participation in the occupation of space in which the occupiers become the agents of execution of the cultures that occupy that space. In polyvalent space, occupiers "participate and manipulate so well that they efface all the meaning one wants to give the operation and put the very infrastructure of the edifice in danger" (Baudrillard 1994, 66).

The questions, of course, that this short consideration of space beg are who (or what bodies) occupy composition? Is composition occupied? Or is composition otherwise occupied, distracted by its occupations? Does composition occupy its own (social) space, or has it become satisfied/complacent (put) in its own place? To what (governing) bodies does composition bow in its occupation, and to what bodies does it stand adjacent? Who determines the content, the orientation, the direction of composition's occupied spaces? How long will this occupation last? There are questions that must be posed of composition's freedom in the occupation of its places and questions that must not be ignored about the complacency and conservatism composition has adopted in its settlement of/with safe places.

Notes

1. Here I am thinking of "life" not in a biological sense, but in the sense that Michael Payne and John Schad question the idea of life as it is bound with the idea of theory in their book *life.after.theory*.
2. Here I intentionally use the term "position"—the place where a thing is located—to indicate that the definitions of *occupation* themselves occupy a particular epistemological space within this paper and within an understanding of space.
3. Of course, Perec does not follow through with the exercise at this point in his discussion by then identifying the function of the space of, say, the bed, as defined by the (to borrow from Soja) secondspace of the bed and its occupation.
4. While making this criticism is crucial, I must own up to the fact that I am guilty of participating in/forwarding such conversations as much as anyone else. I do not mean to imply that having the

conversation about composition's "identity" is an inappropriate conversation to have.

5. In saying that Crowley's book is a spatial argument, I mean to suggest that it is an argument about occupation, about how FYC occupies a given space within the American university system.
6. Minnesota, Florida, and Brodkey all refer to "events" during which forces from beyond the boundaries of composition intervened in places thought to be places of composition and forcefully altered how those places were occupied. In the cases of the University of Minnesota and the University of Florida, upper administrations took control of writing programs with little or no consultation with composition faculty in order to impose their own views of what a writing class should accomplish. Linda Brodkey lost her job at the University of Texas specifically because she attempted to create a curriculum within a space she thought to be safe, but that was ultimately controlled by stronger administrative forces.
7. I wish to acknowledge and thank Joe Hardin, Julie Drew, and Raul Sanchez for their incredibly helpful comments on early drafts of this essay.

Works Cited

Bachelard, Gaston. 1994. *The Poetics of Space.* Trans. Maria Jolas. Boston: Beacon Press.

Barthes, Roland. 1977. *Image, Music, Text.* Trans. Stephen Heath. New York: Hill and Wang.

Baudrillard, Jean. 1994. *Simulacra and Simulation.* Ann Arbor: University of Michigan Press.

Berland, Jody. 1992. "Angels Dancing: Cultural Technologies and the Production of Space." In *Cultural Studies,* ed. Lawrence Grossberg, Cary Nelson, and Paula Treichler, 38–55. New York: Routledge.

Berlin, Jim. 1982. "Contemporary Composition: The Major Pedagogical Theories." *College English* 44.8. 765–77.

Bloom, Lynn Z., Donald A. Daiker, and Edward M. White. 1996. *Composition in the Twenty-first Century: Crisis and Change.* Carbondale: Southern Illinois University Press.

Brereton, John C. 1995. *The Origins of Composition Studies in the American College, 1875–1925: A Documentary History.* Pittsburgh: University of Pittsburgh Press.

Calvino, Italo. 1965. *Cosmicomics*. New York: Harcourt Brace.
———. 1979. *If on a Winter's Night a Traveler*. New York: Harcourt Brace Jovanovich.
Clark, Romy, and Roz Ivanic. 1997. *The Politics of Writing*. New York: Routledge.
Connors, Robert J. 1997. *Composition-Rhetoric: Backgrounds, Theory, and Pedagogy*. Pittsburgh: University of Pittsburgh Press.
Crowley, Sharon. 1998. *Composition in the University: Historical and Polemical Essays*. Pittsburgh: University of Pittsburgh Press.
de Certeau, Michel. 1984. *The Practice of Everyday Life*. Berkeley and Los Angeles: University of California Press.
Deleuze, Gilles, and Felix Guattari. 1987. *Kafka: Toward a Minor Literature*. Trans. D. Polan. Minneapolis: University of Minnesota Press.
Foucault, Michel. 1984. "Space, Knowledge, and Power." In *The Foucault Reader*, ed. Paul Rabinow, 239–56. New York: Pantheon.
———. 1986. "Of Other Spaces." *Diacritics* 16 (Spring): 22–27.
Fulkerson, Richard 1979. "Four Philosophies of Composition." *CCC* 30 (December): 343–48.
Hardt, Michael and Antonio Negri. 2001. *Empire*. Cambridge. MA: Harvard University Press.
Harris, Joe. 1997. *A Teaching Subject: Composition since 1966*. Upper Saddle River, NJ: Prentice Hall.
Kant, Immanuel. 2001. *Basic Writings*. Ed. Allen Wood. New York: Modern Library.
Lefebvre, Henri. 1976. *The Survival of Capitalism: Reproduction of the Relations of Production*. Trans. Frank Bryant. London: Allison & Busby.
———. 1991. *The Production of Space*. Blackwell.
Miller, Susan. 1991. "The Feminization of Composition." *The Politics of Writing Instruction: Postsecondary*. Eds. Richard Bullock and John Trimbur, 39–53. Portsmouth, NH: Boynton.
———. 2004. *Rescuing the Subject: A Critical Introduction to Rhetoric and the Writer*. Carbondale: Southern Illinois University Press.
Miller, Thomas P. 1997. *The Formation of College English: Rhetoric and Belles Lettres in the British Cultural Provinces*. Pittsburgh: University of Pittsburgh Press.
Murphet, Julian. 1999. "Grounding Theory: Literary Theory and the New Geography." In *Post-Theory: New Directions in Criticism*, 200–208. Edinburgh: Edinburgh University Press.
North, Stephen M. 1987. *The Making of Knowledge in Composition: Portrait of an Emerging Field*. New York: Reed/Elsevier.

Payne, Michael, and John Schad, eds. 2003. *life.after.theory*. New York: Continuum.

Perec, Georges. 1999. *Species of Space and Other Pieces*. Trans. John Sturrock. New York: Penguin.

Reynolds, Nedra. 1998. "Composition's Imagined Geographies: the Politics of Space in the Frontier, City, and Cyberspace." *College Composition and Communication* 50, no. 1: 12–35.

———. 2004. *Geographies of Writing: Inhabiting Places and Encountering Difference*. Carbondale: Southern Illinois University Press.

Soja, Edward J. 1996. *Thirdspace: Journeys to Los Angeles and Other Real-and-Imagined Places*. Malden, MA: Blackwell.

Tuan, Yi-Fu. 1977. *Space and Place: The Perspective of Experience*. Minneapolis: University of Minnesota Press.

Ulmer, Gregory L. 1994. *Heuretics: The Logic of Invention*. Baltimore: Johns Hopkins University Press.

2

Composition and the Gentrification of "Public Literacy"

ELIZABETH ERVIN

Several years ago, I presented a paper at the Conference on College Composition and Communication on the subject of public literacy. A graduate school friend congratulated me afterward, noting confidentially that "[a]cademic discourse is over. People are really tired of it. In a couple of years we're all going to be doing public discourse." My friend's comment was prophetic. As Gary A. Olson observes in his foreword to Christian Weisser's 2002 book *Moving Beyond Academic Discourse*, "[P]ublic writing is clearly emerging as a powerful expression of some of the field's most cherished values." As such, it will "most likely lead us all into the new decade" (Olson 2003, ix).

Although part of me is gratified that perhaps I got in on the beginning of a professional trend for a change rather than at the tail end of it, over time I've grown more and more uneasy with the growth of public writing within composition studies. There are, of course, good explanations for this growth as well as worthy motivations behind it. Weisser, for example, sees public writing—rightly, I think—"as an extension of radical composition," which likewise "examine[s] language use as it enables and inhibits participants in their struggles for public democracy and social justice" (Weisser 2002, 55). Susan Wells writes sympathetically on behalf of those compositionists who have propelled this examination—well-meaning literacy professionals who "feel guilty for our absence from the public," believing that we may have, through arrogance or neglect, abandoned this vital space to "political functionaries and spin doctors" (1996, 327). This sense of responsibility for reinvigorating public discourse (however extravagant) has left many in our discipline with a vague desire to "do something" with our knowledge of rhetoric that has an impact beyond the classroom.

Still, my friend's comment lingers: Is it possible that compositionists (myself included) have shifted our focus to public and community contexts less out of civic-minded beneficence than out of disciplinary ennui? In the context of the academy, such a decision would be analogous, I think, to historians claiming that they are tired of "doing" the past and want to shift their focus to something really sexy, like the present. "The present" is, of course, a legitimate context for historical study, one that is continuous with the past; to talk about "today" is to talk about the past. Similarly, "the public" is a legitimate site of discourse and therefore (arguably) a legitimate focus of composition. Academic spaces are often public spaces, and the classroom has been widely theorized as a public space in microcosm even in exclusive and virtual educational environments (see, e.g., Weisser 2002, 43; Wells 1996, 338; Harris 1996, 323–24). But the "public" of public discourse is not only a location but also a constituency, that is, actual human persons who can be abstracted in various strategic ways in order, as David S. Kaufer puts it, to fill "rhetorical slots" (2004, 153)—among them the speaker or writer's claim to stand "as a representative of a community's felt condition" (154). Claims to representativeness may also be motivated by personal and disciplinary aspirations, the kind that manifest what Deepika Bahri and Joseph Petraglia describe as a primal "territorial jealousy" (2003, 3).

Conventional wisdom within composition studies holds that our current disciplinary preoccupation with public discourse (including public intellectualism, community literacy, service learning, advocacy, and activism) is not only intellectually and politically responsible, but also—given our roots in rhetoric—historically inevitable, a birthright waiting to be reclaimed (see, e.g., Halloran 1982; Crowley 1998, 263–65). And yet, there is something vaguely imperialistic about this attempt to extend the disciplinary boundaries of composition's influence and representation beyond its accepted sphere (the classroom)—beyond, even, more recent sites of disciplinary interest (the university curriculum, the workplace, and cyberspace). In this essay I would like to offer a critique of this impulse by reading the emergence of public discourse as "a powerful expression of some of the field's most cherished values" in relation to the frequently but tenuously aligned *topoi* of *work* and *democracy*. I argue that when juxtaposed, our scholarly conversations about public discourse and our scholarly conversations about the work-democracy nexus suggest that we compositionists have increasingly turned our gaze to a constituency called "the public" and a place called "the public sphere" at least in part for reasons of self-interest—that is, as a means to establish a public identity that might enhance our professional and material status. I argue, further, that this dynamic can be usefully reflected upon through the concept of gentrification, whereby members of the middle-class "gentry," in the words of Caroline Mills, "do cultural 'work' with symbols of working-class culture" for the purpose of reorganizing the social order (usually) to their own benefit (1993, 158).

Contesting Our Disciplinary Identity

Questions about our disciplinary identity are important; they are personal, and they are fraught with contradictions. Thanks in part to the epistemological claims of feminist standpoint theory (see, e.g., Harding 1991), it is now commonsensical to assert that how we are situated in the world influences what we see and provides grounds for knowledge and value claims. I would like to begin thinking about these issues by noting Dana Polan's remark that English professors, with their demand for "endless interpretations" but seemingly little else, lack any "real identity or significant purpose within public imagery" (1996, 252)—or what Dale M. Bauer describes more bluntly as "the widespread confusion about what English professors actually do" (1998, 309). In the movies, Bauer argues, English teachers are sentimentalized and trivialized, and they exercise only an "aestheticized" version of power. In an extended analysis of the 1996 movie *The Mirror Has Two Faces,* she contends that while classrooms are consistently depicted as "transformative spaces" (309), and while English professors are very often the catalysts of that change, it no longer takes the form of radical teaching or social revolution, but rather of "the gradual alteration of individual style" (310)—in this case, literally, a makeover of a frumpified Barbra Streisand. Such depictions, Bauer concludes, encourage the popular notion that "teaching English is superfluous, that literature of any sort is a luxury, outside the realm of the practical. English teachers . . . pose no threat to bureaucracy because nobody takes them seriously anyway" (304).

Of course, composition does not even enjoy literature's status as a quaintly benign academic relic, or creative writing's status as a hotbed of personal (often erotic) revelation. Rather, it is virtually invisible within popular culture, and when it *is* visible it is usually depicted in ways unrecognizable or unpalatable to its practitioners: either as leftist posturing wholly unrelated to language and writing (see, e.g., George Will, "Feel-good College Feds Flush Literacy Away," *Wilmington Star-News*, July 2, 1995), or as the lifeless drilling of skills utterly devoid of—even hostile to—inspiration or intellectual content. Frustratingly, these negative depictions of composition seem to be more enduring than any alternative visions enacted in our classrooms and other professional forums. Perhaps even more frustratingly, however, they dramatize a troublesome truth. On the one hand, as Christina Crosby observes, "The professionalization of English in institutions of higher learning depends on the creation of specialized knowledge *that the public accepts as a good*" (2003, 639; my emphasis). That is, part of our disciplinary identity requires that people who are not compositionists recognize and value what we do. But on the other hand, what the public (conceived not only as nonacademic taxpayers but also as our students and probably as most colleagues in other disciplines, including literature and creative writing) most clearly accepts as good is our instrumentalism—the practical uses to which our knowledge and skills can be put, generally understood as correct, conventional, functionally substantive prose. Compositionists value instrumentalism, too. While we seldom acknowledge it and while its particulars may differ from what noncompositionists value *about* us, this instrumentalism nevertheless represents not only professional capital (for many of us, it is the reason our jobs exist) but also a significant part of our disciplinary identity. As Russell Durst writes:

> I want to be successful in my work partly for intrinsic reasons of personal satisfaction in promoting my ideas about composition teaching, which I have worked hard to develop and believe in strongly. I want to be successful partly for political reasons in hopes that my work will benefit students from all backgrounds and possibly even contribute to a more just social order. But I also want to be successful partly for reasons of ambition. I readily confess to a desire to do well in my career, write successful books, be respected in my field, raise my salary, better provide for my family. I do not think such careerism is wrong, particularly when balanced with these other goals, and I think many other people in the field share this view. (1999, 174)

Certainly many composition scholars *do* share Durst's view, from the lofty political ends right down to the advantages of an enhanced paycheck. But still others not only disagree with this view but openly disdain it as the epitome of what Sharon O'Dair calls, devastatingly, "the bad faith of the middle-class professoriate" (2003, 593).

How to address this tension between the demand for public relevance and the desire for professional status? Many compositionists have responded by invoking strategic claims of representativeness: of a constituency that Ellen Cushman calls "the underserved public" (2003, 180), whose contributions, abilities, and aspirations are often depreciated or co-opted by those who hold more power; and of a constituency that develops specialized knowledge about and for that same underserved public and that circulates this knowledge through traditional disciplinary publishing outlets in the hopes of garnering the acknowledgment and esteem of noncompositionists, both in and beyond the academy. In other words, by redefining "them" (both the adjudicators and the supposedly disenfranchised) as "us" (the experts, the subjects) and vice versa, we attempt to satisfy, through our work as compositionists, both the genuinely egalitarian (if not radical) and "the middle-class basis of our motives: to be fulfilled, to be acknowledged, to be liked, to be paid" (Bauer 1998, 313).

Public Discourse and Democratic Work: Exploring a Scholarly Intersection

At this point I would like to sketch the parameters of scholarship in public discourse and in what might loosely be called "composition as democratic work." I do this in order to illustrate the interrelatedness of this scholarship—sometimes explicit, often not—as well as to tease out some of its more problematic assumptions. I'll begin with public discourse because it is so commonly, and so casually, "located" in a place, a place called "the public sphere" that, as Wells acknowledges, "is so intensely imagined"—and so urgently desired—"that we think it must be real" (1996, 326). For the purposes of this discussion, I consider "public discourse" research and teaching that engage directly, primarily through textual production (specifically writing) but also through consumption (i.e., reading and analysis), with the world outside the university and other institutional contexts. This includes service learning, local and community literacies, public intellectualism, political discourse, activism and advocacy, and publicity theory.

The relocation of composition's disciplinary focus to a place called "the public sphere" can be seen as both a continuity and a disruption. It is, as noted earlier, consistent with decades-old trends toward looking at discourse as a social phenomenon, and centuries-old traditions of regarding civic discourse as the ultimate purpose of rhetorical education—indeed, of all education. More recently, however, it represents a shift away from the formerly ubiquitous conceptual vocabulary of *communities* and *contact zones*. As Joseph Harris explains in his book *A Teaching Subject*, those terms enjoyed a relatively short shelf life among compositionists mainly because they backfired in the classroom. They were experienced by many students as "multicultural bazaar[s]" in which they encountered "a series of exotic others"—in other words, as innocuous and utopian discursive interactions among people who in fact have profound and legitimate differences (1997, 119). (Of course, another problem with this view is that it strategically ignores the fact that many of our purported ideological allies outside the classroom actively promote prejudices based on these differences, for example, xenophobia and homophobia.) In any event, although Harris briefly wonders whether a contact zone can function as a physical space or "more like a process or event" (122), he ultimately advocates the creation of "a different sort of social space" (124): a more "cosmopolitan" (109, 119)—even, specifically, "urban" (108)—alternative to the flawed conceptual vocabulary of communities, one that offers a more authentic vision of encounters with "others" and thus highlights the inevitability of conflict as well as the necessity of negotiating that conflict, if only in provisional ways (119). Harris calls such authentic spaces "public spheres" (124).

Harris's proposal was typical of a number of studies published in the mid- to late-1990s—including at least one of my own—that embraced the democratic potential (and practical relevance) of public discourse within composition studies. In "Encouraging Civic Participation among First-Year Students," for example, I wrote buoyantly of teachers' ability to "influence [students'] literate and civic lives, inside and outside the classroom" as long as they do not neglect "those behaviors that embody and engaged participation in civic life in favor of diluted forms of participation and of public that have little resemblance to the unruly world outside the classroom" (Ervin 1997, 398). Edward Schiappa, detailing his own participation in a successful effort to sway his local city council to approve a gay-rights initiative, likewise concludes that "when intellectuals choose to get involved, we can make a difference" (1995, 25). In her acclaimed essay "The Rhetorician as an Agent of Social Change," Ellen Cushman goes so far as to argue that it is our "civic responsibility"—not just a brave new world of pedagogical and rhetorical possibilities—"to make activism part of research and teaching" (1996, 22, 20). And so on.

While there are certainly compelling ethical, political, and pedagogical reasons to engage with public discourse in the composition classroom (and no doubt compelling personal reasons as well), in retrospect such comments seem to manifest democracy nostalgia more than the reclaiming of an intellectual legacy. Like Stanley Fish's notion of "theory hope" (1989, 354), this nostalgia manifests an acute desire to believe that our work does in fact have a reality and a purpose and a status in the public imagination, that rhetoric and literacy are *by definition* integral to the realization of democratic ideals. But the fact of the matter is that there is no clear evidence to support the notion that public-spirited arrangements in the writing classroom, however earnestly conceived or thoughtfully executed, have a lasting effect on political conditions outside the classroom; nor is there evidence that those among us who forgo the activities described above are shirking our civic responsibilities; nor, as I shall discuss further below, is there evidence that the classroom is a more "authentic" environment in which to experiment with egalitarian political structures. Which is why, at worst, theoretical and pedagogical expressions of democracy nostalgia might do the opposite of what they intend—namely, participate in a commodification of "the public sphere" (and its presumably marginalized, disorganized, and "voiceless" members) that serves our professional interests and salves anxieties about our bourgeois "bad faith."

Democracy nostalgia is one thing that connects scholarship related to public discourse to scholarship that seeks to articulate our disciplinary commitment to deeply democratic ideals and practices and to the organizations and people who work to sustain them (and, perhaps, our desire for those organizations—unions, for example—to identify with us). This is exemplified by, among other things, an explicit sympathy with leftist ideologies, particularly as expressed by working classness, and, relatedly, with ardent reflection on the material conditions of composition and compositionists, including what Crosby labels "the ethic of work," that is, the network of social and economic obligations that teaching and writing imply (2003, 628). Composition in American higher education has embraced a leftist, working-class ethos since at least the 1960s, during the earliest days of open admissions, basic writing, and "students' right to their own language." However, this ethos has consolidated in the last decade or so, during which time we have seen the publication of such texts as Karen Fitts and Alan France's *Left Margins: Cultural Studies and Composition Pedagogy*; Alan Shepard, John

McMillan, and Gary Tate's *Coming to Class: Pedagogy and the Social Class of Teachers*; Bruce Horner's *Terms of Work for Composition: A Materialist Critique*; and Eileen E. Schell and Patricia Lambert Stock's *Moving a Mountain: Transforming the Role of Contingent Faculty in Composition Studies and Higher Education*. As these and other texts reveal, our disciplinary sentiments about class and work are complex, and often contradictory.

Let me illustrate this tension by looking more closely at two texts that grapple with the implications of social class and the work of teaching writing: Eileen E. Schell's *Gypsy Academics and Mother-Teachers: Gender, Contingent Labor, and Writing Instruction* and Patricia A. Sullivan's "Passing: A Family Dissemblance" (in *Coming to Class*). Both Schell and Sullivan "confess" working-class origins and their resulting struggles negotiating academic success. Both acknowledge that the very middle-class comforts they desire are also—literally, even physically—discomforting; Sullivan, for example, admits that the students for whom she feels "a visceral antipathy," those who regard "higher education as a simple birthright" also live "the very sort of life, give or take a few ideologies, I might wish for my own daughter" (1998, 244, 246). Both express frustration that, as Schell puts it, despite the "sense that composition studies—as a field of inquiry, a set of pedagogical practices, a series of introductory courses—possesses a liberatory, emancipatory dimension. . . . [t]he rhetoric of 'empowerment' and 'liberation' becomes a vexed proposition in light of the vulnerable institutional position of those who predominantly teach introductory writing courses: teaching assistants, part-time faculty, and temporary non-tenure-track faculty" (1998, 4). Exhorting compositionists at every point in the labor hierarchy to recognize the "connection between [our] intellectual work and [our] status as worker[s]" (119), Schell decries the naive and potentially self-destructive form of "higher education illiteracy" (119) that makes these connections invisible, and she calls for compositionists to "act on the democratic principles so many of us espouse in our teaching and scholarship" (120). Finally, both express the democratic-nostalgic hope that, in Sullivan's words, the presence and labors of class-conscious academics "will matter to more than those few individuals we have had the good fortune to meet. That our writing will thus do important work in this world" (1998, 251). Schell prefaces her call to action with the self-consciously nostalgic disclaimer "At the risk of sounding a note of democratic idealism . . ." (1998, 119).

Although Schell and Sullivan illustrate the ambivalence many compositionists feel about socioeconomic class and our status as workers, it is Horner's discussion that is most relevant for my purposes, because it carefully examines the *consequences* of teaching and engaging in democratic work, specifically public writing, from within an academic context—for example, through service learning projects or "as" an academic expert (see Ervin 1999); a public intellectual (see Schiappa 1995); or an academic with access to certain kinds of resources, both intellectual and material (see Cushman 1996). As Horner explains it, when these sorts of engagements with public discourse involve students, they are typically rationalized as "apprenticeships." More generally, however, they are described as "bridges" to "the real world," a distinction that both accepts and reifies a binary in which academic spaces—specifically classrooms but also more abstract, "professional" spaces such as journals and conferences—are by default less authentic, less important, less "real." The effect, Horner argues, is that "[t]he assumptions governing both the teachers' and the students' perceptions of the greater reality of certain types of writing seem to rehearse dominant notions of writing as a pure commodity" (2000, 68). In response to these perceptions, public writing taught through composition courses seems to seek to increase "the exchange value of the writing as commodity by increasing the range of its circulation, indeed by circulating both the [writers] and their writing outside the realm of the classroom" (68). Horner warns, however, that it is unwise for us to assume that anything "defined as 'political,' 'public,' or 'social'" (55), anything "associate[d] . . . with the realm of the community," is "inherently authentic" (160). Classrooms, he insists, are "real" places, just as academic writing is "real"—and are no less so because of their academic locations. To deny the authenticity and potential of the academic context is to fall prey to a reductive thinking that "dematerializes" writing and in the process denies the potential of intellectual work conducted in academic locations to function in both hegemonic and counterhegemonic ways (55–56).

My point here is not to flagellate those of us who desire a wider audience for our ideas or a broader context for our work. Nor do I wish to imply that composition's "will to public" is disingenuous, even if we acknowledge our self-interest in engaging with nonacademic literacies. I do suggest, however, that because of our discipline's longstanding devotion to democratic ideals and practices, both the motives and the consequences of this will to public may have become obscured. For years we have articulated our disciplinary goals and values in such a way that they are thoroughly compatible with, in some cases identical to, the ideals of democratic work. Is it conceivable, then, that we may unconsciously equate the two—that is, associate our professional influence and esteem (i.e., the significance of our work) with the triumph of democracy?

We can learn from the fate of other recent trends in composition as we consider this possibility. Peter Vandenberg, for example, contends that two decades ago, multiculturalism provided a similarly self-legitimating "institutional momentum" for composition's "scholarly machinery" (1999, 564, 565). "In linking *multiculturalism* with *literacy*," Vandenberg writes, "composition's textbooks and scholarship implicitly make the promises of the former (whatever they are said to be) crucially dependent on the latter. . . . When yoked to the sorting process by which one does or does not acquire writing, a primary means of cultural production, the transformative potential of multiculturalism is fully tamed" (565; italics in original). In short, when composition embraces innovative ideological movements and the agents and locations associated with those movements, the effect can be domestication rather than liberation. Clearly, even the most "democratic" and well-intentioned innovations in our disciplinary practices have multiple motivations, and we need to be self-conscious not only about these motivations but about their consequences—in this case, the possibility that scholarship on public discourse and scholarship on composition as democratic work are on the brink of merging into a mutually sustaining academic industry that traffics in what Graham Huggan describes as "a commodified discourse of cultural marginality" (2001, 20).

Recent critiques of postcolonial scholarship can assist us in this process of reflection. Drawing primarily from Huggan's book *The Postcolonial Exotic*, I suggest that we should be especially concerned with three hazards. The first is privileging the conceptual and interpersonal dynamics of "global *metropolitan* culture" (Huggan 2001, 9; emphasis in original), which privileges cities over families and neighborhoods (and ordinary classrooms), excludes anyone who does not have easy access to urban centers, and thus represents the theoretical manifestation of what Aijaz Ahmad elsewhere calls an "imperial geography" (1992, 217). The second hazard is exoticizing the object or location of our gaze, which includes not just perceptions of cultural difference but also "the sympathetic identification" with those differences (17). And the third is engaging in "rhetorics of liberation" that "run the risk of being seen both as presuming to speak for [supposedly marginal cultural groups] and as daring to make intellectual capital out of their material disadvantage" (21). Within a global marketplace, Huggan says, these practices—when unchecked—inevitably replicate and perpetuate the very inequalities that are being addressed. Certainly, compositionists have not been oblivious to these concerns. Cushman, for example, expresses similar cautions when she writes, "Many critical theorists portray themselves as brokers of emancipatory power, a stance that garners them status at the expense of students" (1996, 23). Thus, it seems equally certain that those public discourse scholars who have a stake in their own professional success likewise have a stake in reifying and exploiting locations and constituencies that are urban, exotic, and disenfranchised. And we do this through claims of representativeness that are frequently antagonistic, if not incompatible.

Composition and Gentrification

I have been inching toward the proposition that the rise of public discourse within composition studies emanates from our disciplinary anxieties about class locations—locations that are both physical (spaces such as class*rooms* and their perceived boundaries and constraints) and personal (socioeconomic class and the ways in which it manifests our status as workers, our "place" in the hierarchy of academic professionals, our identities). Thus, the dynamic I have outlined here—the relationship between composition studies, public discourse, and democratic work—is perhaps more closely analogous to gentrification than to colonization. Gentrification is typically understood in its narrowest sense: as the appropriation and "recommodification" of urban, run-down neighborhoods by wealthier residents and the resulting changes in the character and property values of the area. However, not only is gentrification not strictly an urban phenomenon (those posh "rural retreats" and hobby homesteads featured in lifestyle magazines used to be working farms, after all), but as the urban geographer Tom Slater notes, it is ultimately less about space than about class, which differentiates it from colonization in important ways (2003, 4). Most relevant to my discussion are the ways in which gentrification functions as "a cultural tactic by which a new geographical space authenticates a new 'place' in the interstices of social structure" (Mills 1993, 157). Whatever their political or ideological impetus, Mills argues, gentrification projects attempt "to naturalize a mythical version of the way the world works" (168). Not surprisingly, gentrifiers typically figure prominently, even heroically, in this myth, mainly because they cast themselves as agents of positive change, bringing resources and stability to "derelict" environments. Simultaneously, of course, they also displace "indigenous" residents and their cultural norms, which is why their status, in Mills's view, is paradoxical: "both emancipatory and elitist" (158).

We need not identify too intimately with the ominous archetype of the righteous but ultimately self-serving "improver" in order to take seriously composition's fraught relationship to public discourse, starting with the phenomenon of displacement. Frank Harold Wilson observes that one consequence of gentrification is the displacement not just of residents but also of social problems and their costs—for example, crime, unemployment, or inadequate municipal infrastructure—into concentrated areas (1996, 162). The displacement about which compositionists must be cautious operates in at least two ways. One is that in our efforts to document "indigenous" public literacy efforts (as well as participate in them or import them into the classroom), we might displace and even pathologize those struggling with illiteracy, functional illiteracy, communication problems related to second-language difficulties, and so on. If only the most resourceful, efficacious examples of public literacy capture the attention of academics, then it is quite possible that the human and material resources needed to teach basic literacy skills will be diverted from academic locations and concentrated instead among community literacy programs, prisons, churches, and other settings that serve large populations of English as Second Language (ESL), General Education Development (GED), and educationally disadvantaged learners. A second kind of displacement could happen in the academy itself. If compositionists increasingly focus on public rather than academic literacies, then the responsibility for teaching the conventions of academic writing are likely to be displaced onto poorly prepared (and probably resentful) faculty in other disciplines. Such practices may "authenticate" a higher profile for composition, but at what cost? As Bahri and Petraglia argue, *no* curricular space might be preferable to one that "effectively *dis*places the desiderata of rhetoric education by ostensibly consolidating it" (2003, 3).

Fortunately, examples of self-reflective academic engagement with public literacy are beginning to emerge, and I would like to highlight two of them here. The first is Derek Owens's *Composition and Sustainability: Teaching for a Threatened Generation*, which attempts to show how writing instructors can take advantage of the "cross-disciplinary flexibility" of composition to assist students in "draw[ing] connections between their needs, their desires, their neighborhoods, their majors, and their future careers" (2001, xiv). Owens actively engages himself and his students in considerations of place and location, including the seemingly detached "landscape of published academic discourse" (37). More significant for my purposes here, though, is Owens's unusual (and on-the-record) decision to put his money where his mouth is—that is, to enact a reciprocal relationship with his students by pledging "all royalties I receive for this manuscript . . . to community revitalization projects and third-sector organizations in their neighborhoods" (vi). A second example is represented by the Winter 2004 issue of *Reflections: A Journal of Writing, Service Learning, and Community Literacy*, a special issue entitled "Prison Literacies, Narratives, and Community Connections," guest coedited by Tobi Jacobi and Patricia E. O'Conner. The issue features the work of incarcerated writers alongside the theoretical and pedagogical essays of writing teachers working in that setting. Notably, the inmates' writing is not exoticized in any of the familiar ways: salacious biographical details, marginalization from the work of "real" authors and intellectuals, and the like. Instead, as Jacobi explains, the texts are "organized according to theme and paired in complementary ways that allow each piece to illustrate the relationship between academic theorizing and insider lived experience," an arrangement that allows readers to approach the text(s) in a linear or nonlinear fashion (2004, 10). These examples represent accepted forms of academic capital, but they also demonstrate how traditional forms of academic success are compatible with our ethical obligations toward the constituencies we purport to represent through our work.

But because such innovations likely indicate an incipient self-consciousness about the ethical consequences of our academic engagements with public literacy, perhaps the time is right for compositionists to begin challenging those traditional forms of academic success rather than simply accommodating them. One step in this direction might be to draft an "intellectual work" document that articulates how we might work in and with the public in ways that are academically rigorous but that minimize exploitation and displacement (whether unintentional or merely rationalized) and maximize reciprocity. Among other things, such a document could contribute to a reconceptualization of academic reward systems that is based on the interrelatedness of teaching, research, and service in outreach projects and other public literacy work. A model for this kind of document is "Evaluating the Intellectual Work of Writing Administration," published in 1998 by the Council of Writing Program Administrators (CWPA) as a means of refiguring program administration as knowledge-generating labor that "derives from and is reinforced by scholarly knowledge and disciplinary understanding" but that "neither derives from nor produces simplistic products or services" (92). The document proposes five categories of intellectual work, four evaluative criteria, and a general framework for implementing their acceptance within English departments; in doing so it simultaneously recognizes and contests the traditional paradigm of intellectual work as academic publishing.

A comparable document for public literacy would likely serve at least two purposes. First, it could function as a kind of ethical blueprint, establishing guidelines designed to assist public literacy scholars and public intellectuals in making appropriate decisions about their work and its dissemination. For example, such guidelines might include statements regarding the importance of collaboration and reciprocity among disciplinary experts and nonexperts as they define and address community problems. Second, an intellectual work document for public literacy could propose an evaluative model that accounts for "the ways that specialized knowledge enters into all roles that the rhetoric educator can undertake when becoming a public intellectual engaged in outreach" (Cushman 2003, 185). The CWPA document was drafted and revised collaboratively over several years by the WPA Executive Committee; the drafting of a public-literacy-as-intellectual-work document might be initiated by the Service Learning and Community Literacy Special Interest Group that has formed under the auspices of the Conference of College Composition and Communication (CCCC).

Until such measures are formalized, however, the questions remain: What should we do about the public? Should we simply ignore those people and worlds that are separate from, if continuous with, our classroom spaces? Should we limit ourselves to the "academic public spheres" of classrooms, conferences, publications, and governance? It would be foolish, of course, to try to draw such rigid boundaries. Instead, I propose that we ask ourselves different questions as we engage in research and teaching related to public discourse. For example, does our work represent public discourse, public spheres, and public writers in pat, one-dimensional ways? If so, then we might be domesticating our subjects, glossing over their complexities in order to document them more easily. Does our work challenge or disrupt the academic system of publishing to circulate cultural capital? If not, then our desire for professional acknowledgment and material reward may be leading us to exploit our subjects. These questions are modest, I acknowledge, for ultimately our concerns must be ethical ones: candidly stated, we must regard our adventures in public discourse less as fodder for our scholarship, or performances of our expertise, or quests for representativeness than as the simple—though, of course, not so [illegible] exercise of citizenship.

Works Cited

Ahmad, Aijaz. 1992. *In Theory: Classes, Nations, Literatures.* London: Verso.

Bahri, Deepika, and Joseph Petraglia. 2003. "Traveling among the Realms: A Tale of Big Rhetoric and Growing Ambitions." In *The Realms of Rhetoric: The Prospects for Rhetoric Education,* ed. Joseph Petraglia and Deepika Bahri, 1–10. Albany: State University of New York Press.

Bauer, Dale M. 1998. "Indecent Proposals: Teachers in the Movies." *College English* 60, no. 3 (March): 301–17.

Council of Writing Program Administrators. 1998. "Evaluating the Intellectual Work of Writing Administration." *WPA* 22, nos. 1 and 2 (Fall/Winter): 85–104.

Crosby, Christina. 2003. "Writer's Block, Merit, and the Market: Working in the University of Excellence." *College English* 65, no. 6 (July): 626–45.

Crowley, Sharon. 1998. *Composition in the University: Historical and Polemical Essays.* Pittsburgh: University of Pittsburgh Press.

Cushman, Ellen. 1996. "The Rhetorician as an Agent of Social Change." *College Composition and Communication* 47, no. 1 (February): 7–28.

———. 2003. "Beyond Specialization: The Public Intellectual, Outreach, and Rhetoric Education." In *The Realms of Rhetoric: The Prospects for Rhetoric Education,* ed. Joseph Petraglia and Deepika Bahri, 171–85. Albany: State University of New York Press.

Durst, Russell. 1999. *Collision Course: Conflict, Negotiation, and Learning in College Composition.* Urbana, IL: NCTE.

Ervin, Elizabeth. 1997. "Encouraging Civic Participation among First-Year Writing Students; or, Why Composition Class Should Be More Like a Bowling Team." *Rhetoric Review* 15, no. 2 (Spring): 382–99.

———. 1999. "Academics and the Negotiation of Local Knowledge." *College English* 61, no. 4 (March): 448–70.

Fish, Stanley. 1989. "Anti-Foundationalism, Theory Hope, and the Teaching of Composition." In *Doing What Comes Naturally: Change, Rhetoric, and the Practice of Theory in Literary and Legal Studies,* 342–55. Durham: Duke University Press.

Fitts, Karen, and Alan France, eds. 1995. *Left Margins: Cultural Studies and Composition Pedagogy.* Albany: State University of New York Press.

Halloran, Michael. 1982. "Rhetoric in the American College Curriculum: The Decline of Public Discourse." *PRE/TEXT* 3: 245–69.

Harding, Sandra. 1991. *Whose Science? Whose Knowledge? Thinking from Women's Lives.* Ithaca, NY: Cornell University Press.

Harris, Joseph. 1996. "Research, Teaching, Public Argument." *College Composition and Communication* 47, no. 3 (October): 323–34.

———. 1997. *A Teaching Subject: Composition since 1966.* Upper Saddle River, NJ: Prentice Hall.

Horner, Bruce. 2000. *Terms of Work for Composition: A Materialist Critique.* Albany: State University of New York Press.

Huggan, Graham. 2001. *The Postcolonial Exotic: Marketing the Margins.* London: Routledge.

Jacobi, Tobi. 2004. "Foreword: 'I'm just gonna let you know how it is': Situating Writing and Literacy Education in Prison." *Reflections: A Journal of Writing, Service Learning, and Community Literacy* 4, no. 1 (Winter): 1–11.

Jacobi, Tobi, and Patricia E. O'Connor, eds. 2004. "Prison Literacies, Narratives, and Community Connections." Special issue, *Reflections: A Journal of Writing, Service Learning, and Community Literacy* 4, no. 1 (Winter).

Kaufer, David S. 2004. "The Influence of Expanded Access to Mass Communication of Public Expression: The Rise of Representatives of the Personal." In *The Private, the Public, and the Published: Reconciling Private Lives and Public Rhetoric,* ed. Barbara Couture and Thomas Kent, 153–63. Logan: Utah State University Press.

Mills, Caroline. 1993. "Myths and Meanings of Gentrification." In *Place/Culture/Representation,* ed. James Duncan and David Ley, 149–70. New York: Routledge.

O'Dair, Sharon. 2003. "Class Work: Site of Egalitarian Activism or Site of Embourgeoisement?" *College English* 65, no. 6 (July): 593–606.

Olson, Gary A. 2002. "Foreword: Public Discourse and the Future of Composition Pedagogy." In *Moving Beyond Academic Discourse: Composition Studies and the Public Sphere,* by Christian R. Weisser, ix–x. Carbondale: Southern Illinois University Press.

Owens, Derek. 2001. *Composition and Sustainability: Teaching for a Threatened Generation.* Urbana, IL: NCTE.

Polan, Dana. 1996. "The Professors of History." In *The Persistence of History,* ed. Vivian Sobchack, 235–56. New York: Routledge.

Schell, Eileen E. 1998. *Gypsy Academics and Mother-Teachers: Gender, Contingent Labor, and Writing Instruction.* Portsmouth, NH: Boynton/Cook.

Schell, Eileen E., and Patricia Lambert Stock, eds. 2000. *Moving a Mountain: Transforming the Role of Contingent Faculty in Composition Studies and Higher Education.* Urbana, IL: NCTE.

Schiappa, Edward. 1995. "Intellectuals and the Place of Cultural Critique." In *Rhetoric, Cultural Studies, and Literacy,* 21–27. Hillsdale, NJ: Lawrence Erlbaum.

Shepard, Alan, John McMillan, and Gary Tate, eds. 1998. *Coming to Class: Pedagogy and the Social Class of Teachers.* Portsmouth, NH: Boynton/Cook.

Slater, Tom. 2003. "What Is Gentrification?" Gentrification Web. April. http://members.lycos.co.uk/gentrification/whatisgent.html (accessed August 5, 2004).

Sullivan, Patricia A. 1998. "Passing: A Family Dissemblance." In *Coming to Class: Pedagogy and the Social Class of Teachers,* ed. Alan Shepard, John McMillan, and Gary Tate, 231–51. Portsmouth, NH: Boynton/Cook.

Vandenberg, Peter. 1999. "Taming Multiculturalism: The Will to Literacy in Composition Studies." *JAC* 19, no. 4: 547–68.

Weisser, Christian R. 2002. *Moving Beyond Academic Discourse: Composition Studies and the Public Sphere.* Carbondale: Southern Illinois University Press.

Wells, Susan. 1996. "Rogue Cops and Health Care: What Do We Want from Public Writing?" *College Composition and Communication* 47, no. 3 (October): 325–41.

Wilson, Frank Harold. 1996. "Urban Redevelopment and the Post-Industrial City: The Persistence of Gentrification in Central Cities, 1980–1990." In *Demographic and Structural Change: The Effects of the 1980s on American Society,* ed. Dennis L. Peck and J. Selwyn Hollingsworth, 142–68. Westport, CT: Greenwood.

3

In Visible Texts

Memory, MOOs, and Momentum: *A Meditatio*

CYNTHIA HAYNES

> Writing is a physical effort, this is not said often enough. One runs the race with the horse that is to say with the thinking in its production. It is not an expressed, mathematical thinking, it's a trail of images. And after all, writing is only the scribe who comes after, and who has an interest in going as fast as possible. To go fast . . . we must vie in force and intelligence with a force that is stronger than ourselves.
>
> —Hélène Cixous

There is something primitive (intuitive) about the way words appear. Conversely, there is something frightening (exhausting) about the way they dis/appear—scrolling upward with alarming speed, with the momentum of history, at the behest of time. In between, we inhabit the scroll bars, the space where movement and moment embrace. We witness language in action, in the languid flow of thought, the lurch of long-winded fragments, and the staccato bursts of out/landish play. We bid farewell to words with each keystroke. Imbuing them with invisible protection, we whisper, "[M]ay the force be with you." We watch as they dwindle and fade from view, dim and distant in the cathode rays of our fluorescent memory. We *imagine* them on their way—they travel as *image.*

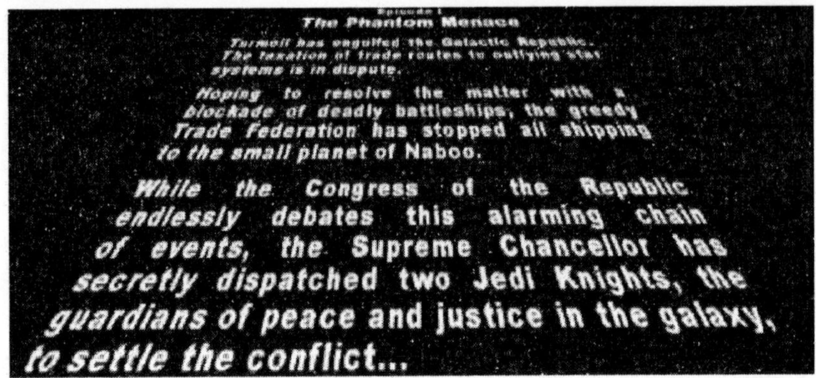

Fig. 3.1. *Star Wars: Episode 1, The Phantom Menace*© Opening Text Crawl

Who can forget the opening scene of *Star Wars*, the text marching into the infinite universe of the Galactic Republic. This filmic device tapped into our cultural experiences of movable type, such as ticker-tape, cinema marquees, and vintage newsreel footage. It joined forces with a simple premise—moving text transforms thought into image and image into memory. It is perhaps uncharacteristic to claim that moving words stay with us longer. But I am interested in the uncharacter that undoes static print—that imagines us caught in a thicket of the thickest thieves: language and motion.

There is, however, a crucial caveat, or noise, in this system: the material action of writing sets language into motion, whether by programming or raw physicality. Composition happens, to riff on Geoffrey Sirc and Jacques Derrida (cf. Sirc's 2002 and Derrida's claim that *deconstruction happens* in Olson 1990, 12). And, as it happens, language speaks us and re-members us at the same time (in the same moment). By some accounts, a focus on writing and motion must start by studying the *parts* of writing we *see*, such as letters and words, that is, printed static texts. John Trimbur argues that "studying and teaching typography as the culturally salient means of producing writing can help locate composers in the labor process and thereby contribute to the larger post-process work of rematerializing literacy" (2002, 192). As "the turn-of-the-century Austrian architect and graphic designer Alfred Loos put it so concisely, 'One cannot *speak* a capital letter'" (Trimber 2002, 191; italics in original). But Trimbur is narrowly focused on the typographical conventions that "[enable] us to *see* writing in material terms as letter-forms, printed pages, posters, computer screens" (192; italics in original), while I am adjusting the focus to capture the images of writing in motion and the momentum that accrues in the backwash of memory. I am further/more interested in the MOO (Multiuser Domain, Object-Oriented) as a primary location of *writing as images in motion.* In other words, the appearance and disappearance of language inside a screen, the limits of which are beyond our vision, turn the scroll bar into a memory pole where words unfurl in the prevailing and transient winds of writing's warp-speed momentum. *Typo*graphy becomes *bio*graphy—the life-world of writing on the fly.

Taking on the notion of typography as (mere) rematerialized literacy (Trimbur), the mixed media-artist Gicheol Lee issues a manifesto that turns materiality into e-*labor*ate labor: "Typorganism is a series of Communication experiments exploring computational interaction design and interactive kinetic typography based on the metaphorical notion of typography. 'Type is a Lifeform,' which lives on the net, responds to user's stimulus, evolves through time, has intelligence powered by computational algorithm. So, this is the showcase for the manifesto: Type is an Organism" (2005, n.p.).

And, I would add, if type is an organism, typorganisms have memories. One such lived space where typorganisms regularly meet is a MOO. Research in Computer-Assisted Language Learning (CALL) flirts with this idea but does not go so far as to assimilate it into its discourse.[1] The closest it comes is when Catherine Doughty and Michael Long lay out the optimal features necessary for language learning in online contexts. Among the methodological principles key to their theory, "elaborate input" ranks highly. Elaborate input is a function of *task-based learning* (versus text-based learning). According to Doughty and Long, "Building lessons around texts (as in most content-based language teaching) means studying language as object, not learning language as a living entity through using it and experiencing its use during task completion" (2003, 56). In other words, "[t]here is a world of difference, for instance, between learning to make a particular kind of social, business, or emergency medical telephone call through acting one out, as in a role play and/or making a real one to given specifications, on the one hand, and on the other, in a text-based program of some kind, listening to or reading a 'dead' script of someone else's effort" (56). The problem of reading a "dead script" is, like committing language to memory versus writing, nowhere more explicitly exposed than in the Platonic dialogue *Phaedrus.* Indeed, this dialogue has long been at the heart of a historical conflict between philosophy and rhetoric. If you recall, Socrates has been lured outside the city to hear Phaedrus recite a speech by Lysias that he has memorized, although Phaedrus holds the written copy hidden beneath his robes. Socrates wishes to hear the speech, but when Phaedrus protests that he cannot recite the speech from memory, Socrates insinuates that, knowing Phaedrus, Phaedrus has taken the speech "and pored over the parts he liked best. He sat reading all morning long, and when he got tired, he went for a walk, having learned—I am quite sure—the whole speech by heart" (*Phaedrus* 228a–b in Plato 1995, 3). In the original Greek text, the last phrase is *exepistamenos ton logon,* meaning "to know thoroughly, to know well" (Plato 2005). It is clear that Socrates privileges this form of learning over written forms.

In contradistinction to this Platonic understanding of writing as "dead," language should be conceived as a living entity (comprised of typorganisms). As such, it requires us to teach writing as *e-laboration.* Doughty and Long explain: "*Elaboration* is the term given to the myriad ways NSs [native speakers] modify discourse (i.e., in language use for non-native speakers [NNSs] to make meaning comprehensible, as revealed by studies of foreigner talk discourse). Most of the modifications occur during negotiation for meaning (i.e., when NS and NNS are focused on achieving communication while working cooperatively on a task)" (2003, 59). When students elaborate on previous written discourse in the MOO, whether their own or another conversant, such elaborations provide additional meaning-making images of text, as well as the supplemental benefit of such input emerging as "elaborate input"—input that is extravagant, detailed, and composed of multiple elements.

The MOO, as locus and instrument of linguistic register and recollection, circum/scribes this composite image of writing and memory. Bruce Gronbeck reminds us that Aristotle makes a clear distinction between memory and recollection and tallies the attributes of recollection in his treatise *De memoria*: "Recalling is always a matter of reconstructing 'movement' or sequences of action" (451b–453a, in McKeon 1941, 140). For Aristotle, memory stems from recollection *as such*: "For remembering [which is the *condicio sine qua non* of recollecting] is the existence, potentially, in the mind of a movement capable of stimulating it to the desired movement, and this, as has been said, in such a way that the person should be moved [prompted to recollection] from within himself, i.e. in consequence of movements wholly contained within himself" (452a, in McKeon 140).

Thus, from an early time our knowledge of how memory works is derived from Aristotle's notion of motion *contained.* In her essay "Habit as Memory Incarnate," Marion Joan Francoz explains the containment model, the hydraulic model, and the physiological models of memory, advocating the latter and its association with habit. According to Francoz, "'Image schemata,' which Lakoff and Johnson propose as dynamic alternatives to abstract schematic representations in memory, find their most basic manifestation in the spatial aspect of the body, 'from our experience of physical containment' (Johnson, *Body* 21)" (Francoz 1999, 14).

But the movement I have in mind must also be a movement that is enduring, that gains momentum from the start, that keeps going. Viewed in this way, writing becomes a force, as Cixous writes, with which we contend and by which we leave our own trail of images. The trajectory of this essay directs us (generally) toward how this force forges a relation between writing *as* image and (specifically) learning in educational MOOs.

Memory

The Chilean artist Robert Matta wrote that "the eye as the agent of memory is a means to simplify." The story goes that in 1938 at the Les Deux Magots café in Paris, Matta was asked to explain his phrase "psychological morphology," whereupon he spoke "with large gestures and using the objects which were at hand, in front of an impassive [André] Breton who declared not to have understood anything of it. He asked Matta to write down his theories. This was difficult for Matta, not due to the fact that he did not have ideas enough, but because it was causing him to lose his momentum. But he succeeded in producing this text" (introduction to Matta 2005, n.p.). In the text, Matta says, "In the area of consciousness, a morphological psychology would be the diagram of ideas. It should be conceived before optical images may give us the form of ideas if we want to stay in the transforming medium. The optical image is only a theoretical section within the morphological fall of the object. The image is retained to calm the anxiety" (Matta 2005, n.p.).

While early explanations of how memory works were derived from Aristotle's containment model, and later on invention and inner dialogues, in time other memory systems emerged, such as the "memory palace" conceived by a sixteenth-century Jesuit, Matteo Ricci, who "recreated the medieval European idea of a memory palace—an edifice you build in your mind and furnish with mnemonic devices. . . . by walking through the rooms and associating information with their contents" (Lienhard 2005, n.p.).[2]

Ideal as an allegory for the building of MOOs, wherein virtual space is rendered in architectural metaphors, a MOO as "memory palace" certainly contains "distinct and dramatic" contents, and all crafted in language (both textual and visual). The MOO is a blend of text and image, and of orality and literacy. It is oral insofar as the interaction among writers/speakers in the MOO reproduces oral conversation via written text, and literate insofar as the writing requires fluency to produce meaning. The interesting, and innovative, aspect of this phenomenon is that in the MOO the tightening (and blurring) the orality/literacy split is achieved visually. In other words, *ars graphē* may have more influence upon *how* we learn than we might otherwise believe.

At Lingua MOO, for example, we combine the textual and graphical registers of meaning production with one window that splits the text side and the graphical side. Rhetorically, the design allows for style to enhance input and for an intertextual-graphical interface to border the space in which learning takes place. The web-based interface also makes many MOO functions easier to learn and execute. But the fact that graphical MOO interfaces such as enCore Xpress (on which Lingua MOO is built) have helped move MOO technology along at a pace in concert with other web-based communication software is not central to the idea I am promoting of *text as image*; we could consider it merely a bonus.[3]

If we extend Matta's explanation a step further, a MOO language *as* image is retained to "calm the anxiety," which evokes emotional registers as well. When we *see* text produced in *real time*, something different happens that triggers several registers of learning. Add to that equation the presence of interactive agents of language, that is, other *languaging* beings, and writing is transformed into learning in *deep time*, inscribed in *deep memory*. This may be explained by another of Doughty and Long's principles, "promoting learning by doing." They argue that the best methods for learning combine memory *and* doing, and suggest that "[a]ctually *doing* a task, or initially a simple version thereof, is more relevant, comprehensible, and memorable than reading about someone else doing it. . . . The basic idea is that a learner on his or her own can gain experience in a simulated environment under conditions of reduced stress and without real consequences to their actions" (Doughty and Long 2003, 58). It is interesting to note that this simple principle was also at the heart of the struggle between the rhetoricians and philosophers. According to George Kennedy, philosophers like Socrates and Aristotle complained that the Sophists (early rhetoricians) used a merely pragmatic method of teaching students to deliver speeches, and this method "consisted only of furnishing speeches to be memorized by students, much as one tried to teach shoemaking by giving the student a collection of shoes" (1980, 28). Philosophy, they would argue, teaches by instilling language and truth into the deeper memory of the soul. In other words, we must "go through" (*dialogos* through words) the heart. Aside from their narrow and derogatory views of rhetoric, against which I do not have the space to argue, our discussion of memory and MOOs benefits from *both* the rhetorical practice of "doing" (*delivery*) as well as the philosophical understanding of the inmost dwelling place of knowledge and the role of language as the means of taking up residence in the heart.

More contemporary rhetorical theories have forged new alliances among writing, memory, and the heart; and technologies like MOO provide a single environment in which such theories may be tested. A prime example on which to test this claim is the predominant perception that MOO discourse is merely "chat," and that "chat" is unproductive discourse. But since MOO discourse is conducted entirely in writing, it is necessary to further advance the claim that writing and memory conspire to conduct meaning across the barriers between different languages through the process of rhetorical invention. For example, writers must rely on memory to construct and reconstruct meanings for notes they take while reading (*active*, versus passive, reading), and they must rely on memory to make connections among ideas, and to attend to such things as usage, grammar, and spelling. Then they re-*collect*. In Roman times, recollection was called *meditatio*. Properly speaking, *meditatio* (meditation) involved listening to one's own composing—a kind of inner dialogue. As Ovid's Leander writes, "[H]aving spoken in such words to myself in a low murmur, the rest my right hand talked through with the parchment" (qtd. in Carruthers 1995, 202). In other words, memory is a dynamic process that involves gathering, listening, and dialogue; and learning is "a process of composition, collation, and recollection" (Carruthers 1995, 203). In later times, what Augustine understood as *cogitatio* is the act of bringing memory images together to create "new" knowledge; but knowledge alone is not enough. He says in one sermon, "I know but do not understand" (qtd. in Carruthers 1995, 203). Thus, "[k]nowledge extends understanding not by adding more and more pieces, but because as we compose, our design becomes more capacious, it dilates" (Carruthers 1995, 203).

Such dynamic processes (gathering, listening, and dialogue) are still a vital part of learning, and are manifested in MOO activities and tools. Students may use the MOO as a combination workspace, research lab, classroom, or private office, and they may create and utilize a variety of virtual tools such as note objects (that may be encrypted while in draft form), recitable notes (that allow users to "recite" something by prompting a scrolling version of the text set at three-second delay for each line), note boards (for communal posting of notes, assignments, project storyboard items), recorders (for logging MOO conversations), MOO Web projectors (for displaying a Web page to all users in their MOO graphical window), MOO text slide projectors (for displaying chunks of text on the "talk" side of the MOO window), and so forth. In other words, in the MOO we stay in/on the path of language. As E. M. Forster once wrote, "How do I know what I think, until I see what I say?" Composition *as* image calls for us to suspend our conventional means of connecting the dots, of interpreting mere morphemic syntaxes. It means for us to make meaning out of other phenomena, imagined for us in other media, such as educational MOOs. Pierre Petiot, who translated Matta's essay, further articulates the confluence of memory and language, adding now the computer:

> Although they all have their roots in language, since they are essentially built to fulfill again and again a prediction, never has a machine been so clearly made of language than the computer. Never has a machine been so openly granted the divine power of oracles—at which practitioners of circuitry or program burst of laughter, or irritation or just sadness, as they know what the heart of things is actually made of. . . . And computers also have thrown a new sort of space under our feet. An intermediate space, neither real nor unreal, woven with metaphors and hypothesis of images and computation. A space where possibilities, compatibilities and consistencies are at stake. And as soon as dream and automatism filter in this space, they root there and find their anchors, they melt with it and they provide proof and evidence of themselves. There collapses and vanishes the false dichotomy between reality and thought. (Petiot, in Matta 2005, n.p.)

The upshot of this excursus on Matta suggests that if we reconceive *how* memory functions in composition, we may begin to understand how teletechnologies like MOOs serve as important locations of composition where we may re/invent composition instruction by producing composing spaces that fulfill the promise of memory *in visible texts*—writing with the *force*, so to *speak*.

MOOs

> If one could x-ray-photo-eco-graph a time, an encounter between two people of whatever sex they might be, by some extraordinary means; and if one could conserve the radiation of this encounter in a transparent sphere, and then listen to what is produced in addition to the exchange identifiable in the dialogue—this is what writing tries to do: to keep the record of these invisible events—one would hear the rumor of a great number of messages that are expressed in other ways.
>
> —Hélène Cixous

Eleven years ago I met my husband, Jan Rune Holmevik, in a MOO. It was in spring 1994, on the cusp (*spinode*) of the Internet's infancy. We were half a world apart, jacked into some in/visible, cuspidate electronic arc between Norway and Texas. We came to know one another in language. "Words are the way, I want to say," writes Michael Joyce (2001, 314). Yet it is difficult, if not improper, to write about the way the MOO spawned our relationship. It was both a "home" we could share and one we built for others to enter and build as they saw fit. We were living/writing in a *visible* text. The question of writing became a manifestation of personal and professional discourses, the crossing of which became for us an invisible boundary—we did not distinguish between the space of our longing and the space of our belonging in an academic world. Call it fate. Call it serendipity. It called us into being.

Yet, in citing my own experience I am somewhat torn. On the one hand, I believe the durability of our virtual experience seals the sagacity of my argument (not to mention the *reality* of our lives, which is hardly virtual any longer, though we tend not to make that distinction). On the other hand, the rhetorician in me understands the need for a critical eye. Roland Barthes expressed it in this manner: "[M]y desire to write on Photography corresponded to a discomfort I had always suffered from: the uneasiness of being a subject torn between two languages, one expressive, the other critical; and at the heart of this critical language, between several discourses, those of sociology, of semiology, and of psychoanalysis . . ." (1981, 8). This is how I approach writing about writing in MOOs; like Barthes, I am both "Operator" and "Spectator" (9). "The Photograph belongs to that class of laminated objects whose two leaves cannot be separated without destroying them both: the windowpane and the landscape, and why not: Good and Evil, desire and its object: dualities we can conceive but not perceive" (6).

Barthes is instructive in an additional sense—as purveyor of the line between forms of visibility. I debated whether to display a MOO transcript of conversation and decided against it. I cannot de/pict the motion of text I am de/scribing here in this static form called *print*. Even a "still" image (i.e., screenshot) of some MOO tran/script cannot do justice to the movement experienced as *graphē/flux* (the flux of moving writing). But we can work with the concept of the photo/graph as theorized by Barthes, because he reanimates it in order to ponder our pandemic belief in the invisibility of its animation of *us*. "Whatever it grants to vision and whatever its manner, a photograph is always invisible: it is not it that we see" (6). "In this glum desert, suddenly a specific photograph reaches me; it animates me, and I animate it. So that is how I must name the attraction which makes it exist: an *animation*. The photograph itself is in no way animated (I do not believe in 'lifelike' photographs), but it animates me: this is what creates every adventure" (20; italics in original).

There is, then, something that wants animating, that reveals itself when time and motion call certain features of text into the unconcealedness of typorganisms—of writing on the move. Barthes meets Martin Heidegger at this juncture, redefining the "origin of the *work* of art," following the workness until we can see it *at* work. What Heidegger saw in a pair of worn-out peasant shoes, Barthes sees in the instruments of time and photography: "For me the noise of Time is not sad: I love bells, clocks, watches—and I recall that at first the photographic implements were related to techniques of cabinetmaking and the machinery of precision: cameras, in short, were clocks for seeing, and perhaps in me someone very old still hears in the photographic mechanism the living sound of the wood" (1981, 15). Our questions come into view now. Are MOOs clocks for *seeing* writing? What happens in the *seeing* of composition *as it happens*?

Momentum

> In the eyes of our critics the ozone hole above our heads, the moral law in our hearts, the autonomous text, may each be of interest, but only separately. That a delicate shuttle should have woven together the heavens, industry, texts, souls and moral law—this remains uncanny, unthinkable, unseemly.
>
> —Bruno Latour

It is time—time to move *into* a new topos where momentum gathers itself *unto* itself, where (it turns out) moments are re-turned to time.

Who were we to think we owned them in the first place? We are so bound up in our sense of sovereign subjectivity (more unseemly than the "delicate shuttle" by far) that we dare to preface topos with its own "u"—unbounded topos—*utopia*. But in so doing, we have managed to create every dystopia known to humanity. The MOO is, thankfully, no utopia; it is more along the lines of what Alok Nandi calls a *fluxtopia*. According to Nandi, "Virtu/RE/alities explore the gap between virtuals, ideals and realities. Fluxtopia can only be understood in the act of attempting to achieve the traject of any flow. But how do we achieve what we mean by it if we do not know what it is, except that IT is in constant mutation, flowing apart?" (2005, n.p.). Nandi exploits our collective delusion that we can capture the flow of media by setting up various fluxtopic passages designed to foreground both delusion and passage. The MOO is a portal into this "fluxography"; or, as Geoff Sirc might call it, this "fluxus-inflected practice" (2000a, 3). The key to understanding how momentum assists memory rests not on the rests, or pauses, we inject into writing and reading, but rather in the in/visible border between delusion and passage, one that is (hopefully) not subject to Aristotelian or Platonic border patrols. In synchronous writing environments we are lulled, by the momentum of language, into no complacent region of learning, but rather an active accumulation of meaning we commonly think of as memory. The movement of language, its marching momentum, lulls us into thinking we are pushing things along, when it is more accurate to say we are being pulled into a remembering machine without being aware of it. The question is how momentum and language do this. To underscore how writing in a MOO accomplishes this lulling, we should sample the most basic qualities of flux: *rhetoric, rhythm,* and *reciprocity*.

As a rhetorical machine, the MOO mixes language, writers, and distance, then reconfigures them as *sustained contextual real-time interactivity*. But distance *itself* also figures *within* language. Barthes suggests, as have others over the years, that all language is rhetorical—that is, it is highly *figurative*. There are countless ways we attempt to maintain the distinction between two dimensions of language, the literal and figurative; but in the end, language is all figurative (1988, 82–93). In short, Barthes argues, "the meta-rhetorical expressions which attest to this belief are countless. . . . Aristotle sees in it a taste for alienation: one must 'distance oneself from ordinary locutions . . . : we feel in this respect the same impressions as in the presence of strangers or foreigners: style is to be given a foreign air, for what comes from far away excites admiration'" (88). There is, then, in language itself a dimension of distance, a sense in which words travel across time and distance in order to "mean" something in the here and now. Words exhibit the wear and tear of distance and time, and no amount of antirhetorical rhetoric can undermine this fact. But critics like Paul Virilio misdirect their fears at teletechnologies (like MOOs) in an effort to restore to language (and thus to ourselves) a degree of nearness and sovereignty that seems to have slipped away (when it was never ours to begin with). As Virilio argues, "Between the subjective and objective it seems we have no room for the 'trajective,' that being of movement from here to there, from one to the other, without which we will never achieve a profound understanding of the various regimes of perception of the world that have succeeded each other throughout the ages" (1997, 24). In short, he laments the "loss of the traveller's tale" (25); he longs for the "essence of the path, the journey" (23).

Whereas Nandi's fluxtopia situates the *trajective* within the *work* (i.e., the act) of writing, Virilio situates it in the *achievement* of writing—the *having traveled* along a path. This is precisely the tension at work in the difference between print and electronic texts, something I think Richard Lanham missed in *The Electronic Word*, but not something Joyce missed. In attempting to articulate the pulse of Carolyn Guyer's phrase "tensional momentum," Joyce finds evidence of a missing *rhythm*—a rhythm not present, literally, in print texts. But he is torn, too. "And yet I know, in the way someone watches water slip through sand, that words are being displaced by image in those places where we spend our time online; know as well that images, especially moving ones, have long had their own syntax of the preliminary and the inevitable" (Joyce 2001, 314).

Writing in *visible* texts, like sand and water, flows at a rhythmic (ragged or silken) pace. In the exchange of languaging beings typing along this tempo-trajectory, reciprocity rises up out of the water like Debussy's *Engulfed Cathedral*.[4] The music builds, the waters part, the cathedral rises up with the crescendo caused by the crescent moon, her tides obeying her written wound. It is woven by the "delicate shuttle" of an/*other* interaction—*sustained contextual real-time reciprocal interactivity*. Reciprocal interaction[5] partakes of a fluidity of movement related to (and determined by) tides and time. The backward (*re-*) and forward (*-pro*) movement of the tides, the ebbing and flowing of *Oceanus* in Homer's *Iliad*, lends its sense of fluid and cyclic language to real-time reciprocity. It is constant, continuing without intermission, steadily present, the constancy of real time. Another way to think of it is articulated in Lanham's antidote to the *bistable illusion* of the fixity of language, what he terms "perpetual oscillation" (1993, 161). Because we have based our notions of a stable self on the fixity of language (82), Lanham claims that digital texts foreground how we have deluded ourselves and require that we reactivate what has been active (though hidden) all along, the necessary oscillation between the rhetorical and philosophical consciousness characteristic of the Western literary tradition. By connecting Lanham's oscillation to reciprocity, I am after a sustained and durable notion of how momentum cradles us as we rock back and forth between event and language, beneath the rhythm of the moon and the tidal flow of writing—always, and already, a reciprocity in which we participate with some Other rhythm not of our making.

Joyce, in connecting time, tides, and MOO, puts it best: "Against the commonly cited momentariness of MOO experience and the evanescence of the selves that form within it, there stands the rhythm of recurrence on unknown screens elsewhere; the persistence of certain 'objects' that, like the consumerist flotsam of temporal existence (a brown bottle or a sailboat), mark the swell and surge of lives lived in body, space and time; and the mark of the momentary itself, meaning with meaningfulness not against meaningless" (2001, 314–15). Writing resists slowing down; it has its own force of forward movement. In the MOO this momentum rushes ahead of us, and it settles into a steady (and calming) lullaby of language. We are lulled into learning, rapt into remembering, and scrolled into seeing (and being) so much more than some fragile con/textual existence. We are engulfed by/in visible texts and set in motion by our words—in their current—on their way.

Notes

This essay appears in Cynthia Haynes, *Beta Rhetoric: Writing, Technology, and Deconstruction* (forthcoming from SUNY Press) and is reprinted here with the permission of SUNY Press.

1. For an extended discussion of the connections between memory and MOOs, see Haynes 2005, my essay on MOOs and computer-assisted language learning.
2. For a thorough and fascinating study of the relation between memory and visual and verbal literacies, see Hobbs 2004.
3. The tug of "visual rhetoric" turf would take us outside the parameters of this chapter, and there are ample venues for the explosion of visual rhetoric scholarship in composition theory. For an excellent collection of essays on visual rhetoric, see Handa 2004.
4. The story upon which Debussy's Prelude #10, *La cathedrale engloutie* (The Engulfed Cathedral) is based is an old legend from fifth-century Brittany. To punish the people for their sins, the Cathedral of Ys is engulfed by the sea. Each sunrise the townspeople watch as

the sunken cathedral rises from the water and then sinks slowly into the ocean. The city of Paris takes its name from the town of Ys. For an extended version of the oral legend, as well as an audio of the piano piece itself, see http://www.e-earthborn.com/gallery/photoshop/e_pages/ys.html (accessed June 5, 2005).

5. Tandem language learning uses, among other things, specific principles that the MOO is ideal for enacting. In tandem language learning, two native speakers are paired to interact in their target languages in the MOO, each learning the other's language. As one of the three main principles of "tandem language learning," *learner reciprocity* is considered crucial to the process. According to Klaus Schwienhorst, the principle of reciprocity means that "[e]ach student must benefit equally from the partnership, and can expect to receive as much help as s/he gives. Each student depends on contributions from both students to make the partnership successful" (1997, n.p.). Markus Kötter cites T. Lewis on the subject: "[E]ach partner should benefit equally from the exchange. At its most basic, this can mean simply that an equal amount of time is spent working in each language. On a more sophisticated level, however, it means that learning objectives, and the means of achieving them, are negotiated between partners, so that each feels (s)he is deriving full benefit from the partnership" (qtd. in Kötter 2002, 36).

Works Cited

Barthes, Roland. 1981. *Camera Lucida*. New York: Hill and Wang.

———. 1988. *The Semiotic Challenge*. Trans. Richard Howard. New York: Hill and Wang.

Carruthers, Mary. 1995. "From: The Book of Memory." In *Rhetoric: Concepts, Definitions, Boundaries*, ed. William A. Covino and David A. Jolliffe, 199–212. New York: Allyn & Bacon/Longman.

Cixous, Hélène, and Mireille Calle-Gruber. 1997. *Rootprints: Memory and Life Writing*. Trans. Eric Prenowitz. London: Routledge.

Doughty, Catherine J., and Michael H. Long. 2003. "Optimal Psycholinguistic Environments for Distance Foreign Language Learning." *Language Learning & Technology* 7, no. 3 (September): 50–80.

Francoz, Marion Joan. 1999. "Habit as Memory Incarnate." *College English* 62, no. 1 (September): 11–29.

Gronbeck, Richard. 1993. "The Spoken and the Seen: The Phonocentric and Ocularcentric Dimensions of Rhetorical Discourse." In *Rhetorical Memory and Delivery: Classical Concepts for Contemporary*

Composition and Communication, ed. John Frederick Reynolds, 139–55. Hillsdale, NJ: Lawrence Erlbaum.

Guyer, Carolyn. 2005. "Along the Estuary." *Mother Millennia.* http://www.mothermillennia.org/Carolyn/Estuary.html (accessed June 5, 2005).

Handa, Carolyn. 2004. *Visual Rhetoric in a Digital World: A Critical Sourcebook.* Boston: Bedford/St.Martin's.

Haynes, Cynthia. 1997. "Total ReCall: Memory, MOOs, and Morphology." Keynote address at CALLMOO: Enhancing Language Learning Through Internet Technologies Symposium, University of Bergen, Norway.

———. 2006. "Learning by Heart: Memory, MOOs, and Morphology." In *Changing Language Education through CALL,* ed. Randall P. Donaldson and Margaret A. Haggstrom, 197–228. London: Routledge.

Haynes, Cynthia, and Jan Rune Holmevik. 1998. *High Wired: On the Design, Use, and Theory of Educational MOOs.* 2nd ed. Ann Arbor: University of Michigan Press.

Heidegger, Martin. 1971. "The Origin of the Work of Art." In *Poetry Language Thought,* trans. Albert Hofstadter, 15–86. New York: Harper & Row.

Helfand, Jessica. 1997. "Electronic Typography: The New Visual Language." In *Looking Closer: Classic Writings on Graphic Design,* ed. Michael Bierut, William Drenttel, Steven Heller, and D. K. Holland, 2:49–51. New York: Allworth.

Hobbs, Catherine L. 2004. "Learning from the Past: Verbal and Visual Literacy in Early Modern Rhetoric and Writing Pedagogy." In *Visual Rhetoric in a Digital World,* ed. Carolyn Handa, 55–70. Boston: Bedford/St. Martin's.

Joyce, Michael. 1998. "Songs of Thy Selves: Persistence, Momentariness, and the MOO." In *High Wired: On the Design, Use, and Theory of Educational MOOs,* ed. Cynthia Haynes and Jan Rune Holmevik, 311–23. 2nd ed. Ann Arbor: University of Michigan Press.

Kennedy, George A. 1980. *Classical Rhetoric and Its Christian and Secular Tradition from Ancient to Modern Times.* Chapel Hill: University of North Carolina Press.

Kötter, Markus. 2002. *Tandem Learning on the Internet: Learner Interactions in Virtual Online Environments (MOOs).* Frankfurt am Main: Peter Lang.

Lanham, Richard A. 1993. *The Electronic Word: Democracy, Technology, and the Arts.* Chicago: University of Chicago Press.

Latour, Bruno. 1993. *We Have Never Been Modern.* Trans. Catherine Porter. Cambridge, MA: Harvard University Press.

Lee, Gicheol. 2005. "Typorganism." http://www.typorganism.com (accessed June 5, 2005).

Lienhard, John. 2005. "Ricci's Memory Palace." Episode No. 1226 of "Engines of Our Ingenuity" Radio Program. http://www.uh.edu/engines/epi1226.htm (accessed June 5, 2005).

Lingua MOO. 2005. http://lingua.utdallas.edu:7000 (accessed June 5, 2005).

Matta, Roberto. 2005. "Psychological Morphology." Trans. Pierre Petiot. http://homepage.mac.com/photomorphose/Mattamorph.html (accessed June 5, 2005).

McKeon. Richard. 1941. *The Basic Works of Aristotle.* New York: Random House.

Nandi, Alok B. 2005. http:fluxtopia.com (accessed June 5, 2005).

Olson, Gary A. 1990) "Jacques Derrida on Rhetoric and Composition: A Conversation." *JAC* 10, no. 1: 1–21.

Petiot, Pierre. 2005. "Surrealism and the Machine." http://homepage.mac.com/photomorphose/machine.html (accessed June 5, 2005).

Plato. 1995. *Phaedrus.* Trans. Alexander Nehamas and Paul Woodruff. Indianapolis: Hackett.

———. 2005. *Phaidros.* Perseus Digital Library. http://www.perseus.tufts.edu/cgibin/ptext?doc =Perseus%3Atext%3A1999.01.0173&query=head%3D%234 (accessed June 5, 2005).

Schwienhorst, Klaus. 1997. "Talking on the MOO: Learner autonomy and language learning in tandem." Paper presented at the CALLMOO: Enhancing Language Learning Through Internet Technologies, Bergen, Norway. http://www.tcd.ie/CLCS/assistants/kschwien/Publications/CALLMOOtalk.htm (accessed June 5, 2005).

Sirc, Geoffrey. 2000a. "English Composition as FLUXJOKE." Paper delivered at Conference on College Composition and Communication (CCCC). Chicago.

———. 2002b. *English Composition as a Happening.* Logan: Utah State University Press.

Trimbur, John. 2002. "Delivering the Message: Typography and the Materiality of Writing." In *Rhetoric and Composition as Intellectual Work,* ed. Gary A. Olson, 188–202. Carbondale: Southern Illinois University Press.

Virilio, Paul. 1997. *Open Sky.* Trans. Julie Rose. London: Verso.

4

INVENTION IN THE WILD

On Locating *Kairos* in Space-Time

THOMAS RICKERT

> When it came night, the white waves paced to and fro in the moonlight, and the wind brought the sound of the great sea's voice to the men on shore, and they felt that they could then be interpreters.
>
> —Stephen Crane, "The Open Boat"

James L. Kinneavy's 1986 call for renewed attention to *kairos* has resulted in a substantial amount of work in the years since, but it has not dispelled a peculiar difficulty. *Kairos* resists formalization and mastery, which Kinneavy notes as one reason for its neglect. This mystery is still a theme in much contemporary work—as Eric Charles White puts it, *kairos* "stands for precisely the irrational novelty of the moment that escapes formalization" (1987, 20). Additionally, the meaning of *kairos* is itself murky because of its many and varied usages. Phillip Sipiora lists a dozen meanings for *kairos* that have appeared in classical discourse, including convenience, decorum, due measure, fitness, fruit, occasion, profit, proportion, propriety, symmetry, tact, and wise moderation (2002, 1). He could have added opportunity, balance, harmony, the right and/or proper time, opening, timeliness, and other terms as well. Little wonder that the philologist William H. Race calls the term "elusive" (1981, 197) Nevertheless, in most of the scholarship that has appeared since Kinneavy's call, *kairos* is understood more or less in line with his original definition: *kairos* is "the right or opportune time to do something" (1983, 80). Whether thought in terms of timeliness, decorum, or situation, *kairos* defines a rhetor's relation to a unique opportunity arising from an audience or context, one that calls for a proper response. The art of *kairos*, in short, is invention on the spur of an unpredictable, irrational moment.

In this essay I am primarily concerned with the *context* of *kairos* as a way toward developing a richer understanding of environment and our inventive relationship within it. One might say that I am trying to find a way for *kairos* to take place, to see what happens when we attend to the emplacement and not just the timeliness or decorum of *kairos*. Essentially, without place *kairos* is an empty concept. I should add that this is not meant to be a historical reconstruction, whereby I would claim that Gorgias or other Sophists had a materially rich theory of kairotic situations. In fact, this would be highly dubious; it would assume that our contemporary understandings of environment and situation could be grafted onto ancient Greek thought. Rather, I am satisfied to consider extant scholarship that demonstrates the role of place in early conceptions of *kairos*, and work from there. A key question is what the ancient rhetorical conception of *kairos* can offer us when considered in the light of contemporary discussions of material context, particularly work on environments, ecologies and ecosystems, autopoesis, networks, ambience, and so on. Such discussions emphasize the fundamental if neglected role of place in every aspect of human activity. Furthermore, as we shall see, most studies on *kairos* attend primarily to its temporal, opportunistic, and propitiatory dimensions. Looking to the earliest uses of *kairos*, we see that it originally had a spatial meaning, and, some scholars claim, the temporal meaning came later (Onians 1973; Race 1981). Using the work of Untersteiner, Miller, Vitanza, and contemporary work on ecology and environments, I will attempt to bring out this spatial quality and show its necessity for understanding invention as an ambient and not a subjective activity. *Kairos* is therefore a concept integral for understanding posthuman subjectivity as radically dispersed, suggesting further that invention itself is an emergent process extending far beyond the bounds of an autonomous, willing subject.

Opening, with Arrows

The first appearance of *kairos* is in Homer, but it shows up in the adjectival and not the noun form. In the several uses in the *Iliad*, the term refers to the "deadliest spot" (A. T. Murray's translation of *kairion*) on the body where an arrow finds its mark (see 4.185, 8.84, 8.326, 11.439). Richard Onians suggests that this meaning for *kairos*, the place on the body where penetration (as by an arrow) is easiest, is older than the more familiar meanings like "due measure" or "opportune time" (1973, 344). Race suggests that this early use of *kairos* "denotes a *vital* or *lethal* place on the body" (1981, 197). As far as we know, Kinneavy tells us, the first use of *kairos* in the customary noun form is by Hesiod, who writes, "Observe due measure, and proportion [*kairos*] is best in all things" (Kinneavy 1983, 80). Yet the older meaning of *kairos* as "mark" or "target" with its implications of specific implacement continues to show up in many ancient Greek authors. Onians cites Pindar ("I have lighted upon many themes, hitting the *kairos* with no false word," *Nemean Odes* 1.18), Aeschylus (*Agamemnon* 363ff.), and Euripides ("[men] . . . aiming the bow beyond the *kairos*," *Supplicants* 745f.; cf. *Andromache* 1120), emphasizing that the customary understanding of *kairos* as normative or temporal is absent in these usages. Race also points out that the temporal meaning of *kairos* comes later, though he emphasizes the normative meaning more than Onians (1981, 198 n. 3). Also of significance here is that the Roman translation of *kairos* as *tempus* captures this early, spatial use of *kairos*, as it is the word from which we get "temple" (344). Thus, in keeping with the ancient Greek conception of critical opening, the temples are the weak and easily penetrable points on the skull (Onians 1973, 344 n. 2).

All this suggests that the earliest uses of *kairos* were grounded in a sense of place, but not just any place. As Onians goes on to argue, *kairos* does not just refer to the target at which one aims, but more particularly "a penetrable opening, an aperture, passage through the iron of an axe or rather of twelve axes set at intervals in a straight line" (345). The set of twelve axes was a way for Greek archers to practice by aiming at the openings. This notion of opening is still with us today, and it is easy to see how it can be affiliated with the more dominant understanding of *kairos* as opportunity. "I saw my opening, and I took it," we might say. Onians goes on to link this meaning of opening with the English word "nick," which literally means a shallow cut, notch, or chip in something, but which we also use to refer to a critical moment ("just in the nick of time") (347).

Another sense of *kairos* stems from weaving. Showing up in Homer, Hesychius, Aeschylus, Pindar, and others, *kairos* can refer to the opening in the warp through which the shuttle must pass; the warp only lasts a moment, so the time to make the "shot" through the warp is brief (Onians 1973, 346). The sense of critical time is clear, no doubt. But, just as important, the opening through which the shot must pass is quite clearly a *place*. A relation to fate is also suggested here; Onians remarks that the "belief in the weaving of fate with the length of the warp-threads representing length of time" contributes to the later emergence of the critical, temporal connotation of *kairos* (346–47).

White puts these two meanings of *kairos* together, defining it as "a passing instant when an opening appears which must be driven through with force if success is to be achieved" (1987, 13). For White, this will mean that *kairos* is primarily an inventional concept; success depends on adapting to continually changing circumstances and "newly emergent contexts" (13). By and large, this has been the consensus on *kairos*, especially as it has been explored in terms of the Sophists, for whom *kairos* is held to be a crucial principle. Protagoras and Gorgias in particular are noted for making *kairos* a fundamental principle in their artistry. John Poulakis, for example, holds that *kairos* is one of the key terms for sophistic rhetoric, an art that "seeks to capture in opportune moments that which is appropriate and attempts to suggest what is possible," and observes that Protagoras was first to capitalize fully on "the power of the opportune moment" (1983, 36, 40). He goes on to elaborate on the importance of the temporality of a given situation, in that a rhetor must be fully respectful and cognizant of the right time that emerges to call forth speaking. Susan Jarratt also notes the importance of opportunity, describing the Sophists' ability "to judge the circumstances obtaining at the moment of an oration, its *kairos*," and adds, "but even more essential was the orator/alien's understanding of the local *nomoi*: community-specific customs and laws" (1997, 11). While for Jarratt timeliness and decorum are conjoined in the sophistic arts, she emphasizes the normative over the temporal aspects. But even here, it is a matter of making appropriate or fitting use of the opportunities that arise. Janet Atwill writes that "[d]eploying an art at the 'right moment' in a particular situation is the sign of the true rhetor, yet it is something that cannot be taught by explicit precepts or rules" (1998, 58). She goes on to explain that Isocrates emphasized the need to cultivate a 'sense' for the right time by careful emulation of masters, described as habituation. Howsoever this sense of timing and decorum is inculcated, Atwill continues, "[i]n the mastery of the moment lies the rhetor's best chance to intervene in and transform a situation" (59).

Balancing, with Middles

Michael Carter, looking to Pythagoras and the Pythagoreans, takes a somewhat different path with *kairos*. Deemphasizing but not abandoning the sense of opening or opportunity, he brings together *kairos* and *stasis* in an attempt to theorize a sophistic rhetoric attuned to contemporary concerns with antifoundationalism, relativism, and social constructivism. Carter is specifically interested in the harmonious qualities of *kairos* as theorized in the work of Mario Untersteiner and Richard Leo Enos. Untersteiner states that the Pythagoreans saw a universal law in *kairos*, in which opposites, "bound together by harmony, give life to the universe" (1954, 110–11). Carter notes that Enos's translation of *kairos* as "balance" conveys this important Pythagorean thematic. He then argues that while *kairos* still retained "its ethical dimension and overall sense of rightness—a critical point in time and space—*kairos* took on the more profound connotations of generation: the conflict and resolution of form and matter that initiated the creation of the universe and all that is therein" (2003, 102). From this perspective, *kairos* achieves a robust, active sense of harmony; it is not the palliation of conflicts, but the achievement of workable or probable truths in situations where surety is lacking.

"Balance" in this sense is a way of looking to the situation itself as a guide to navigating differing positions and finding the correct one. Carter goes on to point out that such rhetorical procedures involve far more than adaptation to audiences (105). Though Carter does not explicitly make the claim, we can infer that the reason for this is that audience is only one part of what is given in a situation. Thus, though scholars like Jarratt are quite correct to emphasize the role of local *nomoi* in a situation, such views neglect the full import of a more robust conception of *kairos* that looks beyond the audience. In this regard, some contemporary theories about human comportment shed important insight; for example, Louis Althusser's concept of interpellation suggests that we respond to a given ideological call, or "hail," in conscious and unconscious ways that have little to do with rational decision-making or belief and more to do with the achievement of identity in sociosymbolic roles. One could also look to Michel Foucault's theory of power, which suggests that power has no specific location and cannot be ascribed solely to an individual or group. The point is that it is misleading to suggest that a rhetor is subjectively responsible for how an audience reacts. This is not to say that there is no responsibility on the part of the rhetor, but it is to say that "responsibility"—if we can even continue to use that term—is dispersed throughout the situational environs. Audience adaptation is only one facet, and possibly a very small one depending on specific circumstances, of how a skilled rhetor would respond to *kairos.*

In "Kairotic Encounters" Debra Hawhee addresses *kairos* in a manner at first reminiscent of Carter's. Instead of looking to the

Pythagorean influence and its emphasis on "balance," however, Hawhee directly tackles the subject/object problem variously attended to in postmodern theory, but evaded in the synthetic approach of harmonizing balance described by Carter. "*Kairos*," Hawhee writes, "enables a consideration of 'invention-in-the-middle,' a space-time which marks the emergence of a pro-visional 'subject,' one that works *on*—and is worked on *by*—the situation" (2002, 18; italics in original). Her concept of the middle is a productive attempt to move our understanding of *kairos* beyond the "individualistic motif" (20). In other words, "*kairos* mediates—or goes 'between'—the outside of the self, i.e., the nodes where the 'self' encounters a world, and the discourse or the 'other' that the self encounters" (25). The concept of "middle" designates not a stable realm between poles, but an always on the move, temporally unstable, and emergent moment beyond the control of a self. Indeed, one might say that Hawhee is proposing through her inventive *kairos* a postmodern, dispersed form of subjectity—one that, properly speaking, is no longer the modernist subject at all. Rather than seeking the harmonious balance of opposites, even in the powerfully generative sense Carter propounds, Hawhee abandons what may well strike her as still too dialectical a conception of *kairos* (as is suggested by her use of Gilles Deleuze) in favor of one that scrambles oppositional poles. In this way, Hawhee underscores the necessity of linking *kairos* to the problem of subjectivity, suggesting a posthuman conception that shares affinity with earlier work on kairotic invention beyond the modern subject, work I will now turn to.[1]

Willing, sans The Subject

I would like to turn now to a problem taken up by Scott Consigny in *Gorgias: Sophist and Artist.* While his focus is on Gorgias, *kairos*'s centrality to Gorgias's rhetorical art shows us that Consigny's arguments have wider scope. Consigny breaks down the interpretations of Gorgias into three distinct schools: the subjectivist, empiricist, and antifoundationalist (2001, 26). It will not be my purpose to analyze these divisions. What I do wish to address is the problem of who it is that Consigny places in one of the categories, the "subjectivist"—Mario Untersteiner, Bernard Miller, and Victor Vitanza. Consigny traces the subjectivist reading of Gorgias to Hegel, and describes it as a position denying the possibility of objectivity and upholding the individual fabrication of one's own subjective reality (27). I would argue that in their own ways, Untersteiner, Miller, and Vitanza each address *kairos* as precisely *not* subjectivist, a point fundamental to their posthumanist views of invention. Indeed, setting aside their differences for a moment, we can see that a common theme emerging in their work is the necessity of stepping out of the modernist paradigm of subjectivity that gives rise to a category like "subjectivist" in the first place. While their agendas are different, they nevertheless help lay the groundwork for thinking about *kairos* in ways that reflect its spatial dimension while abandoning the subject-object dichotomy. This is not to say that spatiality is necessarily a concern in their work on *kairos*; it is to say that their thoughts on *kairos* help us to see that it has heretofore remained entirely too enmeshed in an opportunistic frame, one that reinscribes *kairos* continually in a narrative of subjective control or advantage. In their own specific ways, they each point towards a rich conception of kairotic force that shows how we are shaped by external circumstances/situations. We will see that neither the categories of the subjective and objective, nor metaphors like poles and middles, are adequate for thinking *kairos* in this way; rather, an ambient understanding of *kairos* illuminates the more originary, spatial usage of *kairos*, which, as I will conclude, is a position attuned to the concerns of our own age.[2] In rethinking *kairos* along these lines, then, we are not reconstructing it in order to superimpose it back upon the ancient Greeks, but asking ourselves what in their thoughts on *kairos* can be brought forward and made relevant for contemporary rhetorical thought.

Consigny points out that *kairos* is seen by many scholars as the "key to Gorgias' subjectivist epistemology" (2001, 43). The subjectivist position, argues Consigny, sees the kairotic experience as "ephemeral or fleeting, one that is always radically unprecedented and unique . . . the only reality is the present moment" (44). As support for this categorization, Consigny cites Gorgias's aphorism about the *clepsydra,* or waterclock, used to limit a speaker's time: "[O]rators are 'like frogs; for the latter [make] their cry in water and the former before the water clock' (B30)" (Consigny 2001, 44; cf. Sprague 2001, 66).[3] Consigny argues that for Gorgias, this means that the external reality imposed by the clock is artificial, and it is only in attending to one's subjective, kairotic experience that one can transcend the illusory "amphibian" experience. The first question we must ask here, however, is why the kairotic experience is a "radically subjective new moment" (Consigny 2001, 44)? One might well read the aphorism as suggesting that the water clock imposes something artificial, but it does not follow that one's subjective kairotic experience is somehow more real. It makes greater sense to understand the kairotic experience as one that is *broader* than the experience of the water clock, one that encompasses all elements composing the situation. That is, what is radically subjective is one's limitation of the kairotic moment to the water clock. It is the ambient externality of *kairos* in all its discursive/material/psychic bounty that is decisive, and not solely a speaker's subjective experience. This further suggests that the facilitative locus of *kairos* must be carefully considered.

Untersteiner's reading of the Gorgias and *kairos*, shot through with its Nietzschean overtones of tragedy and excess, is often at odds with more traditional scholarly treatises. Nor do I have the space here to delve into the subtle, winding complexities of Untersteiner's marvelous book. Instead, I will single out one key point, oft repeated by Untersteiner: *kairos* is not something that a "subject" takes advantage of. There is, contra Consigny, no "subject" who accedes to cognitive and decisive priority in a rhetorical situation. As Untersteiner writes, in Gorgias "we are not dealing with a mere theoretical precept enjoining the observance of *kairos* on orators"; rather, "it is always a question of an act of cognition which, not being able to embrace in one conceptual synthesis the antithetical extremes, the ethical *dissoi logoi*, chooses one of these: in the present case the virtue which the 'occasion' (given by the time and the circumstances) renders inevitable" (1954, 180–81). Untersteiner's meaning may not be immediately transparent, but what is clear is that the locus of decision is quite dispersed. First, there is a disjunction between a rhetor and the situation: there is no rational synthesis possible that would make sense of all the contraries suffusing a situation. Second, this disjunction, rather than being an impediment for a rational, willing subject to take decisive advantage of the kairotic moment, is actually generative, a catalyst. Recall earlier that when Carter described these antitheses, he also called them generative; however, there is a key difference between what Carter and Untersteiner do (and this despite the fact that Carter cites Untersteiner extensively). Carter looks to the Pythagorean *kairos* and its emphasis on the achievement of harmony. And while scholars agree that this notion of *kairos* certainly informs the Gorgian notion of *kairos* (see De Vogel 1966, for example), Untersteiner points to a crucial distinction. Choice is rendered "inevitable" by the occasion itself. As Untersteiner says in several different permutations, a rhetor's decision is "willed by *kairos*" (1954, 181; cf. 177).

Bernard Miller makes much of Untersteiner's argument, using it to differentiate between the Platonic and Gorgian versions of *kairos*. Plato's *kairos* is one of a rhetor taking advantage of a momentary opportunity in a given situation; it becomes a matter of gaining subjective advantage over one's audience, of mastering the moment, or at least properly adapting one's words for the occasion (1987, 169). Miller notes that the Platonic *kairos* establishes the split between subject and object (171). Untersteiner, by contrast, establishes that the Gorgian *kairos* fuses subject and object, creating a "meditative correspondence" that slams shut the ontological difference opened by Plato (Miller 1987, 177). Miller is able to connect this understanding of *kairos* with Heidegger's notion of being-in-the-world, in which Being becomes an encounter; further, he discusses Heidegger's oft-quoted, oft-misunderstood idea that language is the "house of being" (Miller 1987, 178–79; Heidegger 1982, 63). To simplify, language is in a sense an abode in that through language, beings—*Dasein* in Heidegger's terminology, meaning "being-there"—come to be what they are. In the instant of any given situation, what Heidegger calls the *Augenblick*, the world is disclosed, and this instant is akin to *kairos.* Miller explains that "the situation is not something we create or something pre-existing that we stand against . . . rather, situation subsists in the temporality of *Dasein*, and their mutual implication anchors us in the awareness of the simple 'that it is'" (1987, 181). *Kairos* marks an abiding, not a grasping, and a trigger for language's concernful disclosure.

Vitanza, while sympathetic to Miller's reading of *kairos*, nevertheless finds the reliance on Heidegger to be problematic. Vitanza links *kairos* with invention, the middle voice, and the will to power in order to see it as a "dispersive power," which will mean, among other things, a moment neither of crisis/renewal (theological *kairos*) nor opportunity (traditional, or Platonic *kairos*) but "*many competing, contradictory voices*" (1957, 289; italics in original). Vitanza cites from the final aphorism in Nietzsche's collected notebooks, *The Will to Power*, to flesh out the connection between *kairos* and will to power qua dispersion; I quote the selection here, but with additional lines that underscore Nietzsche's attention to space:

> And do you know what "the world" is to me? This world: a monster of energy without beginning, without end . . . not something blurry or wasted, not something endlessly extended, but set in a definite space as a definite force, and not a space that might be "empty" here or there, but rather as force throughout, as a play of forces and waves of forces, at the same time one and many, increasing here and at the same time decreasing there; a sea of forces flowing and rushing together, eternally changing, eternally flooding back . . . blessing itself as that which must recur eternally, as a becoming that knows no satiety, no disgust, no weariness: this is my

> *Dionysian* world of the eternally self-creating, the eternally self-destroying . . . without goal, unless the joy of the circle is itself a goal. . . . *This world is the will to power—and nothing besides!* (Nietzsche 1968, 550; italics in original)

Nietzsche, a brilliant stylist whose words shine even in translation, is difficult to improve upon. But it is clear enough, I think, that this world, a world of eternal, flowing, entangling, changing, clashing *becoming* (and many more gerunds besides could be supplied) is what Vitanza sees as *kairos*. It is the perpetual, always burbling right *there* possibility for creating something new, something irrational (Vitanza 1997, 291). "Don't you miss it, don't you miss it / Some 'a you people just about missed it!" sings David Byrne in the Talking Heads song "Born under Punches (The Heat Goes On)," and he could easily be talking about the Vitanzan *kairos*, the sense that it is always happening, *not* as the opportune moment that we could capitalize on (with the full economic valuation that implies), but as something happening, happening now, to us, within the turbulence and play of forces. And it is not just happening to us; as Nietzsche says in the very last line of this aphorism, not only is the world the will to power and nothing besides, but also we are the will to power—and nothing besides (1968, 550).

It is beyond the scope of this essay to unpack all the differences between Miller's Heideggerian and Vitanza's Nietzschean conceptions of *kairos*, except to mention that there is an implicit goal, a sense of proper comportment and attitude, that suffuses Heidegger's incessant talk of the call and authenticity, and this is something Vitanza is keen to jettison as limiting and dangerous, nostalgic and guilty (see Vitanza 1997, 172–73, 187–88, 242–43, 287–94; cf. Miller 1987, 181–82). Perhaps an even clearer sense of the difference between the two hinges on where they conclude. Miller winds down with a meditation on a response to the call of being, with *kairos* providing passage (1987, 182). Vitanza exhorts us to the new, to the unthought, to invention. In this, Vitanza's take on *kairos* is remarkably similar to that of White and Hawhee. All of them are interested in *kairos* as a form of invention, just as they are all keen to see this invention happening in the middle voice. Where Vitanza differs from White and Hawhee, and where he curiously enough is closer to Miller, is in his assimilation and repurposing of Untersteiner's claim that *kairos* wills us, and not the other way around. In this sense, Vitanza is also *with* Heidegger, but wanting to push him further toward a radically dispersed subjectivity of flows without blockages, temporalities without nostalgia, and places without boundaries.[4]

Ultimately, all this shows the extent to which Consigny's claim that Untersteiner, Miller, and Vitanza can be grouped under the category of subjectivism is significantly flawed. Rather than subjectivism, these three variously give priority to the outside world while abandoning the subject-object dichotomy. As a consequence, they deny that we can control, manipulate, or otherwise avail ourselves of the *kairos*, suggesting instead that in some way, the *kairos* does what it does *to* us. What I will do in the next section is explain what that might mean for us, and specifically, why thinking of the *kairos* in this way puts us back onto the path to place. *Kairos*, that is, needs to be thought of in terms of what Heidegger termed the *Umwelt*, or the surrounding world, which further suggests that invention is ultimately spatially enmeshed.

Placing, with Aircraft

Philostratus claims in *Lives of the Sophists* that Gorgias initiated extemporary oratory. Entering a theater of Athenians, he recounts, Gorgias "had the boldness to say 'suggest a subject,' and he was the first to proclaim himself willing to take this chance, showing apparently that he knew everything and would trust to the moment (*toi kairoi*) to speak on any subject" (Sprague 2001, 31). It is common to see Gorgias as boastful, as Philostratus himself intimates. And, certainly, this would be the proper reception in light of the Platonic understanding of *kairos*. We have a subject who is skilled and knowledgeable enough to take advantage of *kairos* at will. However, as we have seen above, such a view is significantly at odds with what many recent scholars have suggested for the Gorgian *kairos*. Nevertheless, I have so far been working with two seemingly different takes on *kairos*, and now is the right time for them to come together. *Kairos*, I argued above, originally had a spatial dimension, though this early usage was gradually lost in favor of meanings like opportunity and decorum, among others, and most of which are keyed to a subject who is an active, willing, conscious agent. Next, I looked at some contemporary reexaminations of *kairos*, focusing in particular on Gorgias, in order to demonstrate that this subjective *kairos* is largely a Platonic legacy, and that the Gorgian *kairos* is better understood as itself having a kind of agency—it is not so much that we avail ourselves of kairotic opportunities as it is that our words and actions emerge as willed by *kairos*. But we must tread carefully here. Am I saying that there is no free will, that our actions and words are somehow predetermined, or legislated by a mysterious, uncanny, exterior force to which we conveniently give a comforting but still obscurantist label? Everything about the Gorgian *kairos* suggests otherwise, pointing instead to a highly nuanced set of relations among language, environment, and people, relations that Gorgias viewed with an affirmative, inventive eye.

Of course, we well know that invention and *kairos* have long been linked. And yet, focusing on the opportunistic or decorous aspects of *kairos* brings with it a particular sort of audience-driven stance, linking it thereby with persuasion, effectiveness, even agonistics, and making invention a subjective act. Viewing *kairos* sans the autonomous, willing subject—or what we have been calling posthuman subjectivity—suggests kinds of invention less attuned to advantage or success *over* an audience than working with what an audience in a material situation brings forth. In part, this will entail moving away from certain kinds of metaphors like poles, middles, and harmony that have a tendency to reinscribe the traditional subject. Perhaps it is that I am looking for ways to theorize a posthuman subjectivity in terms of immersion rather than connection, flow rather than node. A posthuman subject is one that might be described, in Andy Clark's words, as "a spatio-temporally extended process not limited to the tenuous envelope of skin and skull" (1997, 221).

A relevant example from a study of air traffic controllers can help make all this more concrete. Paul Dourish, a researcher in computer and information science, connects contemporary computer engineering issues with the phenomenological efforts of Husserl and Heidegger. Working out of Heidegger, Dourish writes that "the meaningfulness of everyday experience lies not in the head, but in the world. It is a consequence of our mode of being, of the way we exist in the world" (2001, 107). What is fundamental here is the attention to the material world, and specifically place, in human work and interaction; the usefulness of Heidegger is that his existential analytic has concrete consequences for how we view human activity in the world. Dourish provides several examples to illustrate his theories about the centrality of place and social interaction in human activity, and I will discuss one here, the air traffic control center. In a 1995 ethnographic study, it was found that air traffic controllers rely on thin plastic strips lying in a bay on their instrument console to aid them in managing airspace. Dourish points out that this is not a case of simple representation; rather, "the controllers *manage the airspace by managing the strips*" (Dourish 2001, 65; italics in original). Dourish continues: the controllers "transform some of the work of managing airspace into a physical process of monitoring and managing the set of strips corresponding to the current traffic. . . .

The work of managing the space becomes the embodied performance of physical activity, arising around the specific details of the work site itself" (66–67). The controllers work in groups, so that in managing the strips, they are also managing the airspace *for the other controllers.* The strips provide a quick and easy summary of the current work state, "manifested as part of the immediate environment" (67). Dourish concludes from this that we should not understand information as decontextualized, and further, that we should begin to see the environment not simply as the location where information shows up, but the very medium by which work can be conducted (67–68).[5]

We can draw still more conclusions from Dourish's example. First, while we cannot say that there is an abstract unity of controllers, aircraft, instrumentation, strips, and work activity, we equally cannot say that there is anything resembling poles, a middle, or—a point I will return to in my conclusion—irrationality. The controllers are not simply adapting to an environment, but (despite their job designation) they are not simply controlling it, either. The air traffic control center is a series of events in a specific environs, of kairotic moments in a generative place, which form an ambient whole. Subjectivity takes form as radically dispersed throughout the environs. No "subject controls" what occurs—actions emerge as willed by the situation. However, the environs here are not just a material reality to which we adapt or which somehow "determine" us. Instead, the environs are what enable us, but they enable *inclusively* of human beings, insofar as human beings are part of the environs. Thus, the emplacement of the controllers is essential to their activity, for the context makes all that occurs possible. It is not that the controllers do not make choices; it is that their choices are already immersed in the context in which they get played out. To deny the fundamentally constitutive role of place, then, is to suggest that somehow we are back to a subject-object relationship, which, even worse, drags us yet again into the depressing morass of subjectivism.

Inventing, with Verbal

Such insights, while perhaps changing our views of air traffic controllers, may not seem so relevant to invention. Customarily, it has been understood as something a human subject does, causes, or wills. Kairotic invention in this sense simply refers to an opportunity we can capitalize on. I would like to begin closing this essay by showing how *kairos* too might be thought in terms of its ambient environs, just as the air traffic control center is, and how such a redescription likewise disperses our customary understanding of subjective activity. *Kairos* is thus the will to invent suggested by White and Vitanza, yet it is such only when we also displace agentive force away from the subject and toward *kairos* itself, as suggested by Untersteiner, Miller, and Vitanza. We are not far from White's definition of *kairos* as a "radical principle of occasionality establishing the living present as point of departure for rhetorical invention" (1987, 161). What I am adding to the mix is the necessity of melding this sense of *kairos* to a rich, material sense of place; it is only the emplacement of *kairos* that explains how the situational environs can be a "willing" and inventive agent in line with Gorgias's trust in the moment itself to supply what was necessary for speaking.

The film *The Usual Suspects* (dir. Bryan Singer, Gramercy Pictures, 1995) can demonstrate these ideas with an economy stemming in part from the immersive qualities of film itself, and in part because as David Blakesley points out, the film is "explicitly about rhetoric as a social and verbal art" (2003, 234). I would add that my use of the film to write about the emplacement of kairotic invention also exemplifies the very theory I am modeling, which will perhaps have its own immersive appeal. The film takes place as a series of flashbacks constructed from the narrative given by a seemingly innocuous criminal suspect, Roger "Verbal" Kint (Kevin Spacey), under interrogation by a police detective, Dave Kujan (Chazz Palminteri). Kujan is convinced that a former detective gone bad, Dean Keaton (Gabriel Byrne), has masterminded a major drug deal that involved the destruction of a freighter and many deaths. He interrogates Verbal brusquely, extracting the story of how Keaton and the others in his crew, after meeting in a police lineup, began a new wave of criminal escapades. However, Kujan becomes privy to other information, including the involvement of one of the FBI's top criminal suspects, the mysterious Keyser Söse. Verbal, under duress from Kujan, tells all. Or so it seems. At the end of the film, we see that Verbal was Söse all along, though not the Söse of mythic will, coldness, and destruction he relates to Kujan. Through a brilliant montage of panoramic camera shots while Verbal/Söse makes his getaway, we are led to see that many of the names and events Verbal gives to Kujan in fact come from the bulletin board in the interrogation office, from the desk, and even from the manufacturer's name on the coffee cup Kujan uses (Kobayashi, whom Verbal names as Söse's associate). Furthermore, during the course of the film, Kujan himself continually provides Verbal with added information and prompts; "convince me," he says over and over in various permutations.

We might be led to understand the film as demonstrating the most traditional notion of kairotic invention, or even Socratic dialectic.

Verbal, aka Keyser Söse (a German/Turkish hybrid phrase loosely meaning "King Talk Too Much") would in this view be a clever tale-spinner simply taking advantage of his situation. He capitalizes on his seeming misfortune and is able to slip away unscathed. Such a reading, however, is only convincing due to its familiarity; the film takes great pains to suggest otherwise. Kujan, for example, is integral to the creation of the tale: he sets up the interrogation, supplies necessary information, creates the narrative framework concerning Keaton's guilt that gives Verbal a good deal of wiggle room, and presents crucial facial cues. So at the very least, the kairotic situation cannot be adequately explained without taking account of such interaction. But the film goes further; in showing how Verbal picks up cues from the office environment—names, faces, events—and weaves them into his tale, the film suggests the office space itself is a coinventor. We might say that the lesson here is that the environment is always situating us in arrangements that simultaneously unleash some possibilities and foreclose on others. A lesson of the film, then, is that the ambient environs invent us in kairotic moments.

This dispersal of the inventive subject, or the advent of the posthuman "subject," cannot be reinscribed within a subject-object dichotomy where the environment determines the individual, for the individual is already a part of the environment, a complex folding within other complex foldings of material and discursive force. *The Usual Suspects* conveys such an idea in yet another way. During the course of the film, it is shown that while the various characters certainly make choices, such choices are always orchestrated from afar. Not predetermined, I emphasize, but it is clear that there is little or no subjective autonomy or control. The exception appears to be Verbal, who in the end is the only one to get what he wants. But even here, appearances are somewhat deceiving. Verbal is presented throughout the film as a passive, unprepossessing character.[6] A patsy. When asked to do something, or say something, he is the model of cooperation. In the end, Verbal is invented by *kairos* itself, but only when we consider *kairos* in terms of place. Verbal's cleverness is one of inventive passivity before the ambient environs in which he is immersed. Thus, Verbal is a kind of latter-day Sophist, one who invents through attunement to audience and place in much the same way Gorgias trusted to do.[7] Thinking place kairotically, and *kairos* spatially, thereby moves us from a subjectivity of semiautonomous, willing agents to something like subjectivity as a condensation of probabilities realized in movement, materialized in space, and invented in place.

This further suggests that *kairos* can no longer be thought of as in any way irrational. Rather, insofar as *kairos* is emplaced, it is the most rational of concepts. Given that the tradition has judged *kairos* as irrational heretofore, and levied mistrust toward asystematic inventional forms, we might well reconsider these prior conceptions of rationality. If, as Hegel once claimed, we need an adequate definition of reason, the work now ongoing on the importance of place and the dispersal of subjectivity, knowledge, and activity throughout the ambient environs points to a rebeginning for what rationality is or can become, a rebeginning that builds on—though as Vitanza shows, it must also go beyond—Heidegger's existential analytic. Hegel's dictum that the rational is actual and the actual is rational (Hegel 1952), which in miniature glosses Hegel's philosophy of rationality as dialectical progression, is implicitly both challenged and validated by an emplaced *kairos.* Challenged, because dialectical reason as the *aufgehoben* of opposites like subject and object is no longer a conception adequate for understanding kairotic space-time; and yet validated, for our posthuman-being-in-the-world is also an inventional attunement to an emplaced, dispersed, and perhaps therefore uncanny rationality. As Brooke suggests, this in part means a revaluing of partiality and an abandonment of the drive for mastery and control through the will to knowledge (2000, 791). What a conception of kairotic environs shows is that such an abandonment is equally an embracement, and one with quite ancient roots.

Notes

1. For useful overviews of the term "posthuman," see Hayles 1999 and *JAC* 20, no. 4 (2000), a special issue on posthuman rhetorics edited by John Muckelbauer and Debra Hawhee; see in particular Brooke (2000), who distinguishes between posthumanism and postmodernism.
2. I have previously written on ambience in the essay "In the House of Doing: Rhetoric and the *Kairos* of Ambience," *JAC* 24, no. 4 (2004): 901–27.
3. It should be noted that this aphorism is possibly inauthentic; see Sprague 2001, 66.
4. Vitanza points out that Untersteiner also falls into nostalgia, as when he asserts that, in regards to Gorgias's *Encomium*, it must be thought that a decision is carried out by Helen. In this way, Untersteiner himself falls away from the consequences of his own arguments concerning the will of *kairos*, lapsing into what Vitanza

characterizes as homesickness, a nostalgia for being at home in the *logos* (1997, 291).

5. There is a growing body of work scattered across many fields that explores similar issues concerning the material environment and human activity. Of particular relevance here are, from a scientific orientation, Clark 1997 and Hutchins 1995; Johnson 2001 provides a populist account. In the humanities, Hayles 1999 and Taylor 2001 are useful. In rhetoric and composition, Syverson 1999 discusses composition as an ecology, while Dobrin and Weisser have been ardent advocates of an environmental approach to composition, producing a monograph (Dobrin and Weisser 2002) and an edited collection (Weisser and Dobrin 2001).
6. For an illuminating discussion of the role of passivity in contemporary thought, see Wall 1999.
7. My reading here has some similarities with Blakesley's, who argues that in a first time viewing the audience typically attributes the narrative to Verbal, while a close, second viewing suggests that it is more probably Kujan's narrative, constructed from a variety of sources, including his own knowledge and biases, with very little coming from Verbal (Blakesley 2003, 238). Blakesley's reading, then, also depends on a notion of subjectivity dispersed throughout an environs, suggesting that at some level there is ambiguity about the locus of invention, even if he finally settles on Kujan as the primary contributor.

Works Cited

Althusser, Louis. 1994. "Ideology and Ideological State Apparatuses (Notes towards an Investigation)." In *Mapping Ideology*, ed. Slavoj Žižek, 100–140. New York: Verso.

Atwill, Janet M. 1998. *Rhetoric Reclaimed: Aristotle and the Liberal Arts Tradition.* Ithaca, NY: Cornell University Press.

Blakesley, David. 2003. "Sophistry, Magic, and the Vilifying Rhetoric of *The Usual Suspects.*" In *The Terministic Screen: Rhetorical Perspectives on Film*, ed. David Blakesley, 234–45. Carbondale: Southern Illinois University Press.

Brooke, Collin Gifford. 2000. "Forgetting to Be (Post)Human: Media and Memory in a Kairotic Age." *JAC* 20, no. 4: 775–95.

Carter, Michael. 1988. "*Stasis* and *Kairos*: Principles of Social Construction in Classical Rhetoric." *Rhetoric Review* 7, no. 1: 97–112.

Clark, Andy. 1997. *Being There: Putting Brain, Body, and World Together Again.* Cambridge, MA: MIT Press.

Consigny, Scott. 2001. *Gorgias: Sophist and Artist.* Columbia: South Carolina University Press.

De Vogel, C. J. 1966. *Pythagoras and Early Pythagoreanism.* Assen: Van Gorcum.

Dobrin, Sidney I., and Christian R. Weisser. 2001. *Natural Discourse: Toward Ecocomposition.* Albany: State University of New York Press.

Dourish, Paul. 2001. *Where the Action Is: The Foundations of Embodied Interaction.* Cambridge, MA: MIT Press.

Foucault, Michel. 1978. *The History of Sexuality: An Introduction.* Trans. Robert Hurley. New York: Vintage.

Hawhee, Debra. 2002. "Kairotic Encounters." In *Perspectives on Rhetorical Invention,* ed. Janet M. Atwill and Janice M. Lauer, 16–35. Knoxville: University of Tennessee Press.

Hayles, Katherine N. 1999. *How We Became Posthuman.* Chicago: University of Chicago Press.

Hegel, G. W. F. 1952. *Philosophy of Right.* Trans. T. M. Knox. New York: Oxford University Press.

Heidegger, Martin. 1982. *On the Way to Language.* Trans. Peter D. Hertz. New York: Harper and Row.

Homer. 1924. *The Iliad.* Trans. A. T. Murray. Cambridge, MA: Harvard University Press.

Hutchins, Edwin. 1995. *Cognition in the Wild.* Cambridge, MA: MIT Press.

Jarratt, Susan. 1997. *ReReading the Sophists: Classical Rhetoric Refigured.* Carbondale, IL: Southern Illinois University Press.

Johnson, Steven. 2001. *Emergence: The Connected Lives of Ants, Brains, Cities, and Software.* New York: Scribner.

Kinneavy, James L. 1983. "*Kairos*: A Neglected Concept in Classical Rhetoric." In *Rhetoric and Praxis: The Contribution of Classical Rhetoric to Practical Reasoning,* ed. Jean Dietz Moss, 79–105. Washington, DC: Catholic University of America Press.

Miller, Bernard A. 1987. "Heidegger and the Gorgian *Kairos*." In *Visions of Rhetoric,* ed. Charles W. Kneupper, 169–84. Arlington, TX: RSA.

Nietzsche, Friedrich. 1968. *The Will to Power.* New York: Vintage.

Onians, Richard Broxton. 1973. *The Origins of European Thought.* New York: Arno Press.

Poulakis, John. 1983. "Toward a Sophistic Definition of Rhetoric." *Philosophy and Rhetoric* 16:35–48.

Race, William. 1981. "The Word *Kairos* in Greek Drama." *Transactions of the American Philological Association* 111: 197–213.

Sipiora, Phillip. 2002. "The Ancient Concept of *Kairos*." In *Rhetoric and* Kairos*: Essays in History, Theory, and Praxis*, ed. Phillip Sipiora and James S. Baumlin, 1–22. Albany: State University of New York Press.

Sprague, Rosamond Kent, ed. 2001. *The Older Sophists.* Indianapolis: Hackett.

Syverson, Margaret A. 1999. *The Wealth of Reality: An Ecology of Composition.* Carbondale: Southern Illinois University Press.

Taylor, Mark C. 2001. *The Moment of Complexity: Emerging Network Culture.* Chicago: University of Chicago Press.

Untersteiner, Mario. 1954. *The Sophists.* Trans. Kathleen Freeman. Oxford: Basil Blackwell.

Vitanza, Victor J. 1997. *Negation, Subjectivity, and the History of Rhetoric.* Albany: State University of New York Press.

Wall, Thomas Carl. 1999. *Radical Passivity.* Albany: State University of New York Press.

Weisser, Christian R., and Sidney I. Dobrin, eds. 2001. *Ecocomposition: Theoretical and Pedagogical Approaches.* Albany: State University of New York Press.

White, Eric Charles. 1987. *Kaironomia: On the Will-to-Invent.* Ithaca, NY: Cornell University Press.

5

LOOKING FOR LOCATION WHERE IT CAN'T BE FOUND

Possibilities for Graduate Pedagogy in Rhetoric and Composition

PETER VANDENBERG
AND JENNIFER CLARY-LEMON

> Begin with the material. Pick up again the long struggle against lofty and privileged abstraction.
>
> —Adrienne Rich

It is fundamental to postprocess conceptions of composition that the act of writing is unavoidably a product of place. As Thomas Kent has it, "Writers are never nowhere" (1997, 3). Theories of location are grounded in the belief that a sense of place or scene is crucial to understanding rhetorical contexts. Such thinking also helps foreground awareness of the possibilities and limitations created by location, how social control or power is "structured" by the design and maintenance of public and institutional space, and how often power differentials among various social actors are naturalized or held "in place." By recognizing that meaning is a product of the social, theories of location recognize the "situatedness" of individuals among other language users, in the physical sites they occupy; foregrounding this situated connectivity between writer, reader, and scene reveals the extent to which language is bound up with material circumstances, what David Bleich calls "[t]he principle of the materiality of language" (1998, 228).

We hope to show here, however, that the overwhelming commitment to scholarly writing as virtuoso performance in graduate training in composition studies effectively abstracts future writing teachers from material location into the hyperreality of a professional discourse that recognizes an obligation to little more than effective generalization. We propose a movement into the dynamic realm of social interest and localized realities as a check against this displacement. Community-based graduate education complicates the notion that literate practices are intrinsically valuable, and it resists locating graduate students and their writing as isolated, privileged, theory-laden objects. Instead, it promotes mutuality and connectedness, both to lived (rather than imagined) communities and to material contexts that shape how, why, and for whom writing is valuable.

Writing and the Ideology of Research

Influenced by Adrienne Rich's powerful 1984 essay, "Notes toward a Politics of Location," feminist authors began foregrounding the physical body as a material center, *the* place where theory is actualized; one's body defines a point of location in relation to others, a sense of *where* out of which one can act. "To write 'my body,'" Rich explains, "plunges me into lived experience" (1987, 215). The physical, "personal" sites of language use are never self-evident, however, and never wholly personal. How individuals demarcate space, define its use, and delimit action within it foregrounds *location* as an inseparable combination of the material, the social, and the conceptual. As Richard Vatz pointed out more than three decades ago, "No situation can have a nature independent of the perception of its interpreter or independent of the rhetoric with which he chooses to characterize it" (1973, 154). The rhetoric used to define a situation, one might say today, is not always a matter of choice. Indeed, rhetorical action often depends on one's interpretation of and attitude toward the space in which one acts, and much public and institutional discourse is engaged—tacitly or otherwise—in endorsing particular ideas about place and the role individuals should play in it (Mauk 2003). Possibilities and limitations for speaking and acting in specific places are often the product of larger, often unrecognized or naturalized, social processes.

"[I]t is not enough to claim the personal," Gesa Kirsch and Joy Ritchie argue. "Instead," they propose, scholars in rhetoric and composition ought to "theorize their locations by examining their experiences as reflections of ideology and culture, by reinterpreting their own experiences through the eyes of others . . ." (1995, 8). The notion that how one is situated profoundly influences the values directing inquiry and the claims that follow from it has fueled nearly a decade of self-conscious attention to the effects of cultural structuring on "how we do our research" and "who we are in our work" (9). Indeed, when seen as a function of location, scholarly writing itself becomes evident as an institutional practice or mode of labor rather than a disinterested "search for truth" (Kent 1997). Seen as a situated material-conceptual practice, a product of location, modes of research serve as mechanisms by which unequal relations of power can be unwittingly substantiated.

Kirsch and Ritchie work against the inertia of "research" as an exercise of power driven by an objectified, naturalized belief in and commitment to a notion of "disinterested study." They passionately argue for a distinctly feminist research practice, one that "actively seeks to understand and change the conditions of women's social and political realities" (1995, 20). Aware of the limitations of their goal, Kirsch and Ritchie suggest that self-awareness is not equivalent to abandoning the authority to name, define, and order research subjects along a standard of value imposed by the researcher. What passes for "research" in any academic field wears the legacy of a colonialist project of assimilation, a science of categorization and incorporation no less important to the European conquest of the other than Christianity and capitalism. The only sure way to avoid exploiting others, or representing them within the conceptual schema we use to make them visible, may be to "leave some data unpublished, or even abandon a research project" (20).

No doubt. For it is finally in the act of writing that the project-ion of a researcher's conceptual schema on some segment of materiality is fully realized. The lessons of historiography are instructive for all that we might name "research" in its final formulation—to write up is to write off (or out). Kirsch and Ritchie can hardly be faulted for missing the impact of writing itself on the oppressive structures about which they intend to be "unrelentingly self-reflective" (10). The use of spatial metaphors to figure *writing* (in both verb and noun forms) as a location is woven into common idioms to the extent that they function like "speech formulas" (Lakoff and Johnson 1980, 51), metaphorically structured concepts so thoroughly normalized that they are routinely taken as literal expressions: "I am caught up *in* this book"; "She can't work her way *out* of that paragraph." Warranted by the ideology of research, which is driven by a commitment to the ameliorative potential of literate action (Vandenberg 1998), Kirsch and Ritchie announce that they "begin this essay by locating ourselves in this writing" (1995, 8); to not engage in literate action is to deny not only "the impulse to write"—structured, they explain, by the disciplinary activity of a Conference on College Composition and Communication (CCCC) workshop (8)—but to risk "falling into inaction and despair" (10).

To *not* write, to *not* engage in project-ing, is to destabilize disciplinary and professional identity. *Writing*, in both its verb and noun forms, is central to who "we" are as compositionists. We rightly say that more than practitioners of other disciplines, we "see" the writing rather than simply the content. But we see writing in particular ways. Perhaps more so than any other discipline, ours is saturated with the tacit legitimation of literate action (Stuckey 1991). Along with Kirsch and Ritchie, "we" may be best recognizable as a collective by our tendency to "begin . . . by locating ourselves in . . . writing" (Kirsch and Ritchie 1995, 8). By way of (our) *writing* we have taken on the commitment to instill in others a dedication to its explanatory and corrective promise.

Rewriting the Professoriate

Even as rhetoric and composition has interrogated the assimilative potential of literacy instruction and its tendency to elide differences by promoting linguistic similarities, relatively few have contested the rather uniform process of preparing a doctoral candidate almost exclusively through an encounter with the field's published scholarship. A review of syllabi for "gateway courses" in seventeen PhD programs in rhetoric and composition during the mid-1990s shows that reading published scholarship and producing texts that mirror its conventions have been the dominant pedagogical model (Bolin et al. 1995). The acquisition of expertise is bound up, at the doctoral level, with the acquisition of facility in the "genre set that orchestrates a graduate student's chosen field" (Swales and Lindemann 2002, 105).[1] Theories of location and the use of spatial metaphors to describe acts of writing, research, and professionalization perhaps encourage a second look at the implications of the old "gatekeeper" cliché, and the problematic role of graduate faculty in "admitting emerging scholars to the conversation" (Olson 1989, 20).

Juanita Comfort shows the extent to which the implicit expectations of "canonical modeling" can neutralize critical differences, engender an attitude of compliance to subjugation, and leave some composition PhD students feeling "more controlled by conventional discourses than able to take control of them" (2001, 98). Comfort uses metaphors of boundary and location to relate the experience of Tanya, one of the PhD students about whom she writes; Tanya "had not been able to come to the academic table as an African-American woman scholar, but instead . . . had been placed at the table by her instructors to be(come) what she called a 'generic' scholar" (97–98). Tanya's experience, as Comfort presents it, is not unlike the non-Western art about which Gloria Anzaldúa writes, which is both dulcified and *dislocated*, "transported into an alien aesthetic system. . . . Taken over" (1999, 32–33).

Of course, as Anzaldúa implies, no such act of displacement removes one from material-discursive space; it simply relocates one within an unfamiliar set of relations. How well graduate students adapt to their reorientation will have serious consequences for their ability to reap the benefits of their new location. The "crippling disjunctions" African-American women experience within spaces they occupy both in and outside school (Comfort 2001, 98) emerge as a consequence of the material-discursive processes at work in the university. The irony of such disjunctions, as Daniel Mahala and Jody Swilky explain, is that the rupture of a border does not necessarily allow freedom of movement, but rather recomposes groups along newly segmented boundaries. For some graduate students—perhaps in particular those lacking long-term engagement with the discursive space of dominant social institutions—the more significant boundary is the one between physical and theoretical loci. There is a "connection between geography and consciousness" (Mauk 2003, 383), yet scholarly writing is "located" only in the most abstract of formulations. When graduate pedagogy turns on canonical modeling as it does for Tanya, success often has everything to do with removing the implications of place—those from which students came, and those from which they now operate as approximations of the discursive ideal.

At the graduate level, academic achievement typically follows the capacity to write one's way into a "hyperreality," a conceptual or transcendent "where" whose authority in some measure derives from the perception of being cut loose from place and time. Canonical modeling implicitly proposes that both student and evaluating faculty member are located not "in place," but within a virtual reality populated by generalizations. Like any scholarly discourse—as it is represented by its written artifacts—composition studies must erase the particularity of place in order to have value in many places. Editors assure, among other things, that the particularities of a scholar's experience or observation are sufficiently generalized so as to make the specific point of their emergence largely inconsequential. Proposal reviewers for the Conference on College Composition and Communication are admonished to make sure that proposals go "beyond merely local reporting." A "standard career template," which foregrounds the publishing "master critic" as an ideal, organizes a hierarchy of faculty expertise and monetary value irrespective of local needs (Sosnoski 1994, 4). This epic emancipation from place is fully naturalized for the most privileged by a vast, national labor market that fully disconnects the qualification of a tenure-line job candidate from the situated acquisition of her training or experience. The more successful one is "in school," the more likely one is to be employed in a location she knows little or nothing about. Thus, the most influential among a "rootless professoriate" (Mahala and Swilky 2003, 771), often unfamiliar with the implications of local political, economic, and cultural conditions, constitute a relatively privatized community that recognizes no obligation to insure that its claims for justice and action have any impact in material space.

Our goal here is not to demonize written scholarship, for we are committed participants in that activity ourselves. Nor do we believe that *academic* discourses are alone in their capacity to dislocate. Indeed, positions constructed within a discourse are necessarily defined relative to opposing discourses (Gee). However, as with other discourses that evolve—and form the identities of their participants—through writing, the effects of displacement are exacerbated. As we compose this essay, we are frustrated by the function of writing in alienating us from our own material locations through the obligation to frame and respond to generalizations. More important, our concern for Comfort's student, Tanya, leaves us sensitive to our role in sustaining boundaries through the use of a conceptual vocabulary and terminology for which some graduate-student readers may have to stretch. Making an argument more "accessible," however, is certain to only mask the larger problem, which is the conditioned reliance within rhetoric and composition on virtuoso performance in the field's grapholect as *the* mark of excellence.[2]

Our point is that writing is as writing does; a consequence of writing's capacity to bring individuals into conceptual alignment is its capacity to create divisions, to resituate individuals in conceptual-material space. In arguing that "location is more than the material," Mauk rightly suggests that "the value of academia for students depends upon their interpretation or creation of academic space. To buy (into) academia (and its attendant postures, behaviors, and perspectives), students must buy (into) a particular conception of the terrain. . . . Students must learn a vast array of cartographic skills which help them gain a sense of location, a sense of *where*" (2003, 368–69; italics in original). True that, as our undergraduates are fond of saying. But the "cartographic skills" that allow one to define such an "intellectual geography" necessarily situates one in something of a hyperreality, an itinerant construct often best perceived by its distance from material locations "outside school."

As Bruce Herzberg (2000) writes, isolation is a consequence of academic expertise. To meaningfully address the observation of Julie Wollman-Bonilla that our research may not matter off the narrow professional roads we travel, we may have to confront the possibility that it is the very act of writing that enables and sustains the material-conceptual demarcations of space that trouble us—and trouble others about us. Our own comfortable habituation to "traditional academic space" (Mauk 2003, 380) and the symbolic action that defines it may be responsible for "the tendency to see the world beyond the academy as a research site" rather than a realm of engagement (Herzberg 2000, 396). Standing as a boundary between the conceptual spaces separately occupied by scholars and students is the very thing we hope will make those boundaries permeable: writing. For many of us who teach it, the material distances that separate our neighborhoods from those we enter in service learning courses are a direct consequence of the privileged literacies to which we are committed (Vandenberg 2004). Writing divides "us" from our best material-political intentions.

The distances we perceive as compositionists between physical and conceptual spaces are written and read in our own language. In the same way that the "built environment" of a university differentiates it from surrounding neighborhoods (Mahala and Swilky 2003), graduate pedagogies that turn predominantly on "canonical modeling" write future faculty members into the isolation about which Herzberg warns. Those most effective at constructing social and psychological distance through adherence to academic discourse conventions and the locations of publication—those we routinely describe in letters of recommendation as "most promising"—risk finding themselves at the furthest remove from the conceptual-material spaces tomorrow's students will occupy.[3] It is crucial, of course, for graduate students to recognize ways in which the scholarship they produce is embedded and constrained, both within and by institutional and disciplinary structures—a task at which we have become very accomplished. However, if we are to avoid reproducing a professoriate best understood by those outside the academic community for its conceptual and material detachment, we propose that graduate students in composition must become aware of ways in which they are (and will always be) spatially located. To achieve the ends of a graduate pedagogy of location, graduate faculty need to situate students in the localized contingencies and relationships that take shape through other practices and vocabularies.

Landing Sites: Research as Service, Research as Social Action

Creating a historical consciousness in our scholars and researchers—that is, having them see that the production and dissemination of knowledge is connected to a wider context of historically imbalanced resources, power distribution, and competing ideologies—makes them more aware of the potential of their scholarship and research to do "good" or "bad." As Derek Owens puts it, "[T]he problem arises when sustained concentration eclipses wide-angle vision (2001, 140)—or when sustained "research," or sustained "service work," positions students to disregard "flows of persons, goods, and information" (Mahala and Swilky 2003, 780). Questions posed out of such wide-angle vision is critical to any sense of sustained and engaged scholarship, yet, as Wollman-Bonilla points out, "in our doctoral programs, where we socialize students into the research culture, we don't teach such questioning as a central step in the research process" (2002, 320). At the stem of reflexive graduate service is learning how to create a critical research practice; but at the root should be an ability "to train the eye towards one's chosen realms of study while not losing sight of the degree to which one is embedded within other informational flows" (Owens 2001, 140).

The reciprocity that Kirsch and Ritchie propose for research practice is important; we agree that composition "researchers," writers of "research reports," should "view dissonances as opportunities to examine deeply held assumptions and to allow multiple voices to emerge" (1995, 19). What goes undisturbed in this suggestion, however, is obedience to the very necessity of "research." The habituation to "study"—an obligation to assume the examiner's stance—constructs a conceptual displacement, endangering the reciprocity that Kirsch and Ritchie desire. The obligation to make "research results" *publishable*—which effectively means to make them meaningful for an audience that does not share the immediate context examined, or how those examined perceive their experience—guarantees the appropriative rewriting of the disempowered that worries bell hooks.

This, of course, is "the trouble with writing," the predicament that makes Kirsch and Ritchie wonder if they "can claim anything for [their] research." Inside the occupation of disciplined research, there may be no way off the horns of this dilemma—to "[fall] into inaction and despair" or to "move forward," albeit with rigorous self-reflexivity (10). As Paul Jude Beauvais has it, "[A] person cannot cast off ideological assumptions through an act of will, even as he or she attempts to study those assumptions" (1989, 18). If our exclusive aim in graduate pedagogy within rhetoric and composition is to make researchers of our students—practitioners of disciplined method and its discursive desideratum, the publishable text—we can be assured that ours will remain a project of creating and enforcing social, conceptual, and material distance. What we have in mind here is an alternative—one not completely untroubled by the tenacity of ideological commitment, but one oriented more toward correspondence than explanation.

"If we want students to move into academic space, if we want them to buy into the real estate," Mauk writes, "it is time for academia to employ and become embodied in the new space of student life" (2003, 386). Doing that at the graduate level may well require recalibrating the means and ends of doctoral training to situate potential, expertise, and competency beyond the practices of research and the production of disciplined publication. In addition to a reform-oriented practice that encourages attention by the researcher to "the *researcher's* location and subjectivity" (Kirsch and Ritchie 1995, 10; italics in original), we propose that graduate students gain an awareness of the limitations of disciplined perspective by a kind of material defamiliarization. We must find ways to get graduate student bodies out into those localized publics—not for the purpose of revealing the other to a disciplined gaze, but to allow an estimation of the limits of a scholarly perspective through the approximation of a perspective marked by difference.

Abstracting Heather

The final project of a graduate seminar taken in fall 2002, entitled "Feminism and Composition," required one of us to move out of the graduate classroom as a student and into the community. The feminism seminar drew from Kirsch et al.'s *Feminism and Composition: A Critical Sourcebook* (2003), as well as a variety of other readings on feminist epistemology, methodology, and theory. In conjunction with a final seminar-paper assignment that required students to inquire into an issue through a lens provided by feminist theory, students were also required to engage in a volunteer activity assignment, in which they were to devote at least six hours to a nonprofit organization that served the needs of women and then to analyze their experience in a course paper to show how it connected to the theoretical discussions taken up by the course.

As a member of this course, Jen volunteered at two specific sites over the course of the semester—at a local Fresh Start women's center, and at the downtown YWCA. Although located about a block from one another, both nonprofit organizations are poised in distinct contrast. Fresh Start, built in 2002, is safely tucked away next to a hospital. Its outside entryway is sheltered and decorated with sculptures; a gardenscape, fitted with comfortable benches, beckons those waiting outside to enjoy the ambience. The indoor lobby is full of light—the entryway itself is encased in glass and spans the two stories of the building. The polite staff quietly encourages visitors to check in. Bronze plaques with donors' names on them—donors who paid for the four-million-dollar construction—are built into the walls. Fresh Start is an agency that refers women to other agencies (it hopes to avoid duplicating services given by other groups), so that it not only refers women to legal services and employment resources, but also offers fitness classes and workshops on personal finance. A top-level agency such as this might be a second- or third-tier service provider; that is, it assumes that women who enter have a place to stay, food to eat, and the wherewithal to take the next step

The YWCA Haven House facility, built in 1989, recalls, by contrast, a service agency stereotype. A transitional housing facility for women who are homeless or abused and their children, its residence wing resembles a college dormitory. Located a block from a major interstate highway, the Haven House can accommodate sixteen families; it has a two-year waiting list. Meant to be a secure site that discourages abusers from visitation, its elevators are operated by key and security code, and the north-facing windows in each room let in little natural light. The YWCA's residence common area is full of children's toys; women come and go with strollers and car seats; television sets compete with the squeals of children. Its services are listed as counseling, case management, access to medical and dental care, and lifeskills training. The building itself is a metaphor—a starting place for women, a place where a woman with nowhere to go might show up and be taken in. Nothing flashy, but a place to gather oneself until one can move on, the YWCA is a world away from the library quiet of the Fresh Start lobby, where children are kept in child-care rooms so that mothers can have respite. Mothers who come to Haven House must pay for child care or have other mothers in residence look after their children as a favor.

Jen's volunteer experience took the form of tutoring a woman named Heather at Haven House who wanted to study for her GED.

Passing the GED is a condition of the medical technician program, and Heather's progress in the program was monitored by Haven House. If she did not pass, she would not be able to get the job she trained for, and would not be able to move out of the YWCA. Although Heather fit the "profile" of a woman who needed assistance (like the four-hour break to study that Fresh Start's child care rooms could have provided her), and even though she knew about the existence of Fresh Start, she had never been there, just one block away.

Heather's writing revealed her priorities. Although she has an eighth-grade education and is in her early twenties, she is concerned about child care at work and has sophisticated reasons for her concern, as one of her essays showed. When asked to write an essay about "the most important decision you have made," she wrote about her choice to go back to school and how it would affect her son's life as well as her own. An essay about "a very important day" revealed how scary it was to move into the YWCA, but how much hope it provided. Heather's most powerful writing drew specifically from place: her locations as a mother, worker, and student; her situatedness as a woman in transition; and her heritage as a Latina. Yet even as the course readings asserted that feminist epistemology begins from women's lived experiences, a disjuncture between what it meant to be "female"—for those who write feminist scholarship, for Heather, and for Jen—insinuated a range of experiential interpretation.

At first glance, course projects like these serve to widen the location of graduate education. Students are confronted with theory that requires reflexivity: questions of essentialized categories, perceptions of difference, and hierarchies of power are made real with experiences outside the classroom. Through what they were reading, students were able to come to the service projects aware that no connection with othered discourse is a neutral one. The readings students did created a space in which to think about ethics and research in a different way, and to view critically the range of feminist theory in composition studies. They enabled students to see service as praxis.

But, although at some level it was possible for Jen to connect and identify with Heather materially—growing up living on food stamps, shopping at the Salvation Army, being a woman in her mid-twenties—at the same time it absolutely was not. Jen is white, and she has benefited from it; further, she is not a mother. Jen's literate practices locate her differently, enabling a range of material potentials and situated practices unavailable to Heather. Most important here, Jen is positioned to appropriate Heather's story, to abstract Heather. Jen's representation of Heather in the writing she did for class risked not only erasing Heather, but also the very material conditions in which the two worked. Without knowing it, women "served" in such classes become part and parcel of someone else's writing without their knowledge, approval, or visible contribution. Jen's disciplined awareness, ratified by evaluation performed well outside the scope of the YWCA, emerged at the expense of Heather's dislocation. The privilege of Jen's positioning provided a backdrop of zero-location, one of class that protects *those who write* from *those who do not*—the ultimate privilege of ignoring material circumstance.

Conclusion

To politicize our locations as teachers and scholars means to take into account the ways we represent ourselves and our work to future generations of those who hope to be academic professionals. How might we want to define our field in the future, and how might we want scholarship to be valued? As Derek Owens suggests in *Composition and Sustainability*, "The issue is not so much to move meaning from one site to another, converting it in the process, but to explore how such migration forces us to rethink those sites and our relationship to them" (2001, 142). Within any location-based pedagogical model, then, we must recognize—and help our graduate students to recognize—the ironic potential of even the most reflexive research to support primarily the privileged discursive-material site of the university and its interests.

Community-based graduate education encourages future teacher-scholars to view themselves in relation to the world around them by engaging a space beyond the classroom. It allows graduate students (and those who teach them) to recognize the ethical implications of literate practices by enabling them to reinterpret their own experiences through the eyes of others situated outside the academy. What we propose here is sure to complicate our lives, our research, and the connection between the academy and the world outside of it, and it is not a quick or simple fix to all that ails us. We do not espouse a simple "add others and stir" approach, but rather the embodiment of a social and historical consciousness that resonates with our sophistic origins in the very public, and very localized, struggle over the quality of human life.

Notes

1. One of us has shown how a "professionalizing approach" to training even undergraduate writing tutors foregrounds awareness of

and facility in the specialized discourse of writing center scholarship as a standard for competence, displacing tutors from the locations of their work and linking their authority to an abstract grapholect in which they have little hope of participating (Vandenberg 1999).

2. Strictly speaking, the term *grapholect* refers to the written form of a spoken language, yet a grapholect differs from a dialect in exactly the ways that make dialects distinct from each other—a grapholect is a representation of abstraction in action, a point that Patricia Bizzell makes implicitly in calling for "mixed forms" of written scholarship (2002, 2).
3. In a report commissioned by the Educational Testing Service, Anthony Carnevale and Richard Fry project that college-age racial and ethnic minorities will increase by 40 percent in the United States over the next dozen years; by 2016, college enrollments will increase by 2.6 million, and minority students will make up 80 percent of this increase.

Works Cited

Anzaldúa, Gloria. 1999 *Borderlands/La Frontera: The New Mestiza.* San Francisco: Aunt Lute Books.

Beauvais, Paul Jude. 1989. "Sartre's Plea and the Purpose of Writing." *Pre/Text* 10, nos. 1 and 2: 11–13.

Bizzell, Patricia. 2002. "The Intellectual Work of 'Mixed' Forms of Academic Discourses." In *Alt/Dis: AlternativeDiscourses and the Academy,* ed. Christopher Schroeder, Helen Fox, and Patricia Bizzell, 1–10. Portsmouth, NH: Heinemann Boynton/Cook.

Bleich, David. 1998. *Know and Tell: A Writing Pedagogy of Disclosure, Genre, and Membership.* Portsmouth, NH: Boynton/Cook-Heinemann.

Bolin, Bill, Beth Burmester, Brenton Faber, and Peter Vandenberg, eds. "Doctoral Pedagogy in Rhetoric and Composition." Special edition, *Composition Studies* 23, no. 2.

Carnevale, Anthony P., and Richard A. Fry. 2004. "Economics, Demography, and the Future of Higher Education Policy." Educational Testing Service. http://www.nga.org/cda/files/ HIGHEREDDEMOECON.pdf (accessed July 5, 2004).

Comfort, Juanita R. 2001. "African-American Women's Rhetorics and the Culture of Eurocentric Scholarly Discourse." In *Contrastive Rhetoric Revisited and Redefined,* ed. Clayann Gilliam Panetta. Mahwah, NJ: Erlbaum.

Gee, James Paul. 2004. *Situated Language and Learning: A Critique of Traditional Schooling.* London: Taylor & Francis.

Herzberg, Bruce. 2000. "Service Learning and Public Discourse." *JAC* 20: 391–404.

Kent, Thomas. 1997. "The Consequences of Theory for the Practice of Writing." In *Publishing in Rhetoric and Composition,* ed. Gary A. Olson and Todd Taylor, 147–62. Albany: State University of New York Press.

———. 1999. Introduction to *Post-Process Theory: Beyond the Writing Process Paradigm,* ed. Thomas Kent, 1–6. Carbondale: Southern Illinois University Press.

Kirsch, Gesa L., and Joy S. Ritchie. 1995. "Beyond the Personal: Theorizing a Politics of Location in Composition Research." *CCC* 46, no. 1: 7–29.

Lakoff, George, and Mark Johnson. 1980. *Metaphors We Live By.* Chicago: University of Chicago Press.

Mahala, Daniel, and Jody Swilky. 2003. "Constructing Disciplinary Space: The Borders, Boundaries, and Zones of English Studies." *JAC* 23: 765–98.

Mauk, Johnathon. 2003. "Location, Location, Location: The 'Real' (E)states of Being, Writing, and Thinking in Composition." *College English* 65, no. 4: 368–88.

Olson, Gary A. 1989. "The Politics of Empowerment: Admitting Emerging Scholars to the Conversation." *Editors' Notes* 8: 20–22.

Owens, Derek. 2001. *Composition and Sustainability: Teaching for a Threatened Generation.* Urbana, IL: NCTE.

Rich, Adrianne. 1987. "Notes toward a Politics of Location." In *Blood, Bread, and Poetry: Selected Prose 1979–1985,* 210–32. London: Virago.

Sosnoski, James. 1994. *Token Professionals and Master Critics: A Critique of Orthodoxy in Literary Studies.* Albany: State University of New York Press.

Stuckey, J. Elspeth. 1991. *The Violence of Literacy.* Portsmouth, NH: Boynton/Cook Heinemann.

Swales, John M., and Stephanie Lindemann. 2002. "Teaching the Literature Review to International Graduate Students." In *Genre in the Classroom: Multiple Perspectives,* ed. Ann M. Johns, 105–20. Mahwah, NJ: Erlbaum.

Vandenberg, Peter. 1998. "Composing Composition Studies: Scholarly Publication and the Practice of Discipline." In *Under Construction: Working at the Intersections of Composition Theory, Research, and*

Practice, ed. Christine Farris and Chris M. Anson, 19–29. Logan: Utah State University Press.

———. 1999. "Lessons of Inscription: Tutor Training and the 'Professional Conversation.'" *Writing Center Journal* 19, no. 2 (Spring/Summer): 59–83.

———. 2004. "Auto/Graphing: Wheels, Writing, and Work." *Writing on the Edge* 14, no. 2 (Spring): 53–70.

Vatz, Richard. 1973. "The Myth of the Rhetorical Situation." *Philosophy and Rhetoric* 6: 154–61.

Wollman-Bonilla, Julie E. 2002. "Does Anybody Really Care? Research and Its Impact on Practice." *Research in the Teaching of English* 36: 311–26.

Part II

Inside the Classroom and Beyond

6

TEACHING THE CAPITAL CITY

JOHN ACKERMAN

In the writings of James Clifford and other social and cultural theorists, such as Caren Kaplan and Derek Gregory, the "capital city" hovers as a real and imaginary location. It is real in the way that cities became real as cultural and economic centers throughout the nineteenth and twentieth centuries. We know that Bismarck is the capital city of North Dakota, and with some accuracy even those like us who do not live there can guess that Bismarck has operated through the twentieth century as an actual center for law, commerce, and community for those who first settled and then built the city and its surrounding areas. The capital city, however, is also imaginary, because Bismarck, like most major American cities, resides somewhere between material fact and conceptual fiction. That is to say that a "capital" city lives in both our geographic and cultural memories: the first may be our sense of a crossroad, topography, or locus of lived experiences in urban life, while the second form of memory transcends the actual, lived, or mapped space. The capital city as a location in a public's imaginary is a place within an ideational and, therefore, ideological landscape. Increasingly disconnected from its material history, a society's legal or cultural center is shaped within a mediated public sphere (see Weisser 2002): it is Fargo that has eclipsed Bismarck in the public imaginary because of the success of a movie.

For Michel de Certeau, a capital city that circulates in our imagination as commoditization becomes a "conceptual city," one of the remarkable achievements of the twentieth century in capitalist societies. In reading de Certeau's chapter "Walking in the City," we are invited to comprehend a material history of lived environments in three distinct phases: centuries of cartography and ownership that produced a sense of an organized world, the rise of a spectacle society in the twentieth century that depended less and less on the material demarcation of an urban space and more and more on its discursive reproduction, and a late twentieth-century decay of the concept city (his example is New York) as a stable, marketable idea in the public imaginary. For de Certeau, the decay of the concept city is the incremental defeat of the rational and progressive process of emplacement in contemporary culture that mapped our quite real cities onto our national landscape and a public consciousness that presumes the reproduction of homogeneous spaces, a timeless sense of inevitability, and "universal and anonymous subject" (1984, 94). Capital cities as concept cities, then, provide an ideological security, for those most in power, with the veneer of universality and continuity. Yet, as I read his words, he inflects this modernist sensibility with a sense of loss—of the public, geographic and ideological map that provided a logic and coherence to contemporary life—and a rediscovery of territorial imperatives, through the "tactical" enactments of new social and discursive spaces.

In day-to-day living, as writers such as Gloria Valdes (1994), Dwight Conguergood (1992), and Raul Villa (2000) have shown, a stable economic and cultural center is desired by some and rejected by others. And it is those with the least cultural capital who often struggle to make a home after migration to the United States, or to survive in the midst of public housing or in the face of urban renewal. In very real terms, many cities are now defined as much by who moves away as by who lives in them and by a person's role in the distribution of economic and cultural capital in a global society. The capital city as a real and imaginary construct may be located somewhere in the middle of what Kaplan (1998) terms the "global-local nexus," but it implies a quite real question of what we mean by *home* or *neighborhood* or *where I am from.* Sometimes we want to believe and to act as if home or neighborhood exist in a particular place and time, so that the local and global are the same, secure, and identifiable locations. And sometimes we want to believe and act as if home and neighborhood are more relative and malleable in a vernacular rhetorical world. Gerald Hauser (1999) proposes that the profundity of vernacular rhetoric can occur within the "reticulate structure" of society. A reticulate life world consists of an interlacing of publics, subjectivities, and materialities; and social well-being could then be manufactured tactically in social and rhetorical spaces if we, as residents, could negotiate the disciplinary and "anti-disciplinary" powers of everyday life, to use de Certeau's term.

The philosopher Giorgio Agamben, in *The Coming Community*, embraces the absence of both a stable symbolic and material center in daily life and a new presence that can be found in a spectacle society, because this society offers a new cultural space, the "place of the neighbor." This place is conceptual and rhetorical as it comprises our ability to perceive and then act with a heightened sense of the limits of our categorical self and thus the terrain of our periphery, as our identities are never universal in the presence of others. Agamben turns to religious allegory to illustrate how a heightened sense of one's peripheral status, and a stronger sense of our proximity to and interdependency with others, engenders a sense of belonging in the world:

> According to the Talmud, two places are reserved for each person, one in Eden and the other in Gehenna. The just person, after being found innocent, receives a place in Eden plus that of a neighbor who was damned. The unjust person, after being judged guilty, receives a place in hell plus that of a neighbor who was saved. . . . In the topology . . . the essential element is not so much the cartographic distinction between Eden and Gehenna, but rather the adjacent place that each person inevitably receives. At the point when one reaches one's final state and fulfills one's own destiny, one finds oneself for that very reason in the place of the neighbor. What is most proper to every creature is thus its substitutability, its being in any case in the place of the other. (1993, 23)

This "place of the neighbor" is derived from our "adjacency" to others and our awareness of our "substitutability," supplanting the indeterminacy of postmodern life with a different "ethos," consisting of a cohabitation—the "space adjacent, the empty place where each can move freely" (25).

For my purposes, I side with Agamben, de Certeau, and others who recognize the contested role of real and imaginary "capitals" in contemporary life and who champion a sense of belonging and a basis for community action in an otherwise transnational and mediated society. I maintain that writing instruction, when it is joined with theories of social geography, and with what I refer to as a georhetorical methodology, can assist students as writers and as members of society with a profound question of everyday life: How do we surmise the certainty and dimensionality of one's own "substitutability" if this depends upon a survey of one's "adjacency" in a social and material world? My work with architects, with urban planners, and with students at a university, indicates that such questions are beyond a single disciplinary or professional mooring, and they cannot be answered by any of us without moral, philosophical, or technical effort. As I will try to establish in this chapter, sociogeographic theories help us to replot the coordinates of our metaphysical centers, but rhetoric and writing, as elements within a uniquely critical and empirical project, give dimension to our adjacency and thus a way to gauge our ethical probability for substitutability. Adjacency, for example, is a keenly critical and empirical project for students at a university, because they must discern the center and periphery of daily living at a complex institution (most often in a foreign town or city) that is premised on hypothetical and deliberative worlds of majors, disciplines, and future employers in imagined constructs, such as a workforce or a national economy.

The ethnocentric bias in modern anthropology ignores the difference between real and imagined places, and the tension between them, by emphasizing "dwelling over relations of travel." We all make this mistake from time to time: we accept as true and representative what our "cognitive maps" say about another person and where and how he or she lives, as Fredrick Jameson would put it. We make our way in our worlds with these biases because we tacitly reject the principle of "substitutability," and we presume that what we see (and name and map) is true, fixed, representative, and encapsulating. We derive *our* notion of *their* capital city by confusing the present with the past, the transient with the resident, and an observable, present terrain with the "preterrain"—"all those places you have to go through and be in relation with just to get to your village or that place of work you will call your field" (Clifford 1997, 23).

My argument in this chapter is that a georhetorical methodology can assist our students to engineer an answer to the ethical question of substitutability through a critical and empirical question of adjacency in everyday life. That method, which will echo the various methodologies found in *The Locations of Composition*, gains its power through the capacity of measurement and the rhetorical authority that place students as writers and as residents in proximal relations to those around them and to the university as one institutional authority among many. As proponents of social geography make clear, one's spatial memory and skills in cultural orienteering equip each of us with a particular kind of cultural authority, different from but related to the preferred skills and dispositions of universities and other cultural institutions. If I sound hopelessly postmodern in my pedagogical assumptions, I am, at least, to the degree that I believe that cultural identities are disputed and shifting, but that a discernment of self-identity—and self-substitutability—are both possible and advisable. In the plainly spoken wisdom of Wallace Stegner, "If you don't know where you are, you don't know who you are" (1992, 199–206). My hope is that students, as residents of the university but also as residents of a community, will manufacture for themselves what Barry Lopez characterizes as "*la querencia* . . . a place on the ground where one feels secure, a place from which one's strength is drawn . . ." (qtd. in Ackerman, 2000, 127) even if that ground is a discursive location in the simulacra or a place that must be painstakingly manufactured by discerning the coordinates of one's adjacency to others in daily living.

For the sake of my argument, I often find it necessary to couple the words "writer" and "resident," because neither captures the full meaning of identity, authority, and action when students operate within social geographies, both real and imagined. For one thing, to write as a sociogeographic practice is more of an act of inscription than of composing, more of a mark upon the ground, in a public sphere, and in a material history. And because classrooms and universities are one site, or sets of sites, within a geographic tableau, I prefer to see an act of writing as a form of action and authority in civic life. With irony noted, I would suggest that a more appropriate term for the practice of composition in a sociogeographic locale may well be *the writer in residence*. To write, to be a student, to practice composition, and so on require (and benefit from) a distinct authority that is derived from and returned to our residences—our social, physical and discursive addresses that produce, for all of us, *querencia*. This is hardly the sole jurisdiction of any classroom or university.

A Georhetorical Method

In order to sustain sociogeographic writing practices at the university and elsewhere, I believe that a methodology is required that is remarkably different from what is found in most composition classrooms. While I do not mean to declare what is or is not rhetorical (or what is or is not composition), I do hope to present what I think are some of the major components of a method that includes a literature of place, terms of art, measurements, institutional locations, documentation, and a landscape event. In the case of sociogeographic writing, there is a deeper issue than how to invigorate a classroom. As Henri Lefebvre argues in *The Production of Space*, social space as we encounter it today has been previously organized and methodized to become at best an artifact of cultural history that is open to critique and reform, and at worst a source of our alienation and disenfranchisement. Any critical engagement of social spaces will therefore require a method that is equal in scope and acuity to at least some forces and instruments that made the world as we find it today. Analytical tools cannot rewrite history, but social geography was "written" differently than textual geographies of universities and disciplines. For Lefebvre, social space is "both a field of action . . . and a basis of action . . . at once a collection of materials . . . and an ensemble of *materiel* (. . . the procedures necessary to make efficient use . . .)" (1991, 191; italics in the original). In all cases, a georhetorical method will struggle against the historical and material precedents that comprise the social geography of a writer as a resident of community.

With that noted, a rhetorical *ensemble de matériel* will include what Lopez has called a *literature of place*, which would include literature and criticism that reject a bifurcation of the two. Lopez recognizes a turn in this writing from an appreciation of nature (and by implication urban spaces) to the consequence of an irreverence toward nature: "The real topic of nature writing . . . is not nature but the evolving structure of communities from which nature has been removed . . . writing concerned with the biological and spiritual fate of those communities. . . . It is my belief that a human imagination is shaped by the architecture it encounters" (1998, 182).

Naturalists and environmentalists have a secure niche in creative nonfiction, and they can be employed in sociogeographic writing as demonstrations of how a writer can remap a location in the world and in their hearts.[1] By naming these places, they offer the possibility of a return—to reclaim what is overlooked in landscapes and cityscapes and what has been bought and sold in the name of civilization. Lefebvre's earliest writings about life in the French countryside were as much lyrical as dialectical, because he witnessed a process of buying and selling of the natural and lived spaces of his homeland. For Lefebvre, the commodification of France described in the *Critique of Everyday Life, Vol. I*, in the moment of reconstruction after World War II, was a personal narrative in search of a theoretical stance. Thus, a literature of place will be coincidentally imaginative, interpretive, and critical as it speaks in emboldened and embodied ways about places lost, found, lived, and loved and where the spirit and the mind are inextricably linked to habitat. These writers speak of boundaries, of the cartographies of nations and states, of owners and occupants, and of the misplaced separation of body, spirit, and homeland. Lopez continues: "It may be more important now to enter into an ethical and reciprocal relationship with everything around us than to continue to work toward the sort of control of the physical world that, until recently, we aspired to" (1998, 184). A literature of place contributes to a subversion of canonical knowledge and a homogenous cultural memory of lived space. Gloria Anzaldúa, for example, identifies with a return to borderlands and signifies this struggle by mixing Spanish, Latino, Anglo, and Chinese languages and philosophies within her text, confounding the reader's expectations that this prose is a stable genre or style.

As other writers in *Locations* demonstrate, there are numerous sociogeographic theories to include in such a literature. Jameson has assessed the worth of such theories as "a new kind of spatial imagination capable of confronting the past in a new way and reading its less tangible secrets off the template of its spatial structures—body, cosmos, city" (1991, 146). Michel Foucault has characterized this theoretical project in terms of time: a "whole history remains to be written of spaces—which at the same time would be a history of power—from the great strategies of geopolitics to the little tactics of the habitat" (1986, 22). Delores Hayden, a feminist, urban historian, and architectural critic, assigns much of the dynamism of this interdisciplinary theoretical work to issues of design but reminds us, as did Lopez, that a sense of place is reclaimed through the stories we tell about the manufacture of lived spaces: "At the intersection of these fields lies the history of the cultural landscape, the production of space, human patterns impressed upon the contours of natural environment. It is the story of how places are planned, designed, built, inhabited, appropriated, celebrated, despoiled, and discarded. Cultural identity, social history, and urban design are here intertwined" (1997, 15).

A literature of place will invariably lead a writer to the question of language and lexicon, and it will produce *terms of art* for teachers and students as members of the public sphere. All specialized courses and practices are replete with a technical vocabulary, and Nedra Reynolds illustrates how the field of composition depends upon a geographic sense of its institutional and discursive vitality. We speak of *centers, domains, communities,* and we seek writing that transcends intellectual boundaries, because our disciplinary disposition posits both time and space as coordinates for discursive practice. *Borderlands, diaspora, displacement, dwelling, exile, nomads, locale, territorialism,* as Kaplan (1998) illustrates, are terms of arts within cultural studies; but the more commonplace ideas, such as *place, location, position, home, work,* and *travel* are ready-made for an instructional lexicon, provided they are taught with political, spiritual, and social intent. In an interview, Foucault confronts the necessity of such language in the making of social analysis: "Well, let's take a look at these geographic metaphors. Territory is no doubt a geographical notion, but it's first of all a juridico-political one: the area controlled by a certain kind of power. Field is an economico-juridicial notion. Displacement: what displaces itself is an army, a squadron, a population. Domain is a juridico-political notion. Soil is a historico-geological notion. Region is a fiscal, administrative, military notion. Horizon is a pictorial, but also a strategic notion" (1977, 68). The lexicon for a pedagogy of place need not be so Latinate, which is why it is important to read Foucault and then Anzaldúa and then Lopez, who writes in *The Rediscovery of North America,* "[t]he discovery of *querencia,* I believe, hinges on the perfection of a sense of place . . . at the very least, knowledge of what is inviolate about the relationship between a people and the place they occupy" (1990, 127).

If there is one key term that belongs in a georhetorical method, it is the idea of the countersite or heterotope. For Lefebvre, the issue is whether a place, imaginary or real, is differentiated across isotopes, heterotopes (or countersite), and utopias. Isotopias are "analogous spaces" that are recognizable through common properties and occurrences, what we might see out our windows as subdivisions, theme restaurants, and supermarts that mystify modern life because they appear normal through repetition. In another time or place, isotopias might be gardens, porches, and avenues that are patterned through everyday living. Isotopias contrast with heterotopias and utopias in that the former are spaces that are "mutually repellent" and the latter are spaces of the imagination (1991, 366). Willfully place a garden in the middle of a government-housing track, and you may have a heterotope, depending on who ascribes its repellent nature.

Site is also a key term (and method) because it presumes that *topes* are discernible. The architect and critic Carol Burns describes sites and their analyses as being confounded by language as much as by the physical elements attributed to a portion of land. Burns points out the number of conflicting terms associated with natural and built space, such as *lot, plot, region,* and *location,* with each word representing a slightly different legal, physical, and philosophical slant on a site and illustrating a codependence on linguistic and spatial cues. Sites are "teachable places" because of "The elastic nature of the breadth and scale of sites semantically, experientially, and temporally. . . . Every site is a unique intersection of land, climate, production, and circulation . . . already constructed by its specific circumstances . . . an artifact of human work that can neither be completed or abandoned" (Burns 1991, 163–165).

Motivated by imaginative and interpretive literatures, and aided by a critical vocabulary, a georhetorical method for a writing class and for action in the world will invite and require a series of *measurements.* These measurements, as Reynolds (2004) points out, need not replicate the Archimedian impulse to circumscribe the world. Following her advice, there exists in these measurements the potential for domination and for complicity and reciprocity. I list my practical favorites to suggest that such measurements might function as a repertoire that would implicate the designer and measurer in the process of representing a material or geographic reality.

- The countersite. As an activity, the countersite blends travel, observation, measurement, and criticism; and to call a space a countersite means to place this space in opposition to a spatial regime. The countersite, I have found, resonates with students, because they know of places, found or invented, that subvert the authority of parents, teachers, or other authorities.
- Pedestrian speech acts. Engaging in pedestrian speech acts is an activity borrowed from de Certeau's chapter "Walking in the City," is an assignment that is both simple and profound. For De Certeau, street life is a physical form of insubordinate inscription that leads to an unraveling of the concept city. Walking and charting urban foot traffic is a method for understanding the physical properties of a speech act that reappropriates social space.
- Place memory. Place memory is an exercise in social memory that relies on storytelling, but a telling that attends to the stabilizing persistence of place as a demarcation of experiences. Place memory is a cognitive theory with a social agenda and depends on the human ability to connect self with both built and natural environments. For instance, Ruth Frankenburg interviewed women who lived and worked in an urban area and concluded that the social geography of race is firmly entrenched in memory and is experientially coded by social and territorial difference. Frankenburg says, a "racial, social geography . . . refers to the racial and ethnic mapping of environments in physical and social terms and enables also the beginning of an understanding of the conceptual mapping of self and other" (1993, 44).

- Mapping. For forty years, urban geographers and historians have applied what Jameson has called "an aesthetic of cognitive mapping." This mapping begins with the exercise of drawing, as best one can, the perimeter and access routes for a city, neighborhood, school, park, and so on. The results of these maps, when stratified across different axes of culture, indicate that there is not one infrastructure for a cultural landscape, just as people do not share the same sense of territoriality with regard to race or economic difference, as Mike Davis (1992) and Raul H. Villa (2000) illustrate in their writing. Kevin Lynch, an urban planner, used this method to study differences between three neighborhoods in Los Angeles: an affluent white neighborhood, an inner-city African American neighborhood, and a mixed neighborhood that has long been a home for immigrants who work in factories or who travel to business downtown.
- Site analysis. Site analysis is a mainstay in architecture, environmental science, and urban planning, and the basics from architecture are adaptable to a writing classroom. The critical work involved is in measuring perimeters, circulation, materials, structures, building placement and proximics, aesthetics and facades, elevation and perspective, and the life-worlds of residents. While many of the tools of architects and planners are beyond casual use, many can be done with some acuity by anyone. Christopher Alexander's monumental compendium, *The Nature of Order*, posits not only that a "pattern language" exists but that it must be comprehended and used to recapture a process of designing and making of "non-living structure: kinds of things, arrangements of matter, buildings, roads, artifacts which do not belong to the class of living structures and which, for the first time, focus our attention on the distinction" (2002, xiv).

A georhetorical method will also require a particular kind of site analysis of the physical imprint and proximity of the institutions that codify social practice. This *institutional location* will be important for the configuration of practices that constitute a "textography," as John Swales terms the textual hierarchies and practices that define university (or other professional) buildings or a spatial semiotic in the way that Elaine Chin documents the functional and political properties of the internal organization in the built environment of profession. The institutional setting can also be interinstitutional, raising the question how the discursive, material, and political properties of one institutional site relate to another and the points of access and traversal that place these relations in tension. Universities tend to occupy an elevated position on the urban, suburban, or rural landscapes, as if the universities' planners—as was often the case throughout the twentieth century in the United States—sought to position the university beside the church and town hall, as close in kind to God and power as terrain, carpenters, and the imagination would allow. Ellen Cushman studied the communities around her home institution of Rensselaer Polytechnic Institute and in particular the "approach" to the university, an expansive, stone staircase that both invites and expels those who do not belong to either the school or the town. Cushman concludes that social divisions are physically represented and marked by a staircase, and they coincide with social distances between, in her case, academics and the everyday. She proposes that critical work can "collapse political binaries by depicting the complex everyday particulars in the middle place where most people live their lives" (1998, 239).

A georhetorical method will include the *documentation* of preserved natural and built public spaces. To historically excavate a city or landscape, one must find, parse, and deconstruct planning documents, newspaper accounts, the notes for town council meetings, master plans, and building codes. Hayden's work is based on historical documentation of the exchange of lands and on county records that illustrate, for example, how redevelopment can erase past communities and ethnic identity. In my teaching, I have asked students to archive a series of letters to the editor or cycles of e-mail and Web postings that constitute one slice of a public conversation that can be, and must be, then triangulated with policy documents created through different media and motives and with local history and students' direct experience with the natural or public space in question. These three documents—as histories, genres, and analytical instruments—will assist anyone to comprehend the role of language in the production and protection of public and natural spaces and the role of these spaces in the production of texts.

The documents that build and preserve may guide inquiry toward the appreciation of both virtual or actual spaces and the design documents that support them. The virtual building or artifact are accepted results in fields such as architecture, geography, or urban planning because of the necessary technical and material gap between designing and building. Documents and drawings carry a status in these fields and in the design of public and natural spaces that is different from the role of texts within the humanities. Patrick Dias, Alvida Freedman, Peter Medway and Andrew Pare (1999) point out that texts appear in customary roles as part of a paper trail that ends with a fork in the road: one way is toward an actual result, and the other is toward the genre of design as an end in itself. Why a given document or drawing is not built depends on many ordinary constraints such as money or politics, but the difference between virtual and actual designs, in the documentation process, also reveals the importance of multimodality, according to Kress and Leeuwen (1991). As Peter Medway (1993) has shown, visual designs can (and often do) hang on a wall, whether the designs are built or not, thereby underscoring the importance for teaching multimodality, visual rhetoric, and interdiscursivity to track the number of and mercurial nature of representational forms aimed at the production of space.

And finally, in all cases, whether for the purpose of university instruction or the purposes of public deliberation, at the heart of the georhetorical method will be a *landscape event*. These events are exceedingly rich, because they exhibit crosscurrents of land, land use, ownership, economic conquest and blight, cultural and ethnic heritage, urban identity, destiny, obligation, community, democracy, and change. Each region in which our universities reside resonates with landscape events, and their selection as critical sites for analysis and engagement will lead to case studies that foster social activism (if that is one's goal) or that fill a semester with inquiry. The number of events that are open for interrogation and interpretation are without limits, if such events are allowed, for the sake of analysis, to span the inconspicuously local (such as the debate over a community garden) or the monumentally regional (such as the debate over access to and the redevelopment of urban frontage on Lake Erie). Both are part of the greater metropolitan discussion of the urban landscape in Cleveland, Ohio, near where I live today. The declaration of a "monumental" landscape event becomes a critical issue as the political and economic machineries are revealed.

The point here is not to favor the grand over the ordinary, but to realize that the dramatic event in a georhetorical method places the grand and the inconspicuous in dialectical tension. In Flagstaff, my prior residence and a much smaller city in a very different region of the United States, the ordinary and the extraordinary are linked for many, because how one lives, day in and day out in a small city, and how one plans to live from one century to the next (via urban planning) are viscerally linked. On the Colorado Plateau, there are many landscape events: policies toward national forests, controlled forest burning, and tourism that translated into the sounds and smells of residents' backyards. There are nearby disputes over jointly claimed lands on Hopi and Navajo nations that have sparked arguments over national sovereignty as far away as western Europe. In the Sonoran desert, Phoenix has become the fifth largest city in the United States and is facing growth restrictions as well as the politics of water conservation. And in a large city, such as Cleveland, the debate over the economic "concept" of the city is over whether the city can remap its preindustrial attitude toward the "forgotten valley," the Cuyahoga River basin, and pursue a reclamation project that fuses histories of land, ethnicity, and industry with mixed-use philosophy and regional planning. A bike path through this valley will require a major rethinking of industrial territories and civic identities, but when finished would link Lake Erie to my current neighborhood in Kent, some fifty miles to the south.

My clustering of *place-based literatures, terms of art, measurements, institutional locations, documentation,* and *landscape events* as a georhetorical method is my attempt to enable students to join the search for *querencia,* and I would hope that others would gather their own repertoires. What then makes such a composite method rhetorical? One answer may be the interdisciplinary nature of the methods in this collection, since they are derived from fields such as literature, urban planning, architecture, cultural theory, and discourse studies. As Derek Owens (2000) points out, social and environmental sustainability requires an interdisciplinary method and a multidisciplinary audience and motive. Rhetoric, by its nature, would lean toward the expropriation of available and appropriate tools for analysis through the nature of its interdisciplinary and transdisciplinary practice.

A quiver of found tools, however appropriate to a social geography or a landscape event, does not by itself confer rhetorical status. Rhetorical status results from the practice of rhetoric. This sounds circular, but it is what Richard Lanham argued some years ago in understanding how and when rhetoric appears as an organizing principle on a cultural landscape: "The rhetorical view of life . . . conceives reality as fundamentally dramatic. . . . The contribution rhetorical reality makes to Western reality as a whole is greatest when it is most uncompromisingly itself, [and] insists most strenuously on its own coordinates" (1976, 4–6). Lanham reminds us that rhetoric has no claim to sustainability in and by itself, no claim to irrevocability in the territory of human experience. It has to be made and remade, over and over again; and the motive and parameters to act are all that we can say is permanent.

Georhetorical Authority

The writers in this volume assume as I do that there is a rhetorical capacity in social geographic methods. The gathering and using of these methods produce a distinctive kind of authority and text in relation to university and other professional domains. In this chapter I cannot illustrate all of the many ways that georhetorical methods can be used for rhetorical purposes, but I would like to revisit a piece of writing that was produced with the help of some of these methods.

In an entry-level writing class, I required for the second paper a study of multiple perspectives, asking students to consider how "all lands are jointly occupied, but someone currently resides" (Ackerman, 2000, 101). The methods used for this paper involved memory, return, walking, maps, and records, and a goal for the writer was to determine one's "standpoint" in relation to others in any physical, natural, or cultural landscape. Luis Leon[2] wrote an essay titled, "One Mirror: Two Reflections," a paper that interlaces two voices as two perspectives on his neighborhood. Leon implicitly argues that you or me, the outsider, cannot so easily see the textures of life that comprise his home and are not to be easily fooled by what we see and hear. Here is a series of excerpts of the call and refrain that structures his essay—first his voice and then the voice of the outsider:

> *The sky is clear, not a bird or pigeon is in the sky, the humidity has taken care of that. . . . The thick, wooden door is placed between two glass windows, that are surrounded by round bars . . . the shady trees on the grassless lawns are no longer giving off shade, instead they keep it for themselves.*
>
> > The sky is clear. The oppressive hot sun shines its sweltering heat on dully constructed, rectangular brick houses. . . . Windows, imprisoned by metal bars are positioned at each end. . . . Tall trees take up space, but for what, they provide no shade.
>
> *Four men, two Latinos and two Blacks are on the driveway gathered around a table playing dominoes. . . . Three plastic buckets and a plastic mile-crate provide the chairs, but they don't mind. . . .*
>
> > Four men, all minorities, are gathered uselessly on the porch around a makeshift table, gambling . . . the heat is unbearable. . . . They are probably too drunk to know the difference. . . .
>
> *Behind a building lies a huge block fence. . . . The fence serves as a wall of fame. . . . Names that have lived, seen and passed. . . . Two*

> *hands one light-skin and one dark-skin, come together to form an handshake. . . .*
>
> Behind a building lies a huge block fence. . . . It is graffitied . . . a wall of shame. . . . Malicious defacement of private property, vandalism at its worst. . . .
>
> *This is where we live. This is how we live. This is who we are, and we will be here forever. Ask anyone who lives here; they will tell you.* (qtd. in Ackerman 2000, 103–5)

On the surface, this text is not so remarkable as it uses dialogue to create the dramatic tension between insider and outsider. When this text is read from the cultural and geographic locations of Luis Leon, the writer who lives in a neighborhood in East Phoenix, the text expands its rhetorical boundaries. If the text is read as a temporal and spatial record, then the writer is providing the reader with a particular map of a neighborhood and with directions for how to traverse this neighborhood. If this text is read as an artifact, the reader considers the georhetorical methods that led to it, and that are propelled by it. When I read Leon's text, I find a motivation to map and populate my own neighborhood similarly and to search for a method to do so. The text maps onto a place, and this place maps into this text, and both become the basis for this writer's socio-geographic authority. What I also find remarkable about this text is the nature of this authority for a first-year writer so young in age and experience, evidenced in the integrity of information measured and marshaled and the voice that carries it forward. "Perspective" is not an easy notion, in spatial design or in textual analysis, but Luis Leon appears to me to have mastered both to a degree that is commensurate with the landscape event. He could now draw or walk this terrain again, aided by a fusion of visual, embodied, spatial, and textual demarcations. And that is a rhetorical principle from which we can gauge the value of a writer's words in the world. We do not see his actual maps, but we know they are there and we know that an archaeology of this text is possible by working through the methods and measurements he used to produce it.

Writing and residence are closely aligned but are difficult for the traveler to achieve, leading the field of rhetoric and composition to term the tertiary practices of writing at the university "invented." This is because, as David Bartholomae pointed out some years ago, the university must be invented or appropriated, and because writers often have no residential or textual residue from which to work. If the idea of residency within a discourse community is what our field desires, then I suggest that residency in location is what we teach as a form of rhetorical authority, because residency within the location of a text, embroiled in place, and vice versa, is an available means of persuasion for all entering students and can be a bridging authority in relation to the authority of universities and other social institutions. I propose that if rhetorical authority is to have a material, residential capacity, then we may as well begin with social geography in natural and design spaces, suggesting that body, space, and text fruitfully occur as learnable phenomena and in that curricular order. In keeping with Lanham's idea of determinants for rhetorical practice, it will be the return to body, space, and text that makes the practice of writing rhetorical. We are used to thinking that the rhetorical situation is comprised of audience, constraint, and exigence, which conspire in a logocentric universe, but with a georhetorical method and a sociogeographic motive the exigence may productively emerge from the synapse of an embodied, material, and historical location.

Substitutability

I end this chapter by returning to the question of substitutability and the interpretive challenge of responding to the capital city as a one representation (of many) of how someone occupies a cultural location. Agamben's philosophical writing may seem to pull students further and further away from the tangible, traceable locations of a human geography that are determined by walking, observing, mapping, and writing. But his philosophical study is one of ethos, finally, and the search for the possibility of belonging in a world that militates against our participation through the symbolic allure of the capital city. Agamben's joyful proposal is that, in this age of simulation and mechanical reproduction, there is room for the extremes of culture that were not possible in the previous cycles of emplacement that map geographies, communities, and collective will through the production of conceptual categories.

The coming community is one in which the residents, occupants, and participants "co-belong without any representable condition of belonging" (Agamben 1993, 86). The death of the example as a stable placeholder for state, nation, citizen, people, and so on fosters a renewed sense of belonging and a social responsibility: "To appropriate the historical transformation of human nature that capitalism wants to limit to spectacle, to link together image and body in a space where they can no longer be separated, and thus to forge the *whatever* body, whose physis is resemblance—this is the good that humanity must learn to wrest from commodities in their decline" (50; italics in the original).

Agamben eradicates the terrain of the capital city by eradicating the powers of the example (that is, the official Web site of Bismarck, North Dakota, is emptied of meaning). He offers the idea that the actuality of living, with a sense of harmony or purpose, depends upon the discovery of "adjacency" as a fundamental ethical principle, "the empty place where each can move freely . . . the very place of love" (25). I am saying that adjacency is a populated, situated project as well as an emancipatory philosophy. We gauge our adjacencies in life by measuring and remembering and inscribing the coordinates of our proximities.

What I find important, in addition to Agamben's mediation on private and public life in our times, is the insertion of an ethics of adjacency into rhetorical practice, which has always been about the definition of the polis and the relations between where one lives and what one says or does to sustain that place. Teaching "a sense of place" and employing georhetorical methods, I believe, may assist the return of both the teacher and the student to adjacency in embodied, material, and historical locations at the center and periphery of lived environments. Place-based writing instruction, wherever it resides in the university curriculum or in societal practice, has the potential to honor the "preterrain," as Clifford termed the territory of another's life that escapes the observer's gaze. Adjacency, as the practice of measurements and analysis, forces our attention to the time and distance between people and places, in much the way that Mikhail Bakhtin recognized the "transgredient" nature of dialogue as the measurement by distance and the acuity of our vision. It is less the issue of seeing and hearing another person and more the issue of judging the distance between and developing an ocularity to define these relations.

Adjacency is one admirable result of georhetorical methods, and another is the achievement of substitutability as a new conception of ethos, as finding oneself in the place of the neighbor. Substitutability is, for Agamben, the place of freedom and love, but it also a necessary ingredient in achieving other social goals aligned with sociogeographic theories of the life-world. Owens's ethic of sustainability "eventually requires one to synthesize a variety of disciplines" placing the rhetorical labor to synthesize, at least potentially, in an adjacent relation to other corridors of power and practice in and around the university (2001, xv). Sustainability is most fundamentally based on the understanding that a people live in a ecological network that may be construed differently as a disciplinary milieu, a public sphere, and as the equilibrium in an ecology. In all venues, substitutability helps to explain the mutual dependency and consequentiality of shared existence. Substitutability is certainly a goal in the work in and around architectural practices

(Ackerman 1997). My borrowing of disciplinary tools led to a morphing of practices, offering the architect (as collaborator) a hybrid methodology that borrowed much from my training in the humanities and social sciences, and offering the rhetorician (as collaborator) a hybrid methodology that I have partially illustrated this chapter as a georhetorical method.

Adjacency and substitutability can also support new allegiances within a region. A favorite example of mine is the Temple University composition program, which kept, but softened, an interest in basic skills and writing across the curriculum and strengthened the connection with local agencies through New City Writing devoted to art, writing, activism, and community development. This type of educational confederation does not, as I see it, foreground basic linguistic skill as *exemplary* so much as the adjacent spaces where "each can move freely," to borrow Agamben's phrase once more. This is not possible without a regional allegiance, and not possible in a university or curriculum modeled on the nation state or an enclosed domicile of interdisciplinarity. Sociogeographic writing opens many possibilities for sustainable relations between cultural locations as interinstitutional dialogue and intercommunity dialogue that are built upon (but not limited to) geography, environmental and urban studies, creative writing, native and ethnic studies, architecture, women's studies, sociology, local art, and the residence requirements of a school and community.

The principle of substitutability is an intensely ethical question for any individual, but it also suggests, as Bill Readings concludes in *The University in Ruins,* a prospective stance for a university that "holds open the question of whether and how thoughts fit together" (1996, 191). Sociogeographic writing can help to find and sustain the allegiances that may prove mandatory for sustaining the project of rhetoric at the university, if that is our goal, and for sustaining composition as material practice in the lives of students. How else will we build a bridge between writing and the city, composition and the university, or a practice of literacy—in Hannah Arendt's words, as *vita activa* in the polis—unless we define writing as a practice of adjacency and substitutability in the twenty-first century?

Notes

1. Numerous collections of ecoliterature and ecocriticism exist as well, as collections on the rhetoric of public and natural spaces

(e.g., Herndl and Brown 1996). With my colleagues at Northern Arizona University, I produced an edited collection entitled *A Sense of Place* (2000) that gathers writing classified elsewhere as postcolonial writing, anthropology, architecture, fiction, national policy debate, poetry, naturalism, creative nonfiction, and the writing of entry-level students. We gathered these diverse forms of writing quite purposefully to disintegrate the boundaries between genres and to build a spatial and rhetorical pedagogy for entering students at a public university.

2. Luis Leon granted permission to reproduce his writing for the textbook *A Sense of Place*, and for all future scholarly or educational publications. We invited students to publish their work so that other students and readers could benefit from their efforts and success with what am I calling here georhetorical methods and place-based writing and inquiry.

Works Cited

Ackerman, John. 1997. "The Space Between: Reflexivity and Essentialism in Multidisciplinary Work." Paper delivered at the Conference on College Composition and Communication, Phoenix, AZ, March 13.

———. 2000. *A Sense of Place: Physical, Natural and Cultural Environments*. 3rd ed. Boston: Houghton Mifflin.

Ackerman, John, and Scott Oates. 1996. "Image, Text, and Power in Workplace Writing." In *Multidisciplinary Research in Workplace Writing: Challenging the Boundaries*, ed. Anne Duin and Craig Hansen, 81–121. Hillsdale, NJ: Erlbaum.

Agamben, Giorgio. 1993. *The Coming Community*. Trans. Michael Hardt. Minneapolis: University of Minnesota Press.

Alexander, Christopher. 2002. Author's Note: The Concept of Living Structure. In *The Process of Creating Life: Book Two, The Nature of Order*, 1–15. Berkeley, CA: Center for Environmental Structure.

Anzaldúa, Gloria. 1987. *Borderland/La Frontera: The New Mestiza*. San Francisco: Aunt Lute Books.

Arendt, Hannah. 1958. *The Human Condition*. Chicago: University of Chicago Press.

Bakhtin, Mikhail. 1981. *The Dialogic Imagination*. Ed. Michael Holquist. Austin: University of Texas Press.

Bartholomae, David. 1988. "Inventing the University." In *Perspectives on Literacy*, ed. Elaine Kingten, Barry Kroll and Mike Rose, 273–85. Carbondale: Southern Illinois University Press.

Bitzer, Lloyd, F. 1968. "The Rhetorical Situation." *Philosophy and Rhetoric* 1: 1–14.

Burns, Carol. 1991. "On Site: Architectural Preoccupation." In *Drawing/Building/Text*, ed. Andrea Kahn, 148–58. New York: Princeton Architectural Press.

Chin, Elaine. 1994. "Redefining 'Context' in Research on Writing." *Written Communication* 11: 445–82.

Clifford, James. 1997. *Routes: Travel and Translation in the Late Twentieth Century*. Cambridge, MA: Harvard University Press.

Conquergood, Dwight. 1992. "Life in Big Red: Struggles and Accommodations in a Chicago Polyethnic Tenement." In *Structuring Diversity: Ethnographic Perspectives on the New Immigration*, ed. Louise Lamphere, . Chicago: University of Chicago Press.

Cushman, Ellyn. 1998. *The Struggle and the Tools: Oral and Literate Strategies in an Inner City Community*. Albany: State University of New York Press.

Davis, Mike. 1992. *City of Quartz: Excavating the Future in Los Angeles*. New York: Vintage.

de Certeau, Michel. 1984. *The Practice of Everyday Life*. Trans. Steven Rendall. Berkeley and Los Angeles: University of California Press.

Dias, Patrick, Alvida Freedman, Peter Medway, and Andrew Pare. 1999. *Worlds Apart: Acting and Writing in Academic and Workplace Contexts*. Mahwah, NJ: Erlbaum.

Foucault, Michel. 1977. *Power/Knowlege: Selected Interviews & Other Writings*. Ed. C. Gordon. New York: Pantheon Books.

———. 1986. "Of Other Spaces." Trans. J. Kiskowiec. *Diacritics* 16: 22–27.

Frankenburg, Ruth. 1993. *White Women, Race Matters: The Social Construction of Whiteness*. Minneapolis: University of Minnesota Press.

Gee, James, Colin Lankshear, and Glynda Hull. 1997. *The New Work Order: Behind the Language of the New Capitalism*. Boulder, CO: Westview Press.

Gregory, Derek. 1993. *Geographical Imaginations*. New York: Basil Blackwell.

Hauser, Gerald. 1999. *Vernacular Voices: The Rhetoric of Publics and Public Spheres*. Columbia: University of South Carolina Press.

Hayden, Delores. 1997. *The Power of Place: Urban Landscapes as Public History*. Cambridge, MA: MIT Press.

Herndl, Carl, and Steven Brown, eds. 1996. *Green Culture: Rhetorical Analyses of Environmental Discourse.* Madison: University of Wisconsin Press.

Jameson, Fredric. 1991. *Postmodernism, or The Cultural Logic of Late Capitalism.* London: Verso.

Kaplan, Caren. 1998. *Questions of Travel: Postmodern Discourses of Displacement.* Durham: Duke University Press.

Kress, Guther, and Theo Van Leeuwen. 1991. *Multi-modal Discourse: The Modes and Media of Contemporary Communication.* London: Edward Arnold.

Lanham, Richard. 1976. *The Motives of Eloquence: Literary Rhetoric of Renaissance.* New Haven, CT: Yale University Press.

Lefebvre, H. 1947. *Critique of Everyday Life, Volume 1.* Trans. John Moore. London: Verso. Originally published as *Critique de la vie quotidienne 1: Introduction* (Paris: Grasset,).

———. 1991. *The Production of Space.* Trans. Donald Nicholson-Smith. Oxford: Basil Blackwell.

Lopez, Barry. 1990. *The Rediscovery of North America.* New York: Vintage Books.

———. 1998. *The Literature of Place.* The EnviroLink Network. http://arts.envirolink.org/ literary_arts/BarryLopez_LitofPlace.html.

Lynch, Kevin. 1960. *The Image of the City.* Cambridge, MA: MIT Press.

Medway, Peter. 1993. Virtual and Material Buildings: Construction and Constructivism in Architecture and Writing. *Written Communication* 13: 473–514.

Owens, Derek. 2001. *Composition and Sustainability: Teaching for a Threatened Generation.* Urbana, IL: NCTE.

Readings, Bill. 1996. *The University in Ruins.* Cambridge, MA: Harvard University Press.

Reynolds, Nedra. 1998. "Composition's Imagined Geographies: The Politics of Space in Frontier, City, and Cyberspace." *College Composition and Communication* 50: 12–35.

———. 2004. *Geographies of Writing: Inhabiting Places and Encountering Difference.* Carbondale: Southern Illinois University Press.

Stegner, Wallace. 1992. *Where the Bluebird Sings to the Lemonade Springs: Living and Writing in the West.* New York: Penguin Books.

Swales, John. 1998. *Other Floors, Other Voices: A Textography of a Small University Building.* Mahwah, NJ: Lawrence Erlbaum.

Valdes, Gloria. 1994. *Con respècto: Bridging the Distances between Culturally Diverse Families and Schools.* New York: Teachers College Press.

Villa, Raul H. 2000. *Barrio-logos: Space and Place in Urban Chicano Literature and Culture.* Austin: University of Texas Press.

Weisser, Christian. 2002. *Moving Beyond Academic Discourses: Composition Studies and the Public Sphere.* Carbondale: Southern Illinois University Press.

7

DEEP MAPS

Teaching Rhetorical Engagement through Place-Conscious Education

ROBERT BROOKE AND JASON MCINTOSH

What Deep Maps Are

> Writing is not a search for explanations but a ramble in quest of what informs a place.
>
> —William Least Heat-Moon

For several years now, we have been using deep maps as an invention exercise in our undergraduate composition program at the University of Nebraska-Lincoln and in our Summer Institutes for the Nebraska Writing Project. Deep maps aren't road maps like state highway maps, but are drawings of psychological locations (both literal and abstract) created by writers to represent their relationship to place. We borrowed the term "deep map" from William Least Heat-Moon, who used it to describe his rendering of the history, geobotany, cultural significance, and personal significance of one county in Kansas. But as our teaching has developed, we have informally used the term to refer to a variety of drawings that represent different relationships to place, including "mental maps" (Lynch) of our internal perception of a specific place, "conceptual maps" (Aberley) of the defining exercise of power in shaping our use of a place, "heart maps" (Heard) that give territorial shape to our emotional engagements, and "bioregional maps" (Thayer) that represent explicitly our commitments within a place. Informally the term "deep maps" has drifted on us to cover all such pictorial representations of individuals' psychological locations. Used early in a college semester or institute, these hand-drawn representations serve several purposes:

- They provide each writer with a guided inventory of possible writing topics, much like Donald Murray's authority lists or Linda Rief's life graphs.
- The collective act of drawing and sharing one's location on big sheets of art paper helps establish a climate of creative experimentation.
- The intellectual work of drawing a deep map is a start toward the work of place-conscious writing.

For these reasons, deep maps have proved useful for many composition classrooms, and many of our program's new teaching assistants lead their classes through some version of this exercise because it is a good way to start class writing.

But beyond these important invention and class-climate purposes, deep maps can serve as centering metaphors for the work of a place-conscious writing classroom. For us, the goals of such a classroom are all related to how writers visualize their relationship to place:

1. Initially, writers need to become accustomed to seeing themselves *in a place*; that is, they need to become aware of the various ways location (literal and mental) creates their understanding of landscape, culture, class, race, and gender, and surrounds them with local issues and local possibilities. Often this initial writing tends toward description, rendering the locations around them.
2. Once writers see themselves as located in a place, they can explore their relationships *to a place*, that is, the personal responsibilities, commitments, choices, and influences they see in themselves from the places where they dwell. Often, such writing explores personal conflict or struggle—for instance a poem or personal essay from a rural student might acknowledge conflicting desires to preserve rural heritage and to migrate to Chicago for a career in engineering.
3. Some writers, after exploring their relationship to a place, may go on to write *for their place*, that is, to undertake writing projects that attempt to improve the community or

> region in which they dwell. Such projects often merge critique and visionary thinking, as in proposals to the local fraternity/sorority system to buy foodstuffs from local growers, or in photo-text collage essays published in the Journalism School's newsletter celebrating the Gay Pride community parade. Such writing has at its core the desire to use rhetoric to make the region more habitable for the writer and more sustainable for community members.

As a set of classroom practices, deep maps can help writers in each of these core tasks of a place-conscious classroom. In this article, we are particularly interested in two ways to use deep maps: to develop considered space and to encourage civic participation.

Considered space: The use of deep maps emphasizes how the cognitive work of mapping makes writers *consider* the spaces they inhabit—making place something to reflect on and opening mental maps to analysis. Jason frequently quotes the bioregionalist Doug Aberley on this point: "In our consumer society, mapping has become an activity primarily reserved for those in power, used to delineate the 'property' of nation states and multinational companies. . . . The result is that although we have great access to maps, we have also lost the ability ourselves to *conceptualize, make and use* images of space" (1993, 3). Aberley suggests that relearning the "conceptualization of space" can create mapping as "a tool of everyday action" (5). Actively conceptualizing the spaces in which we live, and the existing mental maps through which we subconsciously "see" space, can be a step toward taking local action. Such active conceptualization of space is a necessary prerequisite to writing *inside, in relationship to,* or *for* a place.

Civic participation: The use of deep maps also emphasizes how the work of understanding one's psychological location can lead to a specific kind of civic identity. In his 2003 book *Rural Voices*, Robert articulated this idea this way: "Place-conscious citizens should be people who can live well in intradependence—that is, people who know enough about their natural and cultural region to fashion lives that enhance the communities located there. Place-conscious citizens are locally active, engaged in community decision making for their region through their work, schools, local governments, and civic organizations" (Brooke 2003, 13). Understanding one's personal location within the issues in one's surrounding community prompts an exploration of one's *relationship to* a place, and can lead to the critique and vision that generates writing *for* a place.

In this article, we will describe how two forms of the deep map exercise in our classrooms have helped specific students develop writing from considered space and civic participation.

Considered Space: Deep Maps in Writing: Rhetoric as Inquiry

In his freshman writing class, Writing: Rhetoric as Inquiry, Jason asked students to draw maps that conceptualized the spaces students inhabit. This version of the deep map used traditional cartographic elements such as scale, symbols, locator maps, inset maps, and major landmarks to sketch graphical representations of the writer's inhabited space. This emphasis on mapping real places draws inspiration from the fields of human geography and bioregionalism and complements a writing class where place-conscious learning is valued.

The summer 2004 class Jason taught met for an hour and twenty minutes daily for five weeks. The official aim and scope statements for Writing: Rhetoric as Inquiry have students using writing and rhetorical concepts to explore issues that are both important to them and to the communities in which they live. Students in Jason's class were required to complete three major projects and maintain a daily writing journal. Like all of the writing classes in our program, the routine for this class worked to create a conversation-rich environment of writers writing. Writing groups of four or five students were the core site for talk about drafts, and were supplemented by weekly overnight draft exchanges and teacher response. The reading and writing in Jason's class involved investigations into issues of living responsively and responsibly in local places. Class conversations were informed by cultural critics such as Wendell Berry, Paul Gruchow, and Daniel Kemmis, and the local writers Lisa Knopp and Ted Kooser. Guiding terms included "living a rooted life," "living in place," "bioregionalism," "citizenship," and "place-consciousness."

Students chose their three writing projects from a list of six possibilities. In summary, they were:

1. Design a project in which you investigate and write about a community in Lincoln with which you are unfamiliar or only marginally familiar.
2. Design a project that contributes some piece of writing to a community you belong to locally.
3. Investigate and write about one aspect of the Lincoln area (or east/southeast Nebraska) as a bioregion.

4. Write a personal narrative about some aspect of the local area as you know it.
5. Design a project that represents some part of Lincoln, UNL, or this area of Nebraska to an audience who is unfamiliar with the location.
6. Design a project that identifies and explores an issue, challenge, or concern that is important to local residents

During the first week of class, students did some exploratory talk and writing about the words "community," "bioregionalism," and "place-consciousness." The class read from Anne Lammott's *Bird by Bird* (a book that many of our teachers and students find inspiring) as well as a conceptual piece on bioregionalism, and then it explored the Web presence of the Planet Drum Foundation, an electronic meeting place and information clearinghouse for bioregional activists worldwide. It is within this context that students drew, wrote about, and then shared their maps. Jason's version of a deep map was inspired by what cultural geographers call a "mental map": a rendering on paper of a person's internalized map of their lived spaces. The assignment was this:

> On a large sheet of art paper, draw a map that is rich with the places and pathways you inhabit today. Some features you might consider: the place where you currently reside, locations of local people who are important to you, commonly traveled routes, bike or walking trails, parks, locations on campus, sites where memorable events occurred, favorite places, businesses you frequent, a family farm, bodies of water, landmarks, other geographic elements.
>
> Don't worry about accurate measurements, but do try to make your map proportionally consistent. The rest of us should be able to make sense of your map's *scale.* Also consider the *scope* of your map. Is the place you currently inhabit concentrated in one area of Lincoln? Does it extend beyond the city limits? Do you live on campus and spend most of your time around there? You might also draw one or two *detail inset maps* of areas that deserve mapping out in more detail. Or, you might draw a *locator inset map* that positions your local map within some geographically larger area.

The purpose of this map was twofold. It worked as a reflective moment, as writers inventoried and drew the local geographic features (natural and built) that they interacted with most often and knew most intimately: neighborhoods, homes, businesses, parks, streets, schools, crop fields, and backyards. The process of creating the map and the finished product served as a generative moment for the writing prompts, which asked writers to explore the local areas they inhabit, trying to get a richer understanding of those places, the people that inhabit them, and who the writer is in that place. But the prompts also asked writers to push at the boundaries of those familiar places. The map was also a tool for identifying what students *did not* know about their places: the blank spaces of unexplored land, the neighborhoods they lived in but did not know much about, the economies they participated in but did not understand, the flora and fauna they saw every day but whose names and ecology they did not know.

By mapping their daily routes and locations, students were working to answer what the bioregionalist Robert Thayer identifies as our three life questions: "Who am I?" "Where am I?" "What am I supposed to do?" (2003, 1). As Thayer explains, these questions cannot be considered separately, even though we often think of the first question as essentially personal and separate from considerations of place and action. Of considering inhabited space, Thayer writes:

> The question "Where are we?" has a deep, sustaining ring to it. It is a simple question with a deceptively complex answer. To some readers, we are where our address is—our street, city, county, state, and nation. To a few others, we are in some division of territory on earth, perhaps marked by a particular topography and climate. Many others might find the question absurd: How are we to answer? We are at many locations at different times. Planners, landscape architects, geographers, and others occupied with mapping, planning, or designing places are supposedly more aware of "where they are" than most—yet how deeply do any of us really know where we are? (2)

Jason's version of deep mapping helped students begin answering this question by requiring them to draw and then analyze a version of their mental maps. For geographers, the mental map is a way of describing how the spaces we inhabit are cognitively ordered through our experience of those places. Landmarks, buildings, streets, alleys, fields, and trees all work to create a navigable mental image of a place. By drawing it, the mental map became an artifact to be *considered* through reflection and was a step toward place-conscious writing.

To begin this writing about considered space, Jason asked students to draft legends for the deep maps they drew. Each legend was a two- or three-page narrative that, like conventional map legends, acted as a key to the map's images. Students shared their maps in class, so the legend became a tool for guiding readers through the map's imagery. Unlike conventional legends, this narrative worked as a moment of synthesis, because it asked writers to consider both what they *did* know about the places they inhabit as well as what they *did not* know. The set of guiding questions below asked writers to look for patterns, blank spaces, mysteries, and questions on their maps:

- What images and/or locations feature most prominently on your map? What is the centermost "thing" on your map? What is at the edges?
- Is your map predominantly of rural or urban locations?
- What people or groups of people do you associate with different locations on your map?
- What plants and animals inhabit your map (the ones you have seen)?
- What places do you walk, ride, or drive by regularly but never enter (outdoor and indoor places)?
- Who *does not* inhabit your map?
- What is *not* on your map?
- How would you describe the place in which you live to others?
- List three places you would like to know more about so that you could include them on your map.
- What would you title your map?

A Student Example: "Lincoln's Historic Haymarket: From the Past to the Future"

Kate was new to UNL and Lincoln, having moved here recently from Seattle. The majority of the students in Jason's summer class were from Lincoln, Omaha, or neighboring towns, and their maps tended to represent large portions of the city or region; however, Kate's map mainly depicted the UNL campus and the route she took to school each day. "My map has a very limited scope," she wrote in her map legend. "I've been in Lincoln for less than a year, so for starters, I don't have a lot of experience with the area." The images on her map were primarily campus buildings. A set of train tracks, the bane of students late for class, dominated the top portion of her map. At roughly the center was an image of the plaza water fountain outside the student union, a focal

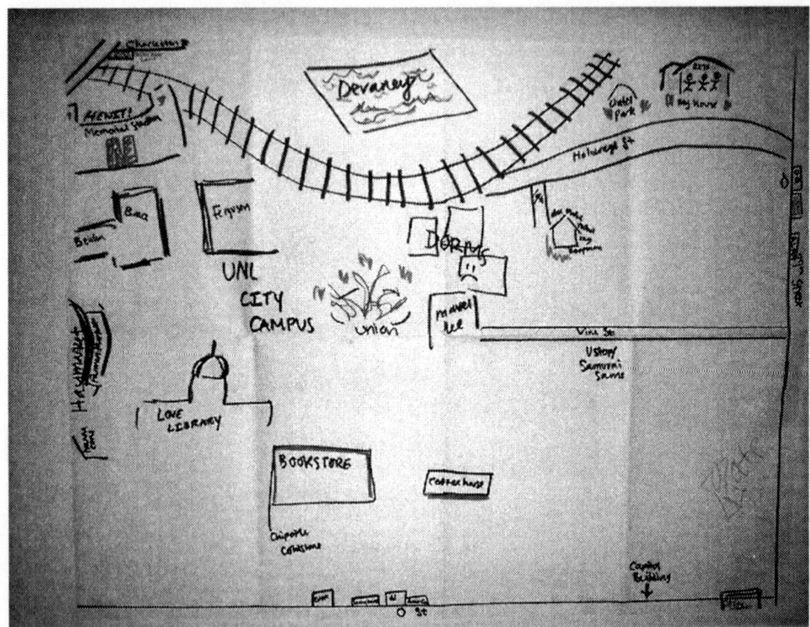

Figure 7.1. Kate's "Considered Space" Deep Map

point for foot traffic on campus. Her map had few roads or pathways drawn, but the ones that were there represent important spaces. Kate wrote:

> I noticed that when I was drawing my map, I didn't include very many roads, because they aren't really a big concern for me. . . . One of the areas I put the most detail into was 27th street. I frequent this area because it's so convenient for me, it's close to my house and has all kinds of stores and restaurants. Also, it feels more familiar to me than many parts of Lincoln because it has lots of ethnic diversity, which makes it feel more like an area I grew up in. So, I spend lots of time on 27th in between Holdrege and Vine, shopping at the Chinese grocery stores, running errands, or just walking around.

As previously stated, Kate's map was dominated by representations of buildings on and near the campus. Kate recognized this after creating her map and later drew on this observation for her third essay, "Lincoln's Historic Haymarket: From the Past to the Future." In the map analysis she wrote during the first week of class, Kate says, "One thing that I noticed was that I included buildings I see a lot or like, even if I never go in them, like Love Library or the Capitol building, or [The] Coffeehouse. . . . I've only been to [The] Coffeehouse three or four times, but it still feels like it should be an important place to me, and I always notice it when I go by." On the left side of Kate's map, taking up a proportionately small amount of space, was a representation of Lincoln's Historic Haymarket, a cultural, shopping and dining area that was once an open-air market, manufacturing district, and railroad hub. "I also included the Haymarket because I really like it down there," she wrote in that same analysis, "especially the Farmer's Market, even though once again I don't get there that often."

With her third essay, Kate drew on her observations of the dominant architectural images on her map and the marginal positioning of the Haymarket and developed an inquiry project that looked at both the history of the buildings in the Haymarket and the city's efforts at preservation in the district. In order to get at this story of architectural preservation versus renovation, Kate looked for both past and present representations of the Haymarket. She read through the Historic Haymarket's Web site which has maps of the district, photos, and descriptions of the current businesses, playhouses, and art galleries. Kate walked the six city blocks that comprise the Historic Haymarket, took photos of many of the buildings, and then wrote about what she saw. The Nebraska State Historic Society, located on the UNL campus, gave her access to early photos of Haymarket buildings as well as newspaper articles and other artifacts documenting the variety of purposes for which the buildings have been used.

After writing and workshopping several drafts of text, Kate created a photo essay that included the pictures she had taken on her walks, as well as those she located in the state historical society. The photo essay's conclusion, which included a quote from the Historic Haymarket Web site, provides a summary of how Kate experienced the project:

> By maintaining the original sense and style of these buildings, the Haymarket Development Council has created a link between the city's present and its past, a bridge between history and the future. The Haymarket is "more than just a tribute to history, it has become a thriving neighborhood," in both the literal sense and in a more abstract way. People do live there, in the Hardy and Grainger buildings, but more

> than that, the Haymarket embodies a feeling of community. Everyone there is a part of something bigger than themselves. Whether you're a store owner, a farmer, a long-time resident, or a teenager on a dinner date, by experiencing the Haymarket, you're experiencing something truly special. The Haymarket's uniqueness has helped it succeed over the years, and it is one of those areas that makes Lincoln more than just a city. It makes it a home.

Kate later struggled to reconcile her fascination with the Haymarket—and the arguments for local sustainable economy put forth by Berry, Gruchow, and Kemmis that she connected with the Haymarket's Farmer's Market—with the financial realities of college life. "It's good to warn people about the hidden costs of buying cheap imports," Kate wrote, "but that doesn't put an extra thirty bucks in my wallet so I can buy something produced locally." But her essay deepened her understanding of her current local place, helping her value its history and current vision and prompting her to name some of the issues involved in living responsibly in such a place. As Kate explains: "We can save the places we call home by making choices. By choosing to create and support a community that includes workers, residents, and the ecology of our place. By choosing to be active in that community, to step down from our roles as consumers and try to be citizens instead." Kate was a recent transplant to Lincoln from Seattle. She did not have the rootedness of many of her Nebraska classmates. But her writing for the class showed her moving through the first two stages of place-conscious writing: writing *in a place,* describing the features of the place she values; and writing *in relationship to a place,* exploring the ways she chooses connection to that place. Even though living in this place was only temporary, as it is with so many college students, Kate was responding to Thayer's question, "What am I supposed to do?"

Considering Kate's essays, the collective work of the class, and the themes explored—"living a rooted life," "place consciousness," "citizenship," "bioregionalism"—we see value in deep maps as artifacts of considered space. "[A] theme I noticed in the reading that really showed up in a lot of the writing our class did," Kate writes in her course reflection, "[is] that our sense of self is inseparable from our sense of place. Who we are is forever tied to where we are." For some students, like Kate, drawing the deep map led directly to essay projects. But for all of the students, it was an exploratory moment that supported a personal context for place-conscious writing. Kate summarized her experience with the map:

> . . . I think the [deep maps] were a good way to get started thinking about all this. I think they made all of us consider more thoroughly the places we inhabit. For me, it showed me some of what I was already aware of—that I don't know a whole lot about Lincoln yet. Part of the reason my map has such a small scope is that I just don't have the options of going to farther places, or reason to do so. However, looking at the maps of my classmates made me want to explore more and get to know about the different places that can make a city a home. If I drew my map again now, the scope of it might not have increased, but I think the depth and detail would have. I now have a greater understanding of how the place I live in functions as part of a larger area, and a greater sense of the community I'm a part of.

Civic Participation and Personal Location: Deep Maps in Rhetorical Practices and Writing Communities

In teaching Nebraska's sophomore writing course, Rhetorical Practices and Writing Communities, Robert emphasizes civic participation. The aim and scope statement for the course focuses on the use of rhetorical principles for action in and investigation of communities. That focus is a direct bridge to two of the goals of place-conscious teaching: the exploration of our relationships *to a place* and the possible development of critical and visionary projects *for a place.* In his summer 2004 course, Robert used several recognized methods for fostering local action (cf. negotiated syllabus, as in Shor, 1996; small groups as in Roskelly, 2003). For this article, the focus will be on using the deep map to explore psychological location as a support for civic participation.

The idea of psychological location is simple: instead of thinking of your "space" as something literally geographical, think of yourself as located psychologically in a "space" composed of generative issues in your life, of people who live in certain places who "represent" those issues to you, and of the actual physical places where you experience those issues most directly. A deep map of personal location, thus, is a representation of those generative "spaces" in your experience. In the handout asking students to draw such deep maps, Robert described the map as follows: "A deep map is a map of the place where you are now, showing what makes up that place, indicating the forces have led you to be the kind of person you are in that place, representing the tensions which create the energy of that place (positive and negative). A deep map represents understanding of location, not just description. A deep map represents celebration and critique of where you locate yourself." This deep map classroom exercise emerged from a sympathetic reading of Least Heat-Moon's monumental *Prairyerth: A Deep Map.* This 624-page tome proposes to represent a single county in Kansas (namely, Chase County) as emblematic of America. The introductory section names the project: "For years, outsiders have considered this prairie place barren, desolate, monotonous, a land of more nothing than almost any other place you can name, but I know I am not here to explore vacuousness at the heart of America. I'm only in search of what *is* here, here in the middle of the Flint Hills of Kansas. I'm in quest of the land and what informs it, and I'm here because of shadows in me, loomings about threats to America that are alive here too, but things I hope will show more clearly in the sparseness of this country" (1991, 10–11; italics in original).

The book's structure attempts to represent what a full understanding of a particular place might entail. Every section of the book takes one quadrant of Chase County and renders

- a collection of quotes from American and European writers that connect with the issues to be gleaned from this quadrant;
- a representation of the historical and cultural conflicts in American history that were played out in the lives of people here;
- a description of the geology, flora, and fauna of this area;
- profiles of several of the place's colorful characters, both living and dead;
- Least Heat-Moon's own presence in the place, as empathetic traveler.

In short, the book takes seriously the complexity of this particular location, offered as an example of the complexity of *any* locale. The overall effect of the book, for those who can manage the extended effort required to read it, is a kind of profound reverence for the saturation of meaning in any given place—and the increase in personal wisdom that comes from knowing any given place deeply. When Robert first developed the deep map drawing exercise in 1998, he hoped that writers might find writing that taps into the saturated reverence and personal wisdom of location. Such writing may be a deep map in Least

Heat-Moon's sense—and such a space should be a generative place for rhetorical action.

In summer 2004, Robert asked his students to draw a representation of their psychological location as a support activity to the major projects they were completing. During the term, students had the choice to complete in any order three major projects from a list of six. During the week focused on psychological location, Robert drew connections most explicitly to two of the possible projects:

> *Project Four: Contributing to the Work of a Community*
> For this project, your task is to write a piece that furthers the work of a community you belong to and address it to an audience in that community. You might, for instance, craft a sermon appropriate to your faith community, or a recommendation for curriculum revision in your major department, or a job description and hiring protocol for the small genetics laboratory where you work, or a useful history of your community. This essay (or equivalent project) requires that you understand the community and the way discourse functions in the community, and then that you can design an effective text for that community.
>
> *Project Five: Analyzing Your Personal History of Moving between Two Communities*
> For this project, your task is to write an analytical narrative of your own movement between two communities, such as moving from family community into your academic discipline, moving from one faith community to another, or shifting political affiliation (you can think of other examples). You should both render this movement so that readers can experience it, and explain the movement using course concepts so that readers can understand it.

Other activities during this unit involved class discussion of Mary Louise Pratt's "Arts of the Contact Zone," Robert Brooke's "Migratory and Regional Identity," and a selection from Gloria Anzaldúa's *Borderlands.* Students also were guided to clarify the kind of change they hoped to achieve in their audience through a writing activity based on Young, Becker, and Pike's *Rhetoric: Discovery and Change.*

In one three-hour class session, students had an hour to draw an initial deep map on large art paper. They posted these maps around the room and explained them to their small writing groups. The class session ended with a period of extended freewriting, in which students were guided to articulate and develop the ideas they were hoping to explore for the next paper (hopefully related to the map activity).

In the context of the course, many students developed projects from this exercise that explored issues of personal location they had identified. For example, three students explored the rural/urban split in Nebraska and the difficulties they face navigating between the urban values of the university and their ranching and farming home communities. One student developed a community handbook for support of special-needs students at Lincoln Northeast High School (using the project to connect with her work as a special education major). All three of the international students in the class took the place-conscious prompt very seriously, producing projects on Spanglish and immigration in Nebraska, a comparison of ecological solid waste management in Brazil and Nebraska, and a personal essay on how a student's understanding of Japanese culture had become more complicated because of her three years at Nebraska. All of these projects wrestled with issues of personal location and civic participation. The writers consciously explored their *relationships to* a place and began the critical and visionary work of writing *for* a place.

Student Example: "The Nebraska Regional Mental Health Center and Personal Responsibility"

One example of place-conscious civic participation in Rhetorical Practices and Writing Communities came from Abby. For this project, Abby addressed a local issue that emerged from her personal location, but then Abby extended her exploration into a direct critique of state governmental policy. Abby's mother worked in the local mental health care industry and her aunt had needed such care, so Abby felt in a position to address a current governmental issue. Her third paper began:

> **April 7, 2004:** Nebraska governor Mike Johanns signs LB1083, the Mental Health Reform Bill, into law. This measure will, in the next year, close two of Nebraska's three mental hospitals in Hastings and Norfolk. In place of these hospitals, communities will implement local mental health services.
> **Benefits:** State hospitals are completely funded by the state. Community-based services are eligible for [compensation] up to 50% from the federal government. This is a huge incentive

Figure 7.2. Abby's "Personal Location" Deep Map

> in light of the serious budget crisis Nebraska is currently facing.
> **Disadvantages:** . . . It is likely that many communities will not be able to meet the needs of their mentally ill citizens, and other agencies, like the police department and private hospitals, will become overburdened.

Abby's paper then described the state of mental health care as her mother experiences it in her job at the Lincoln Regional Center and a "worst-case scenario" for the lack of resources based on an incident in her aunt's life. The paper moves back and forth between these presentational moments from family interviews and an analysis of the current data on Nebraska. As might be expected, her paper ends with a warning: "My aunt's story is not an anomaly. There are thousands of people in Nebraska suffering from a variety of mental illnesses. I fear that under LB1083, there will be many more people suffering like my aunt was. I predict that this will not be the end of the mental health matter. In another ten years the state will be allocating millions of dollars to reopen the facilities in Hastings and Norfolk. In the meantime, the mentally ill in Nebraska will suffer." Abby's pictorial deep map dealt with some of these issues, representing her family members, and the trips she had taken to another state to visit her aunt, as part of a larger collage for her own sense of herself.

In her daily drafting for the week, Abby explored her sense of her own identity as a creative young woman in relation to the female role models offered by her mother and aunt respectively; she wrote a fairly long narrative of a trip she and her mother took one summer to help her aunt with mental health care in Texas; she drew on an interview with her mother to draft an insider's view of the current problems in mental health care at the state's overloaded regional facility. Not all of this writing appeared in her final draft. In conference that week, she and Robert talked at length about the thorny issues of representing personal information from family members in a public essay critiquing civic policy. (Robert had her read his article on this issue, "Personal Experience Narratives: What Are Our Responsibilities as Storytellers?"). Abby chose to deal with these very local audience/responsibility issues by providing her mother and aunt with copies of her paper, and made any alterations they required. Some of these alterations were hard for her to make, but Abby recognized the conflict between her responsibilities to protect the family members she was representing and her desire to change the system. In this case, she consciously chose to privilege protection of her family, toning down many of her most direct calls for change.

An able writer, Abby was quite articulate in her learning letter about how this whole project connected with the course concepts: "I was very much influenced by the 'Borderlands' piece we discussed Tuesday in class. I found the author's concept of language identity interesting and tried to model the way she used her experience to draw grander conclusions about society. . . . I think that some of the issues I have explored in the course of writing this essay (family history, the social contract, my relationship to the characters in the essay, etc.) have potential for later work."

Abby's project is a good example of the possibilities for civic participation that can be supported through the kind of thinking asked for in a deep map. In developing this project, Abby crafted both a written challenge to the Mental Health Reform Bill and engaged in some even more complex reflections about the conflicting responsibilities of writing from family expertise for public purposes, as well as reflections about her own responsibilities as a creative young woman—issues tied to the place-conscious goals of writing *to* and *for* one's place. Abby also sees the "potential for later work" here: with further time and support, she may well be able to craft different documents that go further with both the personal exploration of family and the political campaign to change how Nebraska manages mental health care.

Conclusion: Mapping as Rhetorical Action

In "Settling Down," Scott Russell Sanders offers this striking image of his own mental map of personal location: "I think of my home ground as a series of nested rings, with house and marriage and family at the center, surrounded by the wider and wider hoops of neighborhood and community, the bioregion within walking distance of my door, the wooded hills and karst landscape of southern Indiana, the watershed of the Ohio River, and so on outward—and inward—to the ultimate source. The longing to become an inhabitant rather than a drifter sets me against the current of my culture, which nudges everyone into motion" (1993, 116–17). In asking students to compose with deep maps, to represent their personal locations to themselves, to find the civic issues that energize their lives in those locations, and to wrestle with the shape of their representations themselves, we are unabashedly asking students to begin to think, as Sanders does, of what constitutes "home ground" and how they mean to live there.

Such work, we assert, is at the very core of rhetorical engagement. Rhetorical action comes as much from the choice of *where* to locate one's arguments and emotional appeals as it does from the choice of who to address and what to argue for. Rhetorical action comes into being as the writer shapes a clear understanding of the *place* of the action. Our communities, families, nations, and, increasingly, bioregions have been shaped and altered by the force of people's words. The point of place-conscious education as a whole, and of activities that support it, like the deep map activities advocated in this article, is to make this link between rhetoric and place obvious and present. Once that link is made, then a whole new energy for writing becomes possible—and a whole new energy for shaping the state of the places we will live, and the kinds of places we can help those locations become.

Works Cited

Aberley, Doug. 1993. "The Lure of Mapping: An Introduction." In *Boundaries of Home: Mapping for Local Empowerment.* Philadelphia: New Society.

Anzaldúa, Gloria. 2001. "From *Borderlands*." In *The Rhetorical Tradition*, ed. Patricia Bizzell and Bruce Herzberg, 1585–1599. 2nd ed. Boston: Bedford.

Berry, Wendell. 1997. *The Unsettling of America*. Berkeley, CA: Sierra Club Books.

Brooke, Robert, ed. 2003. *Rural Voices: Place-Conscious Education and the Teaching of Writing*. New York: Teachers College Press.

———. n.d. "Migratory and Regional Identity." In *Identity Papers: Literacy and Power in Higher Education*, ed. Bronwyn T. Williams. Logan: Utah State University Press.

Brooke, Robert, Rochelle Harris, and Jeanine Nyangira. 2003. "Personal Experience Narratives: What Are Our Responsibilities as Storytellers?" In *The Subject is Story*, ed. Wendy Bishop and Hans Ostrom, 78–88. Portsmouth, NH: Heinemann.

Gruchow, Paul. 1995. *Grass Roots: The Universe of Home*. Minneapolis: Milkweed.

Heard, Georgia. 1999. *Awakening the Heart: Exploring Poetry in Elementary and Middle School*. Portsmouth, NH: Heinemann.

Historic Haymarket. 2004. July 28. http://www.historichaymarket.com/

Kemmis, Daniel. 1992. *Community and the Politics of Place*. Norman: University of Oklahoma Press.

Knopp, Lisa. 2002. *The Nature of Home: A Lexicon and Essays*. Lincoln: University of Nebraska Press.

Kooser, Ted. 2002. *Local Wonders: Seasons in the Bohemian Alps*. Lincoln: University of Nebraska Press.

Lamott, Anne. 1995. *Bird by Bird: Some Instructions on Writing and Life*. New York: Anchor.

Least Heat-Moon, William. 1991. *PrairyEryth: A Deep Map*. Boston: Houghton Mifflin.

Lynch, Kevin. 1960. *The Image of the City*. Cambridge, MA: MIT Press.

Murray, Donald. 2004. *A Writer Teaches Writing*. 2nd ed., rev. Boston: Heinle.

Planet Drum. 2004. Planet Drum Foundation. May 20. http://www.planetdrum.org/

Pratt, Mary Louise. 1991. "Arts of the Contact Zone." *Profession* 91: 33–40.

Rief, Linda. 1992. *Seeking Diversity*. Portsmouth, NH: Heinemann.

Roskelly, Hepzibah. 2003. *Breaking (Into) the Circle: Group Work for Change in the English Classroom*. Portsmouth, NH: Heinemann.

Sanders, Scott Russell. 1993. "Settling Down." In *Staying Put: Making a Home in a Restless World*. Boston: Beacon Press.

Shor, Ira. 1996. *When Students Have Power: Negotiating Authority in a Critical Pedagogy.* Chicago: University of Chicago Press.

Thayer, Robert. 2003. *LifePlace: Bioregional Thought and Practice.* Berkeley and Los Angeles: University of California Press.

Young, Richard, Alton Becker, and Kenneth Pike. 1970. *Rhetoric: Discovery and Change.* New York: Harcourt.

8

Between Perception and Articulation

Imageword and a Compassionate Place

KRISTIE FLECKENSTEIN

> They feel like there's no place for them here, like they don't belong here, and you know what the sad thing is? They're right.
>
> —Laura Vedder

> And if going home is denied me then I will have to stand and claim my space, making a new culture—una cultura mestiza—with my own lumber, my own bricks and mortar and my own feminist architecture.
>
> —Gloria Anzaldúa, *Borderlands/La Frontera*

In "The *Tesoros* Literacy Project: An Experiment in Democratic Communities," Todd DeStigter describes the "extreme cases," the displaced students, both Anglo and Latino, who had "checked out" of school, losing class credit through absenteeism and failure to turn in assignments. Called "at risk" and "underachievers" by teachers in the lounge and counselors' office, these students were called "burnouts," "losers," and "trailer trash" in the hallways and cafeteria (DeStigter 1998, 10–11). Alienated by the very public school system designed to serve them, these students, and others like them, were unable to find or create a home for themselves in the classroom. Instead, the classroom constituted an inimical place, one of hopelessness, disconnection, and potential violence. Denied a sense of welcome, or of a sense of faith in the public school, these marginalized students were unable to "stand and claim" their space as Gloria Anzaldúa so fiercely advocates. They were unable to use their own lumber, bricks, mortar, and personal architecture to create a place within which they could connect intellectually and emotionally with one another, with a teacher, and with a subject matter.

The narrative of displacement, of alienation, is a poignant one in our education system. A multifaceted tragedy, the seeds of displacement yield a crop of violence inside and outside the classroom (Twemlow 2004). Affecting any student who comes into the public school situation with an array of "events, artifacts, and ideas" that do not "reflect and perpetuate the values and privileges of the community's most powerful members," displacement inculcates into him or her the belief that these "events, artifacts, and ideas" are both meaningless and valueless (DeStigter 1998, 13). Thus, the student constituted out of these events, artifacts, and ideas is implicitly construed (and self-construed) as equally meaningless and valueless. In Anzaldúa's words, marginalized students blame themselves, hate themselves, and terrorize themselves; and, I would argue, they exile themselves—literally and figuratively—from learning (Anzaldúa 1987, 43). They ghost through places, but they do not inhabit places. They remain "extreme cases," excluded and excluding.

In this chapter, I explore the possibility of creating compassionate classrooms where students experience connection rather than alienation. I argue that the lens of "imageword," a way of knowing comprised of image-making and word making, can fruitfully alter traditional Western orientation to place as something that is static and monolithic. From the perspective of imageword, place can be envisioned as a product of perception and articulation: a sensuous, coproduced, and dynamic reality. I demonstrate the way in which such a vision of place can call inhabitants to act in ways that shape a compassionate rather than an alienating place. While attending to the weave of perception and articulation does not guarantee that a hostile classroom can be automatically transformed into a welcoming one, the perspective of imageword extends the invitation to try. I conclude with a story of one effort to change an alienating environment into a compassionate place by changing students' ways of seeing and speaking.

Place and people are reciprocally linked. As Keith Basso says, they "interanimate": "As places animate the ideas and feelings of persons who attend to them, these same ideas and feelings animate the places on which attention has been bestowed" (1996, 55). Such interanimation, on the one hand, accounts for the alignment of violence and displacement as T. R. Johnson so poignantly captures in "School Sucks." The feedback loop between painful writing in the classroom—the pedagogy, the impossible idealized discourse goals—and individual students results in hatred and resistance, erupting into little and large acts of aggression. On the other hand, interanimation between people and places accounts for the alignment of compassion and emplacement, where, through the sharing of suffering, dreams, and hopes, people offer support and aid rather than violence and cruelty to one another. Mary Rose O'Reilley's dream of a peaceable classroom as well as Nel Nodding's trust in a caring curriculum both testify to the idea (and belief) that the classroom as place, praxis, or subject matter need not be alienating, need not nurture violence. Instead, people and place can mutually engage in the creation, maintenance, and inhabitation of compassionate places.

The necessity of a compassionate place for effective teaching and learning is a pressing concern even for those teachers who advocate a critical writing pedagogy that focuses on "teaching the conflicts," as Gerald Graff (1992) and others recommend.[1] Such praxis cannot be effectively realized without a classroom configured as compassionate. bell hooks concurs. Despite, or perhaps because of, her conviction that teaching should transgress—should critique and challenge status quo ideologies of race, gender, and class by disrupting the "safe" classroom—hooks contends that the classroom must be a place of love. Only when love is present can teacher, and student, be "whole . . . and as a consequence whole hearted" (hooks 1994, 193). Within such an atmosphere of love, students speak out, talk back, and experience the ecstasy of learning. In addition, the need for compassionate places in our schools is becoming more and more crucial as our society and our classrooms are marked (and marred) by increasing desensitization and violence. Without developing what Stuart W. Twemlow, a psychiatrist and the director of the Peaceful Schools and Communities Project, calls "systemic interventions that create safer, more caring and responsive school environments and, optimally, communities as well" (2004, 61), many students will be displaced, barred from participation in the literacy classroom and in the larger public sphere, and vulnerable to physical and emotional violence as both victim and perpetrator.

A compassionate literacy classroom cannot serve as a panacea for all societal ills, nor does it promise to eradicate the massive physical and psychosocial aggression that permeates our school systems. What it can do is provide a starting point for consciously connecting with one another on an affective and intellectual level—for "hold[ing] the other wholly in mind" (Corder 1985, 28)—and an arena within which students and teacher can explore carefully the confluence of school room and community. The question that confronts educators, then, regardless of their pedagogical affiliations, is how we might foster the creation of more caring and responsive literacy classrooms as a necessary prelude to the creation of more caring and responsive communities. I believe that one possible answer begins with conceiving place through the lens of imageword, as a fluid transaction between perception and articulation. This shift in perspective serves as a first step in the effort to reconfigure our classrooms and our communities as places within which we are moved to share joys and succor pain.

Between Perception and Articulation

When place is perceived as fixed and monolithic, a force beyond our control and actions, then inhabitants of a site are rendered passive, overwhelmed by the futility of railing against their environment. However, from the perspective of imageword, all places can be envisioned as a fluid amalgamation of perception and articulation. A major obstacle to transforming places of despair into places of hope is the orientation to place dominant in the West. Throughout the hierarchy of spatial scales—from the cellular to the global—place is traditionally perceived as an immutable reality. Rather than a transaction in which both human and environment are reciprocally constituted, place in the West is conceptualized in Newtonian terms. Place and humans interact like billiard balls: striking each other, thus each changing the path of the other in a balanced cause-effect action, but having no impact on the essential identity of the other. Michel Foucault emphasizes the pervasiveness of this attitude: "Space still tends to be treated as fixed, dead, undialectical; time as richness, life, dialectic, the revealing context for critical social theorizing" (1980, 70).[2] Permeating Western thinking, this static and deterministic view of place is bereft of emotion, activity, and variability, inviting the belief that while people might be *in* place they are not *of* place. Therefore, inhabitants are helpless in the face of place; they are subject to its tyranny, with little or no influence on its reality.

To reshape a hostile place into a compassionate place first requires a conceptual lens that alters this understanding of place. Imageword provides just such an alternative perspective, highlighting the sensuousness, coproduction, and dynamism of all places. This altered understanding empowers people to work consciously toward transforming place. As I argued in *Embodied Literacies*, imageword constitutes a way of knowing that undergirds all meaning; it evolves from the constant movement between image-making and word-making, between perception and articulation. I deliberately fuse the words *image* and *word* to underscore the necessary integration of both in meaning. An image may exist without language, such as in dreams, hallucinations, and proprioception, but we cannot do anything with the image except experience it. As soon as we identify it as an image, however, we have hauled it into the realm of language. In addition, the linguistic formulation of image—that is, naming and/or describing an image—is already an interpretation of an image, which, at the same time, has the potential to change the image. Conversely, the shape—the physical manifestation of, for instance, visible or aural language—is in and of itself an image and has the potential to change the meaning of that language. Meaning and medium are inextricable. Like a Möbius strip, imagery and language comprise a twist of relationships with only a single side. Image and word are mutually constitutive, mutually creative; image and word are not. Imageword is.[3]

The mutuality of imageword is important also for reconceptualizing place, because it points to ways in which a place can be conceived as image, word, and the transaction of both.[4] Place is comprised of a "full range of discursive and nondiscursive modes of expression through which everyday and poetically heightened senses of place are locally articulated," the philosopher Edward S. Casey tells us (1996, 8). So, on the one hand, place can be envisioned as an *image*word, as an image or a network of images, from body-based kinesthetic images by which we biologically map our physical sites to architectural blueprints that literally dictate the construction of those physical sites. On the other hand, place can also be conceptualized as image*word*, as the product of language. This includes a range of words, from specific place-names to greeting and leave-taking rituals to the political edicts that underlie cartography (Kahn 1996; Mignolo 1995), which means that place must also involve habits of language. Finally, place can be conceptualized as imageword, as the transaction between perception and articulation. Such a lens reveals aspects of place important for the creation of compassionate literacy classrooms.

Consider, first, the revelations concerning place afforded by *image*word. An image is the result of our attention shifting from one aspect of random stimuli to another. An image grows out of the contrails of that shifting attention, fashioning a sense of reality by lodging us in the moment, in the experience of relationships. The primary focus of that shifting attention is not subjects, or a "content," but relationships, particularly those between self and other, self and environment. Composed all at once by processes sunk beneath our conscious awareness and inextricable from our embodiment, an image contains no "not," no linguistic markers indicating modality (indicative, imperative, subjunctive), no tenses (except the present), no means to divide elements into classes of elements. As a result, when we have an image, we cannot discriminate between the image and the random reality it orders, because we are caught up in the relationships. Demarcations between external and internal disappear. Thus, when we dream, the dream is the reality. We might assign symbolic value to dream elements after the fact, but, at the moment of experience, at the moment of performance, there is no way that we can separate pattern from reality. Caught within the thrall of relationships, we cannot, as it were, differentiate the dancer from the dance, the body image from the body, the place from the inhabitant.[5]

*Image*word invites us to see place and people as sensuous, as physically experienced, affectively inflected realities. Because image is tied to the body, to the very means by which the biological world constructs itself, it is inextricable from the stimuli that it transforms into meaning. So, too, with place. "To study space," Ioan Davis writes, "is initially to study the eye, the voice, and the hand, and at the same time to conceive of other voices, eyes, hands reworking the space" (1990, 59). Place cannot exist without bodies moving in and out of a site, for those bodies re/produce place in a "bilateral level of knowing bodies and known places" (Casey 1996, 49). As Casey points out: "The lived body is the material condition of possibility for the place-world while being itself a member of that same world. It is basic to place and part of place. Just as there are no places without the bodies that sustain and vivify there, so there are no lived bodies without the places they inhabit and traverse" (24). This embodiment is coupled with a location's physical qualities. Bodies are inextricable from the array of material constraints that allow or disallow certain existences, the development of certain consciousnesses, certain ideologies. Thus, the sensuous nature of the place-body interface affects what Casey, borrowing from Malinowksi, call "the imponderabilia of actual life": such things as "degree of impatience, the understanding of a text, relations with consociates, and so forth" (39). Emotional experiences (good and bad), textual meaning (or meaninglessness), and intimacy (or alienation) emerge out of the sensuous nexus point between place and bodies.

In addition, focusing on *image*word turns our attention to the way in which people and place are coproduced through the sensuality of perception, the process of image-making. Drawing on Merleau-Ponty's work with the phenomenology of perception, Casey underscores the reciprocity of people and place through image-making: "The experience of perceiving . . . requires a corporeal subject who lives *in* a place *through* perception. It also requires a place that is amenable to this body-subject and that extends its own influence back onto this subject. A place, we might even say, has its own 'operative intentionality' that elicits and responds to the corporeal intentionality of the perceiving subject" (22; italics in original).

The creation of place relies on the inhabitants' perception of place, which is influenced by the operative intentionality—physical constraints and configuration—of place. However, those operative intentionalities are, in part, derived from the inhabitants' perceptions of those intentionalities. Places and people are tied together in intricate feedback loops by which they create each other. Places and people interanimate. Place does not produce people, like a lithograph producing a print. Nor do people produce places, like artists painting a landscape in earth tones. Rather, as Steven Feld and Keith Basso argue, "as people fashion places, so, too, do they fashion themselves. People don't just dwell in comfort or misery, in centers or margins, in place or out of place, empowered or disempowered. People everywhere act on the integrity of their dwelling" (1996, 11). Place, then, is coproduced, and that transaction is powered to a large degree by our image-making capacity in perception.

Consider, second, the revelations concerning place afforded by imageword when we focus on word, on image*word*. If the gift of imagery is the gift of *is*, the gift of language is the gift of *is not*. As Kenneth Burke reminds us, "[T]here are no negatives in nature . . . this ingenious addition to the universe is solely a product of human symbol systems" (1966, 9). We are able to generalize because of language's unique ability to make distinctions, to set up boundaries. Like a digital code, discourse enables us to parse, order, and categorize our unruly reality into an infinite number of facets that we can then treat as a substitution for that reality. It gives us a portable reality. With an image, we are tied to an experience; we are a participant carried along on and by the stream flowing through our heads and around us. But, with language, we can step out of the moment and be the observer of our own participation, dipping into that stream of experience at will and reflecting on that stream. Language also offers us a sort of reality-testing capability. Language weaves a tapestry that we call reality (and identity) against which we judge the falsity of all other representations.[6]

The first contribution of image*word* to a reconceptualization of place is to complicate the notion of coproduction afforded by imagery. *Image*word highlights the reciprocity between place and people through perception. Image*word* highlights the reciprocity between people and people through articulation. The interanimation between place and people is effected through the sociality of inhabitants, through people relating emotionally with each other by means of their language practices. The anthropologist Miriam Kahn writes: "Places capture the complex emotional, behavioral, and moral relationships between people and their territory. They represent people, their actions, and their interactions and as such become malleable memorials for negotiating and renegotiating human relationships" (1996, 168). From the vantage point of image*word*, place is revealed not as the creation of a single person but as the joint construction of many people. An important medium of the coproduction of any place, then, is language. People mutually articulate their sense of place, marking, for instance, through leave-taking and arriving rituals, the boundaries of place and their positions within that place. They name place, their actions in that place, and the relationship of one place to another all through language.

Image*word* points to the rich matrix of human relationships—the talk between people—that are necessary for the coproduction of place. The talk by which people create and experience place also highlights the extent to which politics and ideologies infuse place. Image*word* reveals that the spatial segregation imposed by the urban design of buildings, landscapes, and communities is not merely the result of the predispositions of individual inhabitants or groups of community members. Rather, that segregation is "the direct result of a comprehensive system of social oppression. . . . [B]uildings are designed and used to support the social purposes they are meant to serve—including the maintenance of social inequality," Leslie Kanes Weisman asserts (1994, 35). Foucault agrees: "Stones can make people docile and knowable" (1979, 172); "discipline proceeds from the distribution of individuals in space" (141). Sensitivity to image*word* enables us to discern the ideological play of power and politics in any place. It points to the way in which a place credits or discredits a particular construction of self, knowledge, emotion, and reality. It underscores how language itself can invite cruelty and/or compassion through the design of a place.[7]

Focusing on either image or word in imageword reveals the sensuous, coproduced, and ideological nature of place. Focusing on the transaction between image and word reveals the dynamism of place. From the perspective of this mutuality, place can be conceived as dynamic, as a process resulting from the active movement of human attention, which seizes upon one stimulus as significant as opposed to another. Viewed through the lens of imageword, place is stabilized only through the continuous efforts of routinized human actions, including word-making and image-making. Ioan Davis underscores the dynamism intrinsic in place. Place evolves through "the *interplay* between the biologically physical (the tactile, the audible, the visual) and the graphic" (1990, 59; italics added). Place is not an inert container or a stage setting that affords a scene for human actions. Place becomes through the actions of the inhabitants as they respond—visually, verbally, and sensuously—to each other and to particular material facets of the immediate environment. Lovingly recounting the way in which the Wamirans, a people living in a small village on the southeastern tip of Papua New Guinea, made among themselves a place for her, Kahn says she discovered that: "places were not preexisting empty stages to be filled with activity; they took on meaning only when *activity gave them form.* They blossomed into places of significance through my actions and interactions with others. They reverberated with profoundly emotional shared experiences. . . . A meaningful landscape resulted where my actions had taken place and my memory lingered" (1996, 188; italics added). Casey agrees, calling place "more an *event* than a *thing* to be assimilated to known categories" (1996, 26; italics in original). He explains that place is not a definite sort of phenomenon—physical, spiritual, cultural, or social. Instead, place "takes on the qualities of its occupants, reflecting these qualities in its own constitution and description and expressing them in its occurrence as an event: places not only *are,* they *happen*" (27; italics in original). The mutuality of imageword spotlights that dynamism. Place does not exist; people do not exist. Place and people exist together.

Place perceived through the lens of imageword highlights the degree to which all places and people are reciprocally linked both through perception and articulation. It emphasizes that a place is not fixed; instead, places are dynamic coproductions of a sensuous reality inhabited by people who create place as they interact with each other and with their immediate material constraints. This three-dimensionality—the trialectics of sensuousness, coproduction, and dynamism—suggests ways to generate and sustain not just places but also more importantly, compassionate places.

From a New Place to a Compassionate Place

Given the "new place" afforded by the perspective of imageword, teachers working jointly with students have the potential for creating compassionate literacy classrooms. The key to that transformation is determining the kinds of perception and articulation that reciprocally constitute a compassionate place. I believe they are perception as identification and articulation as love.

Perception as identification is what Ernest G. Schachtel calls allocentric perception. Allocentric perception is characterized by a "profound interest in the object, and complete openness and receptivity toward it, a full turning toward the object which makes possible a direct encounter with it" (Schachtel 1959, 220). Rather than focusing on self, on taking away something from the perception to be used in another setting, perception as identification dissolves the boundaries between seer and seen. Knowing occurs through identification. In contrast to the critical distance characteristic of Western habits of perception, perception as identification merges object and perceiver. By practicing perception as identification—a kind of engaged perception that privileges relationships, not content—inhabitants bind place and people, people and people, to each other. In a landmark 1985 essay, Jim Corder alludes to just such a "care-full" mode of perception. He argues that "we have to see each other, to know each other, to be present to each other, to embrace each other" (1985, 23). Seeing connectively obliges us to the "tenderest, strongest care" of each other and our environment (23), for without this mode of image-making we run the risk of injuring one another in the midst of seeking to communicate with one another.

This careful, engaged perception arises out of receptiveness to the bilateral sensuousness of place, both as a body and as the place within which that body has existence. Both levels are important for compassionate places, because compassion is an emotional experience lodged in the body and evoked through the realization that bodies are connected. But, as I argued above, those bodies, and that care-full perception, are linked in feedback loops with the physical constitution of place. Thus, on the one hand, the material quality of a place can potentially erode the mode of perception so necessary for the evocation of a compassionate place. Drawing from his work in the urban wastelands of the Baltimore area, geographer David Harvey emphasizes the degree to which a place can inculcate emotional disconnection on a variety of planes: disconnection from a sense of one's body, one's immediate neighbors, and the specific place itself. On the other hand, the material quality of place functions in conjunction with perception. The physical components of place—such as the dry land, barbwire, and border patrols of Anzaldúa's home space—exist in a feedback relationship with perception. Only when we consider these as intertwined can we understand how perception as identification can flourish in environmentally blasted areas, such as Anzaldúa's borderlands, when inhabitants perceive not the wasteland but their shared suffering and their dreams for alleviating that suffering. Likewise, when people perceive nothing to be shared, no dynamic but disconnection, inhumanity can flourish even in environmentally blessed areas. The physical qualities of place and the care-full perceptions of the individuals embedded in that place are jointly important to the evocation of compassionate place.

A compassionate place relies on particular modes of articulation. All places are coproduced via shared systems of perceptual *and* linguistic habits. To create a compassionate place requires the exercise of a particular array of linguistic habits, which Corder calls commodious language: "Rhetoric is love, and it must speak a commodious language, creating a world full of space and time that will hold our diversities" (1995, 31). As Corder explains, contentious communication has traditionally relied on linguistic habits of display and presentation in which speakers set forth their positions, as if rhetoric consisted of poster boards designed for an audience's perusal. What results always from these language habits is the clash of static positions rather than the negotiation of engaged people. In place of this dead-end language use, Corder advocates argument as "emergence toward the other" (26). This involves going out and "inviting the other to enter a world that the arguer tries to make commodious, inviting the other to emerge as well, but with no assurance of kind or even thoughtful response" (26). For this to happen, language habits "must begin, proceed, and end in love" (28). What results from this loving, commodious language—the time and space such rhetoric creates—is a compassionate place where inhabitants define and negotiate, rather than erase or deride, their differences.

Both perception as identification and articulation as love rely on difference. Neither subverts, annihilates, nor silences difference. Engaged perception and commodious language must have difference to exist. Anzaldúa argues that difference is *necessary* for a compassionate place. Without difference, there is no need of identification, and love without an other is merely narcissism. A compassionate place is compassionate because it neither homogenizes nor elides inhabitants' unique qualities, a dynamic all too possible in situations based on pity (which is an emotional relationship between superior and inferior) instead of compassion (which is an emotional relationship between equals). The role of commodious language in coproduction enables inhabitants to recognize, accept, and celebrate differences as each contributes to the knotting of the connective tissue that binds inhabitants in a compassionate environment. By acknowledging and accepting differences as an inevitable outgrowth of each participant's particular contribution, engaging in what Corder would call commodious world building, community members continually create time and space for each other, creating in the process, I would argue, a compassionate place.

A compassionate place relies on the reciprocity of perception and articulation, for within this reciprocity lies the dynamism characteristic of compassionate place. All places are dynamic; all exist as a particular event or happening. However, the nature of the event—of the happening—differs from place to place. The dynamism characteristic of a compassionate place is that of emergence to the other. Emergence, Corder explains, "requires a readiness to testify to an identity that is always emerging, a willingness to dramatize one's narrative in progress before the other; it calls for an untiring stretch toward the other, a reach toward enfolding the other" (26). The implications of an emergent dynamism for creating a compassionate place are twofold. The existence of place as an event underscores the degree to which place and people can change and the degree to which place and people are coagents of change. Anzaldúa's efforts to create *una cultura mestiza,* a culture in on and out of "this thin edge of / barbwire" demonstrate the agency of people and place (Anzaldúa 1987, 3). Through her feminist architecture, the hemorrhaging borderlands become La Frontera, an exhilarating place of participation and evolution (preface). Furthermore, the dynamism of place highlights that compassion begins to erode when people are no longer able to connect, when they cease to "love before [they] disagree" (Corder 1985, 26). Once evoked, a compassionate place must be maintained through the continual care-full actions, images, and words of its inhabitants emerging toward each other.

Embedded within the reciprocity of perception as identification and articulation as love are the seeds of beneficial action. Both modes of image-making and word-making bind inhabitants to a particular kind of "right action": to do no harm to people or place because all are inextricably intertwined. Thus, what is good for a person or a community is decided by the degree to which an action knots or unknots the connections that bind people to people and people to place. This consideration enables people to determine the point at which, in their congress with each other and with place, they are morally obligated to protest a difference or to cease identifying with each other. An action stops being beneficial when it begins to erode the connectiveness that is key to compassion. The choice between problematic actions is therefore determined by assessing which action injures connectiveness least. Thus, Corder notes the limits of a rhetoric of love, of an emergence toward the other, when the other is a "Captain of Dachau" whose actions systematically destroy the reciprocity between place and person, between person and person. Compassion does not mean an "anything goes," "I'm okay, you're okay" attitude. It means actively looking for points of connection in suffering and hope, which requires an examination of one's own participation in/contribution to both suffering and hope as well as an examination of another's participation in/contribution to both suffering or hope.

Compassionate Classrooms and Caring Communities

By envisioning place through the lens of imageword, we gain a different perspective on place, one that offers the opportunity, the invitation, to create deliberately and consciously a compassionate place by enacting care-full seeing and commodious speaking. The next question that confronts teachers is how we might apply this new perspective to the classroom. One answer lies with what DeStigter calls "empathetic togetherness." DeStigter's work with the Tesoros literacy project illustrates the possibilities for shaping a compassionate place within our literacy classrooms by altering students' ways of seeing and speaking.

DeStigter's literacy project begins with his concern for high school students who fail to find a welcoming place for themselves in the American public school system. To address alienation within the classroom, DeStigter engages with two high school teachers in a ten-week program in which at-risk Anglo students from an American literature class meet with their Spanish-speaking counterparts in an English as a Second Language class. The goals of the program were twofold: to help students succeed academically by building on literacies they already possess and to help students connect with others so that they would "feel as though they actually belonged in the classes they attended" (1998, 13). The process depended on what DeStigter calls "empathetic togetherness," which serves as the core to creating communities where an inclusive participation does not elide difference (17). To achieve this, DeStigter designs activities wherein students share interests, discover common ground, and build affectionate relationships. Perception as identification is core to these activities.

Creating close relationships depends on inculcating the habit of care-full seeing and listening. DeStigter quotes Dewey's saying that empathetic togetherness relies on "a cultivated imagination for what men have in common and a rebellion against what unnecessarily divides them" (23), and this cultivated imagination is enacted when people connect by identifying with each other. Martin L. Hoffman theorizes that empathy, the vicarious emotional response to another person's situation, occurs, for example, when an observer's feelings and those of the sufferer match (1984, 103). The major process by which an individual experiences those matching feelings is care-full perception: imagining oneself in another's place either by visualizing the situation of the other and responding as if that situation were physically perceivable or by picturing oneself as the other, merging identities with the other. DeStigter creates classroom activities that cultivate these kinds of care-full seeing. For instance, Anglo and Latino students begin the ten-week course by constructing a written or graphic introduction that a classmate of the other ethnic group responds to with questions. Responding requires classmates to suspend, if only provisionally, their adherence to a personal, localized situation so that they can construct and inhabit the author/artist's unique position. As a result of this emergence toward the other, DeStigter says that students discovered common ground in the "shared experiences of their families' having been uprooted by poverty" (1998, 20). This experience led to students taking greater and greater risks in revealing personal aspects of their lives in their graphic art created for the class and in their conversations, a shift in habits that indicates their greater and greater trust in the ability of the other to identify empathically with those revelations.

In these activities, care-full seeing worked in tandem with care-full listening. Identification was inextricable from commodious language in creating these affective connections. The epiphany students experienced via the introductions concerning their shared experience of poverty became the basis for a "dialogue that helped them articulate and assess the social realities in which they lived' (23). For instance, following the introduction and the subsequent life narrative, one student shared a poignant photograph of his family, the only one he had of his entire family together (20). During the ensuing discussion, Aaron revealed risky personal details of a painful family dynamic, engaging in a discussion with both Anglo and Latino classmates that created a "level of solidarity that had not existed before that moment" (25). This pattern of commodious language was replicated throughout the course as students participated in activities that aimed at a "free social inquiry . . . indissolubly wedded to the art of full and moving communication" (John Dewey, qtd. in DeStigter 1998, 20).

As Anglo and Latino students acted together, they discovered in their shared marginalized status a basis for solidarity and shared affection, DeStigter points out (1998, 23). However, while affective connections through care-full perception and articulation were important to dispelling the sense of alienation students experienced in the high school at large, they were not sufficient in and of themselves for crafting the empathetic togetherness necessary for a compassionate place. Important to students' sense of emplacement in a compassionate environment was the parallel conviction that differences were important. "Truly democratic communities must not only allow for dissent, but also . . . depend on it," DeStigter argues (36). Therefore, cautious of the "homogenizing and exclusionary potential of communities" (16), DeStigter places affective relationships within a beneficial dialectical tension with the free interplay of difference. This tension emphasizes the common ground among groups (their unity) and the differences between them (their separation). A tentative empathetic togetherness grew out of this "dialectical tension between unity and separation" (17). The web of affective connections enabled the members of the fledgling Tesoros community to encounter difference as "complementary and socially productive rather than threatening" (17).

Again, central to that fruitful tension are care-full perception and articulation. For instance, activities fostered (and depended for success on) care-full perception of images of ethnic identity. DeStigter explains that the Latino students signified and maintained their ethnic identity through the style of clothes they wore and through the symbols on the clothing, ranging from Mexican national identity markers to self-parodying ethnic comics. In addition, Latino students participated in the classroom by contributing experiences and information that validated their ethnic differences, from the music they shared for a popular culture project to the art they created for their "hero" project. Latino students engaged in required course work in such a way that they could make "eloquent statements underscoring their sense of themselves as Mexicans" (34). Crucial to my argument is that such visual and musical performances would not have been possible in a place where the habit of care-full perception was not actively practiced.

Commodious language, too, was intrinsic to honoring ethnic identity. A commodious language is not one in which the speaker carefully excises all evidence of his or her home community so that he or she might better "fit" within the space and time of a different community. Rather, commodious language is one inflected by the speaker's unique position. Therefore, DeStigter explains, the teachers involved in the project sought to "encourage uses of language that recognize speakers and listeners as agents with the power to expand the boundaries of their discourse and to revise the circumstance in which they live" (27) This required providing a forum for the "assertion of a distinctly Latino identity" so that the dominant Anglo voices did not erase Latino differences. Conversation, dialogue, and informal classroom exchanges were marked by expressions of differences, and these expressions were enriching for everyone, Latino or Anglo, because "they were presented in the context of a dialogue that had included . . . students' descriptions of shared marginalization" (38). DeStigter says the "*Tesoros* project suggested to me that if people can begin by emphasizing their connections with each other, they will be more likely to develop the motivation and disposition required to encounter difference as complementary rather than divisive" (38).

The empathetic togetherness that arises from class interactions serves the students well in the classroom. In his conclusion to his narrative of the Tesoros literacy project, DeStigter says the results were grounds for optimism: the project was a beginning, a localized point at which people learned to appreciate their shared ground and to perceive difference as an opportunity to imagine different habits of mind and action (41). Through the intertwining of perception as identification and articulation as love, teachers and students worked jointly to connect emotionally and intellectually across borders. Together they crafted a compassionate place for and out of civic interactions.

Conceiving of place from the perspective of imageword provides an opportunity for changing hostile place into compassionate place, but it does not guarantee that such a transformation will be effected. Even the most valiant efforts can yield at best a limited success with no pledge that even limited success in one environment will promise similar success in another. Such was the discovery that DeStigter later made. A year after the conclusion of the Tesoros project, DeStigter visited some of the student participants, where he found that the lives of many of the project's students had spiraled into violence and despair. DeStigter concludes that communal ties of affection are not enough, regardless of how successful that community is at complementing difference. Identification must be intertwined with commodious language *outside* the classroom. The place of civility must be extended into the place of civic action through the exercise of what DeStigter calls critical empathy: the process of establishing affective connections "while always remembering that such connections are complicated by sociohistorical forces that hinder the equitable, just relationships that we presumably seek" (1999, 240). Critical empathy, he explains, "situates conceptions of community and the public not in opposition to each other, but as complementary, recursive, and mutually-dependent" (239). The combination of affective and social responses leads to prosocial activism: the "sustained action in the service of improving another person's or group's life condition either by working with them or by trying to change society on their behalf" (Hoffman 1989, 65).

DeStigter illustrates the possibilities, and the limits, of critical empathy through the activities, and the death, of Tammi, a young counselor at the Latino Youth Alternative High School in Chicago. Through her work with the students at the alternative school, Tammi established strong affective ties, but these ties had consequences beyond solidifying the sense of community at Latino Youth. Her students extended the reach of a compassionate place by weaving similar ties in the larger public sphere. Almost as a memorial to her life, DeStigter recites a list of civil and civic moments, of instances of how Tammi's students, through her close affinity with them, have shifted compassion into public space: Lisa, a mother of two, plans to attend college as a result of Tammi's influence; Pedro, with Tammi's encouragement, attends a Chicago Public School Board meeting to protest funding cuts to alternative schools; dozens of Latino Youth students, with Tammi's help, organize a rally at Daley Plaza to protest police violence. Her relationships, DeStigter points out, were without a doubt civil, but they also led to civic participation that reshaped an alien public sphere into a place for humane behavior. Her actions testify to the potential of critical empathy for crafting a portable compassionate place. However, Tammi's suicide at the age of twenty-five also testifies to the limits of a compassionate place. Care-full perception and commodious language were not enough to hold Tammi within the web of that affectionate community. We can never totally understand another's position, DeStigter concedes; we can only connect in "partial and mutable ways" (243). Thus, even the strongest compassionate place, where inhabitants share suffering and hope, aid and anguish, is not a curative for daunting array of ills that plague our students, our classrooms, and our communities.

By conceptualizing place through the lens of imageword, we gain insights into the way that any place, caught between perception and articulation, is sensuous, coproduced, and dynamic. In addition, imageword highlights habits of perception and articulation necessary for the creation of compassionate places. Through those insights, we have the hope of crafting a more socially responsible public place that integrates communities; we have the hope of generating an affective and intellectual joining that extends our understanding of one place and one people to another place and another people. An imageword perspective on place does not promise happiness, success, or emplacement for all inhabitants. It does not pledge that fostering care-full perception and articulation will automatically create a compassionate place. It only offers the possibility of compassion, the possibility of emplacement.

However, the possibility of success, even limited success, calls us to care-full seeing and commodious speaking. Such perception and articulation, in turn, invite us to recognize and to redress the inequities that lead to the systematic alienation of people from people and people from place.

Notes

I thank Nancy A. Myers for her patient responses to drafts of this essay. In addition, I am grateful to Christian Weisser and Christopher Keller and the anonymous readers from SUNY Press for their help in shaping and reshaping this chapter.

1. The degree to which any literacy pedagogy (or any pedagogy) might constitute an act of violence has been explored by a variety of scholars. Without a doubt, pedagogy by its nature seeks to effect a change in a group of individuals who may not have acceded to those changes. However, to indict all pedagogies as equally violent leads us to the dangerous conclusion that the only way to alleviate displacement and the results of displacement is to abandon pedagogy, which is a ridiculous position. Rather, as Patricia Bizzell (1986) argues, the onus placed upon teachers, especially literacy teachers who through their pedagogy teach not only a content and a process but also a way of being in the world, is to choose the most ethical pedagogy possible at any given moment. To act otherwise is to succumb to the paralysis of perceiving all choices as equally poor.
2. The Feminist geographer Gillian Rose (1993) argues that as a discipline geography has been dominated by masculinist conceptualizations of space, one of which is the treatment of space as transparent. Thus, what Foucault sees as "dead" space, Rose sees as masculine space.
3. See 22-38.
4. My argument here is that imageword provides a productive *metaphor* for perceiving aspects of place that would be otherwise invisible. For a fuller exploration of the constitution of place as both image and word, see Fleckenstein 2004 and 2003, 61–66.
5. See Fleckenstein 2003, 22–27.
6. See Fleckenstein 2003, 27–29.
7. For an incisive examination of the discursive construction of space, see Walter D. Mignolo's description of the sixteenth-century efforts on the part of Spain to map the Indies, a process that controlled

territories and colonized the imagination of people on both sides of the Atlantic (1995, 281). This process involved the use of written responses to questionnaires, compiled and organized by a *chronista mayor*, and resulted in a distinctive role for writing in the mapping of space. "Looking at them [maps] as social and semiotic interactions and territorial control instead of representations of an ontological space . . . opens up new ways of understanding in which cognitive patterns become embedded in social actions and representations become performances of colonization" (313).

Works Cited

Anzaldúa, Gloria. 1987. *Borderlands/LaFrontera: The New Mestiza*. San Francisco: Aunt Lute Books.

Basso, Keith H. 1996. "Wisdom Sits in Places: Notes on a Western Apache Landscape." In *Senses of Place*, ed. Steven Feld and Keith H. Basso, 53–90. Santa Fe, NM: School of American Research Press.

Bizzell, Patricia. 1986. "Foundation and Anti-Foundationalism in Composition Studies." *PRE/TEXT* 7 (Spring–Summer): 37–58.

Burke, Kenneth. 1966. *Language As Social Action: Essays on Life, Literature, and Method*. Berkeley and Los Angeles: University of California Press.

Casey, Edward S. 1996. "How to Get from Space to Place in a Fairly Short Stretch of Time: Phenomenological Prolegomena." In *Senses of Place*, ed. Steven Feld and Keith H. Basso, 13–52. Santa Fe, NM: School of American Research Press.

Corder, Jim. 1985. "Argument as Emergence, Rhetoric as Love." *Rhetoric Review* 4: 16–32.

Davis, Ioan. 1990. *Writers in Prison*. Oxford: Basil Blackwell.

DeStigter, Todd. 1998. "The *Tesoros* Literacy Project: An Experiment in Democratic Communities." *Research in the Teaching of English* 32: 10–42.

———. 1999. "Public Displays of Affection: Political Community through Critical Empathy." *Research in the Teaching of English* 33: 235–44.

Feld, Steven, and Keith H. Basso, eds. 1996. Introduction to *Senses of Place*, ed. Steven Feld and Keith H. Basso, 3–12. Santa Fe, NM: School of American Research Press.

Fleckenstein, Kristie S. 2003. *Embodied Literacies: Imageword and a Poetics of Teaching*. Carbondale: Southern Illinois University Press.

———. 2004. "Words Made Flesh: Fusing Image and Language in a Polymorphic Literacy." *College English* 66: 612–31.

Foucault, Michel. 1979. *Discipline and Punish: The Birth of the Prison.* Trans. Alan Sheridan. New York: Vintage.

———. 1980 "Questions on Geography." In *Power/Knowledge: Selected Interviews and Other Writings, 1972–1977,* ed. Colin Gordon, 63–77. Trans. Colin Gordon, Leo Marshall, John Mepham, and Kate Soper. New York: Pantheon Books.

Graff, Gerald. 1992. *Beyond the Culture Wars: How Teaching the Conflicts Can Revitalize American Education.* New York: Norton.

Harvey, David. 2000. *Spaces of Hope.* Berkeley and Los Angeles: University of California Press.

Hoffman, Martin. 1984. "Interaction of Affect and Cognition in Empathy." In *Emotions, Cognition, and Behavior,* ed. Carroll E. Izard, Jerome Kagan, Robert B. Zajonc, 103–31. Cambridge: Cambridge University Press.

———. 1989. "Empathy and Prosocial Activism." In *Social and Moral Values: Individual and Societal Perspectives,* ed. Nancy Eisenberg, Janusz Reykowski, and Ervin Staub, 65–85. Hillsdale, NJ: Lawrence Erlbaum.

hooks, bell. 1994. *Teaching to Transgress: Education as the Practice of Freedom.* New York: Routledge.

Johnson, T. R. 2001. "School Sucks." *College Composition and Communication* 52: 620–50.

Kahn, Miriam. 1996. "Your Place or Mine: Sharing Emotional Landscapes in Wamira, Papua New Guinea." In *Senses of Place,* ed. Steven Feld and Keith H. Basso, 167–96. Santa Fe, NM: School of American Research Press.

Mignolo, Walter D. 1995. *The Darker Side of the Renaissance: Literacy, Territoriality, & Colonization.* Ann Arbor: University of Michigan Press.

Noddings, Nel. 1992. *The Challenge to Care in Schools: An Alternative Approach to Education.* New York: Teachers College Press.

O'Reilley, Mary Rose. 1984. "The Peaceable Classroom." *College English* 46: 103–12.

Rose, Gillian. 1993. *Feminism and Geography: The Limits of Geographical Knowledge.* Minneapolis: University of Minnesota Press.

Schachtel, Ernest G. 1959. *Metamorphosis: On the Development of Affect, Perception, Attention, and Memory.* New York: Basic Books.

Twemlow, Stuart W. 2004. "Preventing Violence in Schools." *Psychiatric Times* 21, no. 4: 61–62, 67–68.

Weisman, Leslie Kanes. 1994. *Discrimination by Design: A Feminist Critique of the Man-Made Environment.* Urbana: University of Illinois Press.

9

THE LOCATIONS OF USABILITY

JOHNDAN JOHNSON-EILOLA
AND STUART SELBER

On February 25, 2004, the CCCC Executive Committee adopted a position statement on teaching and learning in digital contexts. This statement outlines several assumptions that to us seem, not surprisingly, to coincide with directions that the subfield of computers and writing has been leading composition toward during the last two decades or so: with increasing frequency, teachers are integrating digital technologies into writing courses; these technologies support a wide range of literate practices, from the conventional to the nonconventional, including drafting print-destined essays, participating in online exchanges, and designing Web sites that involve multiple media. Thus, the focus of writing instruction itself has begun to expand to cover screen as well as print literacies. The position statement also offers a few principles of good practice that can help guide pedagogical efforts: emphasize the constructed nature of digital technologies and their contexts; create activities and assignments that engage significant problems and that require hands-on use of digital technologies; and encourage students to become reflective practitioners, especially people who can critically evaluate digital contexts. In this chapter, we focus on the task of creating reflective practitioners, doing so from a standpoint that is congruent with the assumptions outlined above.

More specifically, we undertake a discussion that introduces compositionists to the subject of usability, one that has intellectual roots in a variety of other fields (e.g., engineering, computer science, cognitive psychology, ergonomics), but that deals explicitly with the assessment of discursive artifacts, especially those designed for digital contexts. Although some in composition studies, particularly teachers of technical and professional writing, have long employed usability methods (see, for example, Doheny-Farina 1988; Schriver 1997; Sullivan 1989), this chapter offers a framework for thinking about the big picture. In other words, as opposed to focusing on procedures for assessment, which are discussed elsewhere in detail (see, for example, Barnum 2002; Nielsen 1993; Dumas and Redish 1993), we map the usability landscape in ways that clarify options, issues, and resources for teachers and theorists of composition.

To begin, we present a discussion of our theoretical framework, which is constructed from several complementary perspectives on space. We then provide a concise overview of usability, historicizing it in ways that are useful to compositionists. The heart of the chapter unpacks a spatial matrix that frames usability in metaphorical, rhetorical, methodological, and pedagogical terms. Key to this task is the explication of usability examples. We conclude by encouraging the field to pursue usability as a significant subject for a digital age.

Theoretical Framework

Our theoretical framework consists of several complementary perspectives on space. The project itself is an attempt to produce what Charlotte Thralls has called a "mapping essay" (Thralls and Blyler 2004, 124). This genre, according to Thralls, asks researchers to consider "an influential movement or concept in order to unpack underlying assumptions, chart trajectories or transformations, and tease out distinctions and implications" (124). Her essay with Nancy Roundy Blyler, "The Social Perspective and Professional Communication: Diversity and Directions in Research," is a paradigmatic example of the genre. Thralls and Blyler unpack the social perspective in professional writing by looking at four key concepts framing discussions of three different social approaches. The result is a matrix that does some general high-level sorting and that helps researchers to better understand the terrain of the social perspective, including important distinctions between the different approaches. Thralls is clear about the inevitable dangers and limits of mapping work, such as partial and incomplete representations, reductiveness, and simplification, but the genre serves to establish broad theoretical categories and significant points of divergence. The matrix is a heuristic device with explanatory power and not a monolithic, all-encompassing system.

LOCATIONS	Heuristic Evaluations	Usability Tests	Contextual Inquiries
Metaphorical	Usability as artifactual examination	Usability as experimentation	Usability as anthropological investigation
Rhetorical	Publication contexts	Writer/designer contexts	Reader/user contexts
Methodological	Analytical	Empirical	Multimodal
Pedagogical	Critical-analysis projects	Peer-review activities	Service-learning projects

Table 9.1. A Spatial Matrix of the Locations of Usability

Our structure involves the following locations: metaphorical, rhetorical, methodological, and pedagogical. These locations situate usability in a productive way for compositionists, covering both practice and theory with disciplinary sensitivity. We plot these locations in a matrix that includes three different types of usability, which are increasingly social and spatial: heuristic evaluations, usability tests, and contextual inquires (see table 9.1). Generally speaking, heuristic evaluations are conducted by usability experts who analyze a digital environment against the best practices reported in the published literature. In heuristic evaluations experts speak to one another about the environment, which is limited to the software itself. Usability tests attempt to open up this controlled feedback loop by asking real users (or user surrogates) to perform a set of authentic tasks that can be observed and measured. Here the actions and reactions of the user-tester, which are psychological and emotional and physical, constitute human layers of the environment. Contextual inquiries flesh out the human context, because they jettison the controlled conditions of tests for the contingencies of user settings. Thus, contextual inquiries attempt to understand a designed artifact as it gets employed in actual settings of work. Contextual inquiries can also involve participatory practices that construct users as codevelopers with a real say in design directions. The discussions in subsequent sections cover these different approaches in more detail, ultimately working through the entire set of usability locations.

Another perspective guiding our project comes from the work of James Berlin. Although postmodernism (and work such as Berlin's influenced by postmodernism) is deeply suspicious of grand narratives that attempt to offer encompassing explanations, Berlin makes the case for contingent metanarratives, for "heuristical" methods of proceeding that "provide connections while never determining in advance exactly what those connections will be" (1996, 74). In this manner, we offer a contingent metanarrative that can help compositionists make some sense, however provisional and partial, of an enormously complex and complicated landscape: usability. Our approach is not meant to be a universal or definitive explanation, but only one useful and informative account of the dynamics and nature of usability work.

Put in different terms, we are not after an objective model of usability here, but rather a relative and fluid framework, an effort at what Fredric Jameson calls "cognitive mapping": the attempt to position oneself contingently within a space that is so large, multiply determined, and fluid that it cannot ever be known completely, a representation that necessarily always fails, but in productive ways (1991, 409). A matrix itself is inherently spatial and indexical, providing a map of spatial relationships that both deconstructs and recontextualizes commonly perceived relationships along different, multiple lines. From the traditional perspective of physical space, the different articulations of usability each focus on successive, expanding constructions of space: from very local articulations focused primarily on the text (heuristic evaluations) to slightly expanded articulations examining individual, relatively isolated users (usability tests) to broad views that take into account complex, real-world contexts of use and users (contextual inquiries) (see figure 9.1).

At the same time, the matrix offers other potential spatial organizations that map against this simple (but useful) framework: the constructs of metaphorical, rhetorical, methodological, and pedagogical views of composition.

So we see this piece as a mapping essay with the general objective of presenting an overview for people new to usability. It is organized by a framework that is more suggestive than definitive, emphasizing an increasingly spatialized dimension that can be traced across three common forms of usability. This framework should be useful to the assessment practices of composition, in large part because such practices must be expanded to include the genres and contexts for digital work. The contingent matrix that we offer here positions service learning in composition as a form of contextual inquiry, an approach that sees writing and reading as situated, collaborative activities rather than simply as decontextualized surface-level features or isolated (nonuser) peer reviews. Mapping locations of usability against locations of composition (as both text and activity) provides one way of enriching our changing notions of what it means to write and read in the world.

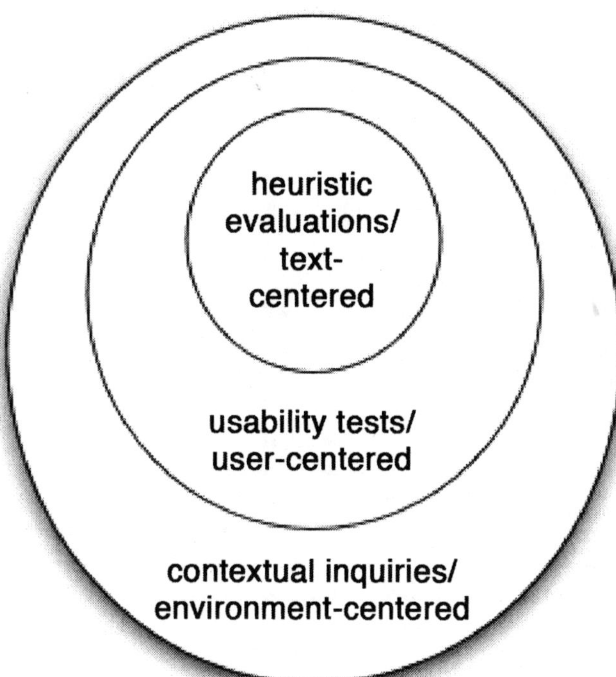

Figure 9.1. The Expanding Scope of Traditional Spatial Contexts in Usability

A Brief Overview of Usability

Usability is not an area of inquiry that is easy to grasp. A major difficulty for researchers is that the scholarship on usability is indexed under a wide variety of keywords (e.g., ergonomics, evaluation, information architecture, experience design, usability engineering), and it is often unclear exactly how those keywords relate to each other. This situation is a result, at least in part, of the fact that usability is something of a metasubject: its content is not a self-contained system, but rather is spread out across numerous disciplines with widely varying perspectives and objects of investigation. Usability, for example, could be considered the domain of automotive engineers, museum curators, software developers, graphic artists, occupational therapists, and technical writers. And it could involve things as disparate as voting systems, home appliances, Web site interfaces, tax forms, and health-care devices.

Usability work draws on research methods ranging from formal experiment and quantitative measurement through ethnographic research and ideological critique. In short, usability is a varied terrain with no single controlling discourse.

Most historians cite World War II as the context within which usability became a more energized and organized enterprise. As John Sedgwick explains, "The field has roots in Frederick Winslow Taylor's time-and-motion studies at the turn of the century, but it first flowered during the Second World War, when the fate of the Allies hinged on soldiers' ability to work complicated machinery" (1993, 99). This factor, perhaps not surprisingly to compositionists, was also instrumental in the historical establishment of technical writing as both a practice and a profession. In fact, the history of technical writing reveals some additional factors that were influential in the development of usability. In his account of the maturation of technical writing, James Souther notes that the field was encouraged and broadened by at least three mandates for more effective public communication of scientific and technical matters: "(a) the environmental legislation, both federal and state, requiring that understandable environmental-impact statements be made available to the public, (b) the consumer movement that increased corporate and governmental responsibility for providing reliable information in plain language, and (c) the advent of the personal computer, which places the usability of software documentation at the center of the marketing strategy" (1989, 2–3).

These mandates reflect several cultural developments that have driven usability work over the last half century or so, including the recognition that scientific and bureaucratic practices should be demystified in democratic contexts and the realization that both work and play are increasingly mediated through a range of digital environments. As in the case of technical writing, the mandates position usability somewhere between experts and users, attempting to make their relationship less hierarchical and more respectful, participatory, and human-centered.

One of the most frequently cited definitions of usability comes from Jakob Nielsen. According to Nielsen, usability is commonly concerned with five key areas: learnability, efficiency, memorability, errors, and user satisfaction (1993, 26). That is, how easily can users learn a digital environment? Once they learn it, can they use it efficiently? Can they remember how the features work over time, even if they only use them sporadically? Do users make errors using the digital environment? And are users personally satisfied with how the environment looks and feels? These are certainly useful inquiries, and we would encourage compositionists to take them seriously as a question set that focuses to a large extent on instructional versus technical considerations. However, from our point of view, this definition is a bit too artifact-centered, neglecting larger social contexts and relationships. It is, in the words of Clay Spinuzzi, a definition that tends to "bleac[h] out the very things that make us human: culture, society, history, interpretation" (2001, 42).

Spinuzzi conducted a study of four decades' worth of writing and communication activities surrounding a traffic accident location and analysis system at the Iowa Department of Transportation. Drawing on constructivist and genre theory, he shows how users of this particular system were governed not only by its built-in features but also by a dynamic activity network that included various actors, communities, texts, noncomputer tools, and objectives. Studies like this trace the constellations of cultural-historical forces that invariably influence the direction and appropriation of a technological artifact, promoting a model of usability that is distributed across time and space rather than localized in a specific digital environment (see also Johnson 1998; Mirel 2002; Grice and Hart-Davidson 2002). The summary point is that usability is evolving into an evaluative activity that is increasingly interested in the situatedness, politics, and social embedding of digital environments. Thus space- and place-centered pedagogies, theories, and epistemologies will become ever more vital to usability efforts.

In our rough mapping, then, we offer a framework for understanding usability structured according to spatial aspects. In this map, heuristic evaluations focus primarily on isolated texts (as should be evident, we consider the interfaces of digital environments to be texts). Usability specialists rely on generalized theoretical and research-based guidelines in order to evaluate the likely success of a text. Formal usability testing, the second method we examine, extends the scope of usability to include multiple users of a text as they attempt to make their way through specific key tasks. In contextual inquiry, the third method we consider, usability practices move outward in the spatial/social frame in order to look at users operating within the contextually situated structures and processes of their actual work. Researchers in this method leave the usability testing lab and visit users "in the wild," observing people doing their everyday work. These three focal ranges each provide usability researchers with important feedback about the ability of texts to support users.

Heuristic Evaluations

In this section, we suggest that heuristic evaluations are similar to the critical-analysis projects already used in composition classrooms. In terms of the spatial component, this approach works within a relatively contracted intertextual space, one that basically involves a text-in-process and what the published literature tells us about creating effective texts.

In a heuristic evaluation, a usability specialist employs a research-based framework in order to assess a digital environment. It is a type of usability inspection method that involves artifacts in various phases of development and evaluators who understand usability principles and who ideally understand the domains supported by the artifacts. Of the available approaches, heuristic evaluations are considered to be relatively quick and inexpensive: They do not require labs or special pieces of equipment, nor do they call for access to user sites. Moreover, heuristic evaluations are considered to be comparatively easy to perform, assuming the evaluators are trained in the research literature. These are the major advantages of this usability method.

Selber, Johnson-Eilola, and Mehlenbacher (1997) provide an example of a research-based framework that can be used heuristically in order to assess a digital environment. Although it was developed with online support systems in mind, it is applicable to other types of digital spaces. The framework consists of twenty usability principles, focusing on both global and local design issues. A selection of these principles can be found in table 9.2.

These usability principles were derived from an extensive review of the research literature in human-computer interaction, graphic design, technical writing, cognitive psychology, and other disciplines interested in how people interact with designed artifacts. And they reflect the findings of formal empirical studies, theoretical and philosophical analyses, and practical work experiences. So the principles are informed not only by different fields of study, but also by different methodologies and perspectives.

Perhaps the easiest way to explain the steps in a heuristic evaluation is to look at a completed evaluation. Levi and Conrad (2005) report on the results of an assessment that considered a prototype Web site developed by the Bureau of Labor Statistics. The prototype was for a Web site that provides online public access to the massive amounts of economic and statistical data collected by the bureau. Levi and Conrad decided to employ a heuristic evaluation, because the project was constrained by time and resources. In addition, they wanted to determine

GLOBAL ISSUES	USABILITY QUESTIONS
Accessibility	Is the environment easy to access and exit?
Organization	Does the environment have a discernible organizational structure? Is it congruent with the task objectives of users?
Metaphors and Maps	Do the conceptual schemas leverage user knowledge?
Navigation	Does the environment have a logical navigational structure?
User Control	Are users powerless over the environment, or can they modify it in meaningful ways?
Consistency	Is the environment consistent from one screen to another—and across the various features that inhabit those screens?
Reversibility and Error Recovery	Can users reverse their procedures and easily recover from errors?
LOCAL ISSUES	USABILITY QUESTIONS
Chunking	Is the content divided up in ways that help users access, process, and retain information?
Discourse Cues	Are there structures that anchor users in information they have already processed and that they will process in the future?
Iconic Markers	Are there visual items that highlight important information, simplify actions, and help users skim for specific kinds of information?
Typographic Legibility	Do the type styles enhance the reading experiences of users?
Negative Space	Do the surrounding areas, the places without content, make the content easier to access and understand?

Table 9.2. A Heuristic Framework for Text Analysis (from Selber, Johnson-Eilola, and Mehlenbacher 1997)

if this method might be of more general use at the bureau. Thus, in a sense, they were also testing the usability of heuristic evaluation for their work site. The organization of the report actually reflects a standard approach, so let us describe the report in a fairly quick fashion, emphasizing the more important issues.

The report begins with background information on the project, including its rhetorical dimensions. Like so many other Web sites, this one began as a loose collection of electronic documents that were published with little or no attention to the research-based design advice for interactive digital environments. The background discussion clarifies this usability problem, but it also constitutes an explicitly agreed-upon text that can be used to educate evaluators, who will need an initial conversation that discusses objectives, intended audiences, expected usage patterns, and the like. The next section of the report addresses method. Here, Levi and Conrad talk about three tasks: selecting a heuristic, identifying evaluators, and conducting the evaluation itself. What is important to note about the selection process is that Levi and Conrad did not begin with a predetermined heuristic. Instead, they operated more inductively, allowing the situation to suggest an appropriate framework. The other notable point is that several heuristics were combined to create a framework that would be sensitive to the specifics of the project.

To identify evaluators, Levi and Conrad followed conventional wisdom. They enlisted three to five evaluators with significant expertise in both usability practices and the subject matter (economics and statistics). As a rule of thumb, heuristic evaluations do not tend to uncover domain-specific problems, but it is difficult to evaluate form apart from content, which of course are mutually constitutive.

The evaluation process involved three phases. The first phase was an initial meeting in which the evaluators were presented with an overview of the prototype, the method of evaluation, and the heuristic. In the second phase, the evaluators conducted the actual assessment. Although they were given several anticipated usage patterns, the evaluators were encouraged to browse through the prototype, looking for potential usability problems and tying them to specific principles in the heuristic. Levi and Conrad do not mention a critical point here: Evaluators should carry out at least a second systematic inspection, drawing on the overall context developed in the first inspection. The third phase was a debriefing session in which the evaluators were brought together to produce a composite list of findings organized around the usability principles. This is a highly collaborative moment in which evaluators begin to debate improvements to the system. After this session, the composite list was formatted as a ratings form, and each evaluator was asked to rate the severity of the usability problems on a five-point scale, to provide relative weightings, and to sort out the major from minor problems.

The final sections of the report—results and conclusions—present and interpret the findings. The findings were presented in both quantitative and thematic terms, offering more than a single view of the data.

All told, the evaluators found 102 problems that could be identified with eight usability principles. For each principle, the quantitative results note the average severity rating, the standard deviation, and the percentage total of the problems. For example, for the usability principle of chunking, the average severity rating was 3.4, a rating that signaled a serious issue; the standard deviation was .68, which meant that, given this particular set of scores, there was relative agreement among the evaluators; and the percent total was 5 percent, which meant that, while chunking is a serious issue, it was a minor problem in the scheme of things (95 percent of the usability problems were found in different areas). The other view of the data grouped the usability problems according to theme. Staying with the usability principle of chunking, the evaluators noted themes of merging separate topics and splitting the same topic. Tracing themes generated a more concrete description of actual usability violations, providing a structure for action.

The conclusions interpret the findings and make it clear that the data collected in a heuristic evaluation does not speak for itself. Levi and Conrad discuss the strengths and limits of the method, situate the findings within a larger corpus of related work, both at the bureau and in the usability literature, and attempt to account for discrepancies. One of the more interesting things to mention is that the heuristic was revised based on the results. In adding an additional principle and in revising descriptions of several other principles, the evaluators refined their approach, working recursively at the nexus of situated practice and usability theory.

This example-driven discussion illuminates certain parallels between heuristic evaluations and the practices already valued in composition studies. In this mode, the spatial matrix constructs usability as an artifactual examination, a metaphor that emphasizes the critical analysis and evaluation of texts. The rhetorical location is the published research literature, a context that indicates the evolving knowledge base of an interdisciplinary field. This knowledge base gets deployed methodologically through text-analytic heuristic procedures that are alert to local social forces and conditions.

To make the parallels clearer, consider the pedagogical location. In composition courses, students are frequently asked to critically analyze a cultural artifact that is discursive in nature. As part of the assignment, teachers provide students with a heuristic to help them generate ideas and responses. The heuristic derives from what the field knows about the rhetorical aspects of texts, but it has also been tailored to fit the situation. Working together in small groups, students negotiate and produce a critique that distinguishes between major and minor analysis points. The heuristic both enables and constrains the collaborative activities, while a reflective memo serves to further contextualize the dynamics of the project. Although not an exact match, there are considerable parallels between heuristic evaluations as an approach to usability and critical-analysis projects as an approach to composition. Notwithstanding the limitations of the method, the goals, approaches, and priorities should resonate with the field.

The heuristic evaluation approach, then, is one that many composition teachers will recognize in their own classroom practices. Table 9.2 offers classes some additional methods for implementing aspects of heuristic analysis as part of their group critique work. In general, the framework in the table suggests that when composition classes begin evaluating new types of texts such as Web sites and new media documents, students may benefit from understanding the artifact as something that functions in concrete ways for users. Even when the space of analysis focuses on a relatively isolated text, a heuristic evaluation deals explicitly with an intended audience who will use—literally *operate*—the text as they create meaning with it. So issues such as error recovery, navigation, and negative space all gain more importance than traditionally given in composition studies.

In some ways, the challenges for composition will not be metaphorical or methodological or even pedagogical. Rather, they will be rhetorical in that heuristic evaluations require a deep awareness of the different research contexts that contribute design principles and practices for digital environments. As such, heuristic evaluations, like other pedagogical activities, frequently involve the act of helping students learn to work as experts in different domains as they analyze and respond to texts.

Usability Tests

Usability tests traditionally bring in potential users of a text and ask them to interact with it in an environment that allows careful observation (and frequently recording) of user-text interactions. In this characterization, usability tests are akin to peer evaluations, especially those that involve texts written for an audience that the peers belong to (e.g., asking other students to read an essay that proposes a solution to a problem on campus). Notably, usability testing commonly asks for responses from a larger number of users than a traditional, small (three- to five-person) peer-response group. Although the ideal sample size for usability tests is affected by many factors (ranging from complexity of the text to diversity of the audience to budget/time allowed for testing), usability professionals generally recognize eight to ten users as an acceptable sample size. A usability testing approach to peer review would focus the review more tightly by posing specific questions about concrete elements that interrogate how readers have responded to the text.

Unlike heuristic evaluations, this method attempts to collect empirical evidence that can steer and justify design choices. With roots in experimental psychology, usability tests often take place in special lab settings that allow researchers to construct an environment that is conducive to observation and interaction. The artifacts themselves can be in various phases of development, and in fact the different types of tests have been mapped in a rough manner onto the design process. For example, Rubin distinguishes between exploratory tests, which target conceptual models and designer assumptions about users and their tasks; assessment tests, which consider the effectiveness of specific implementation efforts to create features that instantiate the models and assumptions; and validation tests, which examine how well a nearly finished artifact compares to certain usability benchmarks. Although this approach is influenced by the tenets of experimental psychology, it is important to note that, given the generally pragmatic and fast-paced context of software development, most researchers are more concerned with interpreting and understanding findings than with collecting data that offers a seemingly objective window onto the usability of an artifact.

It is also important to note that most usability researchers rely on qualitative as well as quantitative measures. As with other research methods, usability testing procedures represent ways of framing and seeing a problem. Historically, the privileged lenses for examining usability have been experimental: studies are designed for controlled environments, variables defined, and results derived in quantitative terms. And there can be value in this type of empirical project, depending on the questions a researcher is asking. Usability specialists, however, have increasingly embraced qualitative empirical approaches, particularly interviews, surveys, case studies, and ethnographies (we will discuss ethnography in the next section on contextual inquiry). Not only that, but usability specialists have become increasingly sensitive to the nonneutral role of researchers in usability tests (Sullivan and Porter 1997). This is all to say that usability testing should not be unfairly stereotyped as the domain of old-fashioned experimental psychologists with social blinders. Rather, it is more productive and accurate to think of it as one approach that can provide insights into the perspectives of real users and their tasks.

In an attempt to provide a discussion that might speak to a field that has become skeptical of quantitatively oriented empirical approaches, we have selected an example of usability testing that involves qualitative research methods. It comes from a context that is familiar to teachers and theorists of composition—the academic research library—and involves undergraduate students in an effort to understand how well a library Web site supports basic research tasks, including those expected in first-year writing courses. As with our previous discussion of heuristic evaluations, we will gloss the example and stress significant issues in the usability testing process. Importantly, this treatment is much more suggestive than exhaustive: no one example could possibly cover the different test types, which are quite numerous and varied, to say the least.

Battleson, Booth, and Weintrop (2001) discuss their usability test of a library Web site in four parts: setting the goals, designing the test, conducting the test, and evaluating the results. In a sense, this reflects the typified organizational scheme for a scientific article: IMRAD (Introduction, Method, Results, and Discussion). But, their first-person style is more discursive and explanatory than what one tends to find in scientific articles, especially those reporting on quantitative studies, a move that belies the veil of objectivity often associated with the IMRAD format and that humanizes the project in valuable ways, revealing the beliefs and judgments of the researchers.

The section on setting goals is rhetorical in nature. Here Battleson, Booth, and Weintrop address several questions: Who are the users of the Web site? What are their tasks? What types of support should the Web site provide? These might appear to be relatively straightforward questions, but the answers were arrived at through a deliberative process of refinement and negotiation. Needless to say, a library Web site supports many different categories of users who engage in many different kinds of research activities. In attempting to set goals, it became clear to the researchers that they needed to establish priorities, for no one empirical design could possibly take into account even all of the basic issues (for this reason, running multiple tests with different focuses is a key recommendation in the literature on usability testing). After much deliberation, Battleson, Booth, and Weintrop prioritized the audience as undergraduate students with little to no experience with the Web site and delineated three representative tasks to examine: using the site to find an item owned by the library; using the site to find the most appropriate resource for locating journal articles on a specific topic; and using the site to find an appropriate starting point for a specific research project (191). These audience and task definitions, in essence, constitute a goals statement that clarifies the objectives of the usability test.

While the first part of the process entails setting goals, the second part deals with designing the test. The design process for empirical tests in lab environments often begins with the formulation of a hypothesis. Not so in this case (and in many other cases of usability testing). Usability specialists are not typically interested in setting out to prove a hypothesis as either true or false. Instead, they are more concerned with transforming the goals statement into an apparatus that can test design features in meaningful ways with representative audiences and tasks. In our example, the testing apparatus was constrained, in part, by the artifact itself, a situation that highlights one recursive dimension of usability testing: Researchers should not select their method beforehand, but allow the goals and the state of the artifact to help determine the method. According to the framework provided by Rubin, validation tests are appropriate to well-developed artifacts like the library Web site in question. In general, such tests attempt to determine if the features of an artifact have been instantiated in an effective manner. Battleson, Booth, and Weintrop created a validation test with usability benchmarks that echo research-based assumptions about effective human-computer interactions. The design of the testing apparatus was not especially complicated, and this is another reason why we selected this particular example. From a design standpoint, usability tests do not have to be overly rigorous. In reality, researchers learn a great deal not by attempting to isolate and control the so-called variables of the situation, but by observing and listening to real users working on real tasks.

There were roughly two phases to designing the test. In the first phase, the researchers developed a specific set of test questions that students would be asked to perform with the library Web site. The interrelated issues here involved determining an appropriate number of questions, a number that would yield sufficient data without making the test too tedious or time-consuming; wording the questions in ways that limited ambiguity and that made it clear to students that it was the Web site, and not their research skills, that was being tested; and scaffolding the questions so that they could build from each other, a strategy that could help the researchers determine if the Web site is easy to learn and remember. Notably, all of the researchers contributed potential test questions and helped to design the test, a collaborative process that leveraged the various perspectives of the researchers, who came from different areas within the library.

In the second phase, the researchers created a protocol for conducting the test, outlining methods for presenting the questions and capturing the data. Because the researchers were interested in testing for glaring usability problems, they did not employ videotaping, eye-tracking, or other mechanisms that support fine-grained analyses. Instead, given the goals and budget of the project, the researchers decided to use think-aloud procedures, a method familiar to compositionists that asks people to verbalize their thought processes as they interact with an artifact to accomplish real tasks. The protocol provided two researchers for each test, one to conduct the test and interact with the student, the other to record student movements through the Web site and to take written notes. The protocol also included a script to aid the researchers with consistency and to support the note-taking process. For each test question, the script included the ideal response, the least acceptable response, and instructions for when to intervene and when to end the test. It also created a space for a posttest evaluation, which asked students to further comment on the library Web site and on the test itself.

In terms of conducting the test and evaluating the results—two steps with far too many details to mention here—there are just a few broad points to highlight. The first one is that Battleson, Booth, and Weintrop took time to pilot the test, a move that yielded important refinements to both the questions and the script. They also attempted to reduce the bias of any one particular tester by involving many different testers in the process. Multiple perspectives were also involved in evaluating the results. In drawing conclusions about the usability of the Web site, the researchers considered the think-aloud comments; the observations made by the note takers, including notes about body language, facial expressions, and reaction times; the observations made by the testers; and the posttest questionnaires, which in part provided reflections on the research methodology itself. In addition, the researchers triangulated their findings with those in the published research on human-computer interactions. This enabled them to situate the findings in a larger context, to see if the patterns and issues that they noticed were also considered to be problems by the usability community.

Despite the fact that composition studies has generally become less interested in empirical approaches to research, usability testing, at least in the ways we discuss it here, overlaps with certain routine practices in the field. For example, like usability testing, peer-review activities provide important ways for students to gain multiple perspectives on how their texts are read and understood by real readers (especially beyond the teacher, who many students see as a somewhat artificial and detached audience). In addition, unlike heuristic evaluations, which are centered primarily on the artifact itself and can call to mind certain current-traditional practices, usability testing situates artifacts in a slightly larger social space and, by bringing in representative users and tasks, expands that space in rhetorically useful ways. The key, from our perspective, is to think less rigidly about what it means to conduct empirical research. Empirical research is not synonymous with experimental research. That type of research can be useful to usability specialists, but so can a wide range of other systematic approaches that involve observing and listening to users.

Another perspective that usability tests offer to composition is the positioning of texts and users as sites for experimentation. Because usability tests attempt to examine specific, concrete effects of texts on users, student writers can be encouraged to try out different rhetorical and textual strategies, documenting their effects on users. Commonly, peer evaluations are based on a general grid or under a rubric that emphasizes features common to texts produced in the course—sections on, for example, structural organization, textual style, and surface-level issues that fall more into a heuristic evaluation construction of usability. These peer-response activities are obviously beneficial, but might be augmented by a usability testing approach in which students identified (prior to the review) a set of concrete, functional outcomes they expect from readers after interacting with that specific text. Although we would not suggest that readers should be constructed as unitary, obedient machines that invariably respond in simplistic ways to textual prompts, usability testing can reveal important, meaningful trends among actual users. In addition, the results of usability tests typically portray ranges of significant responses to texts, things that student writers learn cannot be simply controlled but nonetheless must be taken into account.

In addition, very brief usability tests might also examine how different textual features encourage or discourage different types of responses among readers. For example, a test might illustrate how readers construct different meanings from different types of high-level organizations such as chronological versus topical. Similar topics are often alluded to in composition classes (active versus passive voice, variations in sentence length, and, increasingly, the use of new media as a rhetorical strategy)—an experimental approach encouraged by usability testing can provide students with concrete, working examples of how those strategies affect reading.

Finally, the perspective of usability testing suggests ways in which students can expand the audiences for their work by bringing in people from outside of the class to provide richer sets of responses for analysis and revision planning (an approach that is expanded on in the following usability perspective).

Contextual Inquiry

The final type of usability work follows, in many ways, a direct methodological genealogy leading from ethnographic and participant research. Such work in composition shows up frequently in service learning projects, with students designing texts for use by local nonprofit agencies. Contextual inquiry emphasizes ongoing interaction with users over the full span of designing a text so that the text responds to concrete features present in the user context (not only physical but also cognitive, social, and temporal).

Contextual inquiry expands the focus of usability to include people employing digital environments within actual working contexts—the office, home, or other locations. This method assumes that the contexts of users are much more complex than can be adequately understood in isolation. Contextual inquiry, then, moves outward from the artifact in isolation and from the usability lab out into the world. In addition, it typically includes aspects of ethnographic participant observation, with usability specialists sitting alongside users, asking the users themselves to illustrate their typical work habits, including things that are not directly located within the artifact being examined: the numerous interruptions, complex flows of social and technical information, and the place of specific tasks within the overall social and institutional frameworks in which the artifacts being ostensibly tested are situated. The location of expertise within contextual inquiry similarly expands; usability experts are, to some extent, just along for the ride, as apprentices, with users themselves as the experts. In one extension of contextual inquiry, participatory design, users are given a voice during the early design stages, helping to construct artifacts that are more fully integrated in usable ways with their own situated needs and demands.

As one might guess, contextual inquiry methods are typically more complex, more time-intensive, and more expensive than heuristic evaluation and usability testing. Proponents of this method point to greatly increased usability, particularly when usability is understood as a contextualized activity rather than as an isolated act. Importantly, an effective usability plan frequently involves multiple methods—heuristic evaluation and usability testing are not negated by the value of contextual inquiry, but augmented by it.

Mary Elizabeth Raven and Alicia Flanders (1996) offer a structure and process for implementing contextual inquiry. While their specific focus is on users of software documentation in corporate sites, the general approach can easily be adapted to running contextual inquiries for nearly any type of artifact use in context. According to Raven and Flanders, contextual inquiry involves three primary principles: researchers gather data in contexts of use; researchers and users work as partners during the inquiry; and the inquiry begins by articulating one or more specific focus areas, rather than a list of interview questions or prespecified, functional tasks. These three principles guide the processes of contextual inquiry, which follow five coordinated steps: identify key sites for inquiry (usually at least three sites, with an attempt to vary sites in order to ensure a diverse range), identify key users at those sites (again, usually at least three varied users per site), set the focus for visits to the sites (usually as a team effort, in brainstorming sessions that identify key concerns about the usability of the artifact in question), visit the sites and meet with specific users in their own workspaces (often also asking users to keep diaries beforehand in which they document the work flow surrounding the use of the artifact; the visit proceeds with an overview, observation, and discussion of key issues involved in the research focus), and analysis of the information gained during the visits. In a commentary on this approach, Barbara Mirel (2002) notes that constructing and revising the focus of contextual inquiry should be a process that is relatively large-grained—not limited to specific functions, for example—and open to ongoing reassessment and revision to ensure that the focus does not overlook issues that arise during the visits.

One useful example of the richness and complexity of contextual inquiry is illustrated in the previously mentioned studies conducted by Spinuzzi with workers at the Iowa Department of Transportation (IDOT) who were using a suite of software packages to understand patterns of accidents on roads and highways in Iowa. In discussing this example, we will omit describing many of the more detailed steps that match up with the formal processes of contextual inquiry. For our purposes, we merely wish to provide some concrete examples of how his research demonstrates the three primary principles of contextual inquiry and how this method provides a rich set of data for understanding the usability of artifacts.

Spinuzzi's research interests lay in understanding how users work with multiple genres of documents (including interfaces, e-mail, print, and other media) to construct hybrid genres over time. In this way, the research follows Mirel's advice to set the focus for the project at a relatively high level—rather than examining a single software interface or an isolated document, the focus of Spinuzzi's research is broad enough to capture relationships among multiple documents and document types across a range of work. His focus in the specific study described here grew out of a series of earlier inquiries, leading him to note possible difficulties caused by new versions of software that mixed older methods for representing data with newer (and possibly very different) methods. His focus, in one segment of the study, was on how users coped with software that displayed accident locations (used, for example, to determine traffic intersections that might require redesigns in order to improve safety).

Like all contextual inquiry, Spinuzzi's main site for research was at the workplace, at IDOT itself, working alongside those who used the software at their jobs, rather than in a separate, specialized usability lab. After asking participants to complete background questionnaires, Spinuzzi observed several users working with a prototype of the new software, taking field notes as well as videotaping sessions for later discussion. Following the sessions, Spinuzzi and the participants engaged in a prompted recall session, with participants providing insight into their thought processes and ongoing decisions as they attempted to use the prototype. In one session, a worker named Sam was attempting to gain a better understanding of the accident history surrounding a specific intersection. In the prompted recall session, Sam notes the benefits of the new software's display of information in geographic form (the earlier version only displayed coordinate data, which then had to be translated to a map manually). He also notes, though, that the data displayed did not agree with his understanding of the history of accidents at that specific location: to his knowledge, the intersection accounted for a larger number of accidents than were being shown in the interface. In discussions with Sam, Spinuzzi traces the discrepancy to differences in how data was stored and used in successive versions of the software; the display functionality behind the two versions called for different types of data to be stored, leading to discrepancies when the data were combined to drive visualizations in the new system.

Contextual inquiry, in these cases, provides information about the design and use of artifacts that would be difficult or impossible to gain simply through heuristic evaluation or usability testing, two methods that are relatively more isolated from complex work processes and real problem solving. By expanding the scope of usability to include actual work sites and processes, researchers can gain a fuller understanding of how artifacts will actually be used.

The usability model described by contextual inquiry thus offers another approach to implementing real-world projects. The structured processes and set of principles documented in work on contextual inquiry are a resource for compositionists to draw on as they engage their students in the complex, contingent, and valuable learning that takes place within real-world projects. By "real-world," we are not suggesting a division between the classroom and "outside" culture. Rather, we are emphasizing the shift in spatial and cultural context to involve not simply isolated texts or even users in isolated situations, but users and texts and authors and the contexts within which they all exist. Contextual inquiry can give composition teachers another useful set of examples for demonstrating the contingency of meaning-making within communities as an active, interconnected activity. We want to reiterate here that contextual inquiry should not be positioned hierarchically above other forms of usability in terms of truth or value. An effective approach to usability, like an effective approach to writing or design, takes multiple stances and is always aware of its own (sometimes multiple) positionality.

Contextual inquiry suggests ways to expand the locations of writing to include readers actively and recursively within the writing process, as participants in not only the use of texts but also in the design of them. We have seen in recent years an important emphasis on service learning as a way of connecting students to communities, both as social action and as a way of making the complexities of writing situations more concrete and immediate for student writers (Cushman 2002). Work in contextual inquiry can provide additional strategies, examples, and resources for writing teachers (and ultimately, provide a corresponding set of strategies, examples, and resources for usability professionals). Drawing on the examples discussed earlier in this section, community service projects might include a structured process of inquiry that involves users in rich and recursive ways. By expanding the spatial location of communication outward from the text and including users in context, students can gain firsthand information about the complexity and contingency of document use in other environments.

Such an approach frequently involves reframing an assignment in more spatially and socially expanded terms: Rather than assigning students to design a Web site for a community service organization, for example, students would work with a client to understand the overall needs of the organization and the people who rely on its services. In our own classes, students have frequently discovered that community organizations require a varied set of documents, of which a Web site might be only a small portion (or not even relevant). In addition, students come to understand the texts they are constructing as living documents that need to be usable over time by people with multiple demands. Issues such as who maintains a Web site (updating it as staff rotates and as service programs change) are brought to the fore.

As we indicated earlier, contextual inquiry can be a time-consuming and complicated activity. However, from a usability perspective, it is a crucial component of learning to design texts that are ultimately valuable to their users.

Contextual inquiry also suggests a productive complication in terms of how we teach writing and text design. Historically (in both composition and technical communication), writing and design were commonly taught at least partially as a modes or genres approach: students learn to write one type of text at a time. In this way, genres can become solutions in search of problems, or the hammers to which everything seems a nail. In contextual inquiry situations, writers and designers must learn to draw on a repertoire of genres that can be applied (and often mixed) to specific, concrete locations of use. One successful approach to this complexity is to structure a class so that students learn a coherent set of text genres or types near the start of the semester, turning to contextual inquiry practices during the final part of the semester. Students can be assisted in connecting particular text genres (or combining hybrid genres or learning new ones) as the contextual inquiry demands—in some cases, identifying unfamiliar genres and learning how to author them on the fly. Given the rapidly shifting nature of genre in contemporary culture, the ability to identify, master, and combine new genres has become an increasingly vital skill.

Conclusion

In this chapter, we have constructed a rough map of the ways concepts and practices developed in the field of usability can inform composition theory and practice. We should reiterate here that usability and composition are not as distantly separated as they might seem at first glance to many writing teachers and theorists. Indeed, many of the theorists we have drawn on are technical communicators trained initially in composition and rhetoric and who continue to work actively (and productively) in both areas. Their work, unfortunately, is only infrequently attended to by people working in other areas of composition. We hope that by making these connections and alliances more specific, by relating usability practices concretely to work in composition, we can reconnect the two somewhat divergent strands.

The three types of usability that we discuss—heuristic evaluations, usability tests, and contextual inquiries—provide a useful framework for considering a complex range of social, cognitive, and technical forces. In considering these three approaches in terms of their spatial locations, compositionists can begin understanding digital environments as concrete, situated, and active locations of use. The contingent matrix we have offered can provide useful ways to understand the different spatial constructions of textual development and use—that is, writing and reading. The matrix itself, as we indicated earlier, is certainly not exhaustive or completely representative, but a set of open positions that should encourage additional, critical constructions.

Works Cited

Barnum, Carol M. 2002. *Usability Testing and Research.* New York: Longman.

Battleson, Brenda, Austin Booth, and Jane Weintrop. 2001. "Usability Testing of an Academic Library Web Site: A Case Study." *Journal of Academic Librarianship* 27: 188–98.

Berlin, James A. 1996. *Rhetorics, Poetics, and Cultures: Refiguring College English Studies.* Urbana, IL: NCTE.

CCCC Position Statement on Teaching, Learning, and Assessing Writing in Digital Environments. 2005. August 30. http://www.ncte.org/groups/cccc/positions/115775.htm.

Cushman, Ellen. 2002. "Sustainable Service Learning Programs." *College Composition and Communication* 54: 40–65.

Doheny-Farina, Stephen, ed. 1988. *Effective Documentation: What We Have Learned from Research.* Cambridge, MA: MIT Press.

Dumas, Joseph S., and Janice C. Redish. 1993. *A Practical Guide to Usability Testing.* Norwood, NJ: Ablex.

Grice, Roger, and Bill Hart-Davidson. 2002. "Mapping the Expanding Landscape of Usability: The Case of Distributed Education." *ACM Journal of Computer Documentation* 26: 159–67.

Jameson, Frederic. 1991. *Postmodernism, Or, the Cultural Logic of Late Capitalism.* Durham, NC: Duke University Press.

Johnson, Robert R. 1998. *User-Centered Technology: A Rhetorical Theory for Computers and Other Mundane Artifacts.* Albany: State University of New York Press.

Levi, Michael D., and Frederick G. Conrad. 2005. "A Heuristic Evaluation of a World Wide Web Prototype." August 30. http://www.bls.gov/ore/htm_papers/st960160.htm.

Mirel, Barbara. 2002. "Advancing a Vision of Usability." In *Reshaping Technical Communication: New Directions and Challenges for the 21st Century*, ed. Barbara Mirel and Rachel Spilka, 165–88. Mahwah, NJ: Lawrence Erlbaum.

Nielsen, Jakob. 1993. *Usability Engineering*. Boston: AP Professional.

Raven, Mary Elizabeth, and Alicia Flanders. 1996. "Using Contextual Inquiry to Learn About Your Audiences." *Journal of Computer Documentation* 20: 1–13.

Rubin, Jeffrey. 1994. *Handbook of Usability Testing: How to Design, Plan, and Conduct Effective Tests*. New York: Wiley.

Schriver, Karen A. 1997. *Dynamics in Document Design*. New York: Wiley.

Sedgwick, John. 1993. "The Complexity Problem." *Atlantic Monthly*, March: 96–100.

Selber, Stuart A., Johndan Johnson-Eilola, and Brad Mehlenbacher. 1997. "On-Line Support Systems: Tutorials, Documentation, and Help." In *The Computer Science and Engineering Handbook*, ed. Allen B. Tucker, 1619–43. Boca Raton, FL: CRC Press.

Souther, James W. 1989. "Teaching Technical Writing: A Retrospective Appraisal." In *Technical Writing: Theory and Practice*, 2–13. New York: MLA.

Spinuzzi, Clay. 2001. "Grappling with Distributed Usability: A Cultural-Historical Examination of Documentation Genres over Four Decades." *Journal of Technical Writing and Communication* 31: 41–59.

Sullivan, Patricia. 1989. "Beyond a Narrow Conception of Usability Testing." *IEEE Transactions on Professional Communication* 32: 256–64.

Sullivan, Patricia, and James E. Porter. 1997. *Opening Spaces: Writing Technologies and Critical Research Practices*. Greenwich, CT: Ablex.

Thralls, Charlotte, and Nancy Roundy Blyler. 2004. "The Social Perspective and Professional Communication: Diversity and Directions in Research." In *Central Works in Technical Communication*, ed. Johndan Johnson-Eilola and Stuart A. Selber, 124–45. New York: Oxford University Press.

10

From Site to Screen, From Screen to Site

Merging Place-based Pedagogy with Web-based Technology

TIM LINDGREN AND DEREK OWENS

A Two-Way Circuit between Biosphere and Technosphere

If de Certeau is right that every story is a form of spatial practice (1984, 115) then this is surely the case for the place-based writing classroom. Any composition course has multiple spatial narratives woven throughout it: the material conditions of the room, not to mention the professor's assigned office space (or lack thereof, as in the case of so many contingent faculty), the various localities referenced in assigned readings, the microenvironments created by students' seating decisions and their relation to the instructor's body in the room, even first-year comp's basement-level status within the hierarchy of the English Department's curricular infrastructure. All of these literal and metaphoric spatial conditions reveal a web of geographic narratives implicit within any writing course. But in a writing course where place takes center stage because of an instructor's interest in, say, regionalism, sustainability, cultural geography, local history, or simply the surrounding local campus and neighborhoods, the resultant writing work space explicitly emphasizes personal and cultural exploration via the investigation and critique of physical sites.

In such classes the contributions of students map the course into being. Students bring their homes and hometowns, their memories of places past and present, into dialogue, and these sites take on personalities as vivid as the students themselves. One student writes of a suburban neighborhood in Staten Island where hundreds of southern Indians have relocated in the past decade, initiating the beginnings of a little India. Conversations about the ongoing evolution of suburbia follow. One student wears his Bronx and Puerto Rican heritage proudly and also literally on his sleeve, and his enthusiastic embrace of his block in the South Bronx surprises others conditioned to think of this borough in a negative and racialized context. Another student writes of being homeless in Hoboken, how he slept beneath the bleachers in his high school gym. Sitting next to him, a student writes of her gated community outside Kansas City, and how safe and happy its security gates make her feel. Another describes a Queens neighborhood she feels is being "overrun" by Korean churches and businesses; another writes of her Queens neighborhood with unbridled passion, declaring that she hopes to remain there until she dies. And so on. A classroom where students investigate their local communities in detail, expanding their narratives and composing extensive place portraits while discussing what makes them, in their eyes, good or bad or boring, on the mend or in decline, is a classroom where writing converges with spatial practice.

Space and place have become two of the more prominent pedagogical metaphors orchestrating writing praxis. In a relatively short period of time compositionists have considered their field under the rubrics of public discourse, ecocomposition, cultural geography, and place-based pedagogy (Mahala and Swilky 1997; Reynolds 2004; Weisser and Dobrin 2001). What has yet to be fully explored, though, is the fecund and, we would argue, now unavoidable relationship between place-based pedagogy and new media technologies providing mechanisms for the articulation, monitoring, and evolution of place.

For some, place and technology might be seen as conceptual realms occupying opposite ends of the spectrum, particularly for those whose identification with the former is informed by ecological concerns. The audiences at the Association for the Study of Literature and the Environment (ASLE), for instance, are not likely to be the ones in attendance at a conference on new media studies at MIT, and vice versa. For a host of reasons, "technology" is still viewed as something residing "outside" of "nature," a tension Stephen Doheny-Farina wrestles with in *The Wired Neighborhood*, where he claims that participation in online "communities" often results in a distancing from one's own physical local environments. To a degree we share this concern; one of our primary goals in this article is to argue for using new media and online technologies in ways that take us outdoors, away from our computers. But the other side of our argument is that we need to take what we find "outside" and feed that information back into our computers. We seek to think of place and technology as nodes within a feedback loop, a circuit where each realm informs and feeds the other.

Joel de Rosnay helps to clarify this position. In *The Symbiotic Man: A New Understanding of the Organization of Life and a Vision of the Future*, de Rosnay moves beyond recent investigations into the status of the posthuman as presented in the work of N. Katherine Hayles (1999) and Donna Haraway (1990), calling for nothing less than the realization and reconstruction of a planetary brain via a "marriage of the biosphere with the technosphere" (de Rosnay 2000, 71). "In order to create a planetary brain, humans will have to communicate with machines through a system analogous to that of the synapses, linking the two distinct worlds and transmitting information in both directions" (78). We are in fact already well en route to such a "symbiotic humanity," de Rosnay argues, as people already live in degrees of symbiotic accord with their homes, cars, and workplaces (77).

> The planetary brain of the cybiont is in the process of emerging. It functions . . . through individual human "neurons" connected by computers and communications networks. The electronic highway provides the nerve pathways of the planetary nervous system, and personal computers . . . are the glial cells that allow the neurons to function and create interfaces. Through interconnected global networks—private, public, commercial, and military—local networks, and networks of networks, a collective brain is being created, a hybrid biological and electronic (and soon biotic) brain with a vastly greater processing capacity than that of our few billion neurons or our most powerful computers. (132)

"I prefer to consider humanity, society, and the technosphere as a *coevolutionary whole*," de Rosnay writes, where the two-way information flow between humans and information networks assists, enhances, and can ultimately maintain and preserve both (96; italics in original).

This cybiont—as de Rosnay calls this planetary macroorganism—has two functions: "*self-preservation* through the linking of ecology and economy and *self-perception* through the emergence of a collective intelligence and consciousness" (119; italics in original). Needless to say, the implications of de Rosnay's vision are staggering. "Humanity has taken on an unprecedented challenge to build a living organism from within—an organism possessing a higher level of organization than its own and one that is destined to become its symbiotic partner. No political theory, philosophy, or even religion has prepared us for this titanic task, which calls into question the sovereignty of humanity and the impact of human action on the world" (113).

This talk of a planetary brain, of humans as the equivalent of neurons within this global Gaianesque mind, might sound as little more than science fiction were it not for de Rosnay's ultimate concern with global self-preservation, manifested in a shift toward ecological economics:

> For real symbiosis to be possible, people must divert part of their individualism into participation in a system that is larger than themselves and from which they can benefit. The traditional economic system is founded on individual reward, and everything—education, advertising, the idea of success, politics—is geared toward stimulating individualism and the achievement of personal goals. The modern economy has become a machine that produces egoists, or "egocitizens." . . . Neither an ecosystem nor symbiotic relationships can function without a collective intelligence that arises from actions involving both individuals and the larger whole. A change from today's top-down approach of political or technocratic plans and programs to a bottom-up approach based on different values and involving membership organizations, community life, and participatory democracy would be a good start toward creating a new sense of community. . . . We need new values and a new ecoethics to be able to move beyond individualism to an organized community that respects individual freedom and personal initiative. (128)

A splendid example of one person's explorations into using contemporary technology for environmental and local awareness is found in Paul Ryan's merging of video art and environmental education. In *Video Mind, Earth Mind: Art, Communications, and Ecology,* a collection of essays from 1968 through 1991, Ryan's project recognizes video technology as a means by which individuals attend to their local environments. Influenced equally by Marshall McLuhan and Gregory Bateson, Ryan draws up a variety of plans, including an "Earthscore curriculum," a New York City "Ecochannel" where community members continually monitor their watersheds, and other educational projects where "all non-private information will be available to anyone at any time and place in any mode he wants" (1993, 31) and each person is his or her own composer: "Give them videotape, audiotape, and film and let them find forms for their own experience and their own environs rather than let the teacher take the data, inform it, and present it as a precooked packet to be warmed over and consumed in the classroom. Self-structuring of unprepared data develops the capacity to be your own information composer" (31).

Ryan's ideas about the revolutionary impact of video are now beginning to be realized in today's online technologies. While technologically dated—this passage was written around 1970—Ryan's goal of making new information technologies available to the widest number of people in order that they might cultivate their local cultures, and in the process discover the means of preserving and sustaining their local ecosystems, presages a host of contemporary online activities where individuals are mapping, recording, critiquing, and calling attention to the status of their local environments. What follows is a closer look at some of these projects.

Place-blogging, Geoannotation, and Other Examples of Environmental Knowing via Locative Media

For those interested in place-based education, it is tempting to think of the Web as a suspect medium, one that tends to disconnect people from actual places and communities; it would seem much more productive to go out and spend time engaging with actual places rather than to be online. The environmental education scholar C. A. Bowers has argued that the more time people spend in cyberspace, the less time they spend cultivating "high context" knowledge and gaining the intimate understanding of ecosystems that we need to preserve the health of our environments, a criticism that would suggest that the Web is particularly ill-suited for teaching place literacy (2000, 65). But the fact is that the Web now mediates much of life, and we frequently go online when we are trying to locate ourselves in various ways.

Among those beginning to develop the place-oriented potential of the Web is a network of bloggers who share an interest in writing intentionally and regularly about the experience of place. One Web site, "Ecotone: Writing about Place" is designed to act as "a meeting spot for a number of webloggers who write extensively about place in their own blogs and were wishing to work more collaboratively, as well as raise awareness to this genre of weblogs" (Ecotone 2005). Like many bloggers, these writers have found a medium to facilitate a daily writing practice that documents their personal experiences and connects this writing with an online community of interested readers. However, if a weblog can be defined as "a Web site organized by time," then a place blog could be described as a *weblog organized by place.* The network of bloggers facilitated by Ecotone represents a transgeographic online community whose goal is not to transcend geography but to engage more deeply with the experience of place. In describing why he began blogging about place, Fred First makes it clear that his blogging grew out of a specific motivation—"Two years ago I began to see myself not so much by what I do for a living as *where it is that I do my living*" (First 2004; italics added). This concern with *whereness* points to what makes place blogging unique as a form of online writing: its concern with the relationship between identity and place.

The technology of blogging lends itself to writing about place in several ways. The chronological organization and ease of publishing facilitate daily writing in a way that supports the habit of daily observation, allowing bloggers to post both their written reflections and their digital photographs without having to be Web designers. The online nature of the Web means the production of local knowledge can be shared either with those next door or those in the next country. Ecotone bloggers write regularly about their places in Fairwater, Wisconsin; Davis, California; Floyd, West Virginia; San Francisco, Bowen Island near Vancouver; London; Tokyo; Newcastle; and Australia. The interplay between this geographic diversity and the place-oriented nature of their writing creates the "edge effect" associated with the concept of the "ecotone," "an area of increased richness and diversity" that emerges where diverse communities are allowed to intermingle in a shared place.

The ecological metaphor is apt, not only as a way to describe the creation of online community, but also to describe the relation between place and technology inherent in the practice of place blogging. Place bloggers appear acutely aware of the productive tensions between the time they spend in front of their computers and the time they spend out in place. Ultimately, they are not interested in virtualization for its own sake or in creating online communities as a way of compensating for the loss of actual communities and environments (Doheny-Farina 1996, 54–55). Rather, Fred First's May 4, 2004, post in *Fragments of Floyd* represents the connections place bloggers tend to make between the health of communities, the ethics of technology, and even issues of global justice. After describing his discovery of a fifty-five-gallon drum of waste oil dumped into Goose Creek, which runs through his property, he concludes his post with this reflection: "There is no way to catch this slug of a human who did this. I would be perfectly willing to accept that this same person left Goose Creek and went back home to their regular job: propagating weblog comment spam. There are facets of human nature with which I am thankfully not often in contact—while some of the prisoners in Iraq have become quite familiar with them, I fear. God help us overcome the varied ways we find to reap pollution, corruption and hatred on the earth and each other" (First 2004).

The intentional, regular engagement with place that characterizes Ecotone bloggers suggests that it is a writing community well situated to reflect on the relationship between place and the Web. In the daily movement from screen to site, place bloggers attend to both the benefits and challenges of using new media to engage with place.

While place blogging represents one effort to use the Web to connect people to places, communication technologies are changing in ways that blur the distinction between online and offline, between site and screen. As the Web matures, users appear less enchanted with the early utopian rhetoric of the Web, which claimed an end to geographic limitations and embodied existence. In reality, of course, we still have bodies, we use the Web in very local ways, and, in the context of frequent mobility and rapid environmental change, more people are looking to online technologies and new media to help them figure out where they are.

The growing prevalence of mobile phones, wireless technologies, handheld computers, GPS (global positioning systems), and online mapping applications has the potential to create another massive cultural shift in our relation to technology. As Howard Rheingold has argued in *Smart Mobs*, the Web challenged our understanding of community, but soon mobile/pervasive computing will begin to challenge our understanding of place (2003, xxii). In *Digital Ground: Architecture, Pervasive Computing, and Environmental Knowing*, Malcolm McCullough asserts that we are experiencing "a paradigm shift from cyberspace to pervasive computing," a transition "from building virtual worlds toward embedding information technology into the ambient social complexities of the physical world" (2004, ix). In McCullough's view, "[i]nstead of pulling us through the looking glass into some sterile, luminous world, digital technology now pours out beyond the screen, into our messy places, under our laws of physics; it is built into our rooms, embedded in our props and devices—everywhere" (9).

This shift is reflected by the emerging field of "locative media," which explores the use of new media technologies to connect information and people with places. In Drew Hemmet's definition, locative media "uses portable, networked, location aware computing devices for user-led mapping and artistic interventions in which geographical space becomes its canvas" (Hemmet 2004). To explore the implications of these technologies, numerous developers, artists, scholars, and theorists around the world have begun to experiment with ways to engage with actual places through new media to "merge virtual spaces and communities . . . with the physical world" (Hankin 2002) and to help users "feel correspondence between 'Information space' and 'Urban space'" (Fujimura 2003). For many projects the basic idea is "to connect pieces of digital information to a specific latitude-longitude coordinate," often by using a mobile device, creating what the Geographiti project describes as "location-dependent messages or media" that can be "accessed by others not by a URL, but by the real location itself" (GPster 2005).

In trying to imagine a World Wide Web organized by place rather than by URL, the metaphors these projects use to describe their visions demonstrate that writing plays an important role, both literally and figuratively, in the development of locative media. For example, the online mapping project MapHub: Shared Urban Storytelling evokes traditional writing technologies when it offers users "pen and paper to record their unique and situated perspectives and then deliver that documentation to others" (MapHub 2005). For other projects like Geostickies and Geonotes, this "paper" turns out to be something like a sticky note designed to give users "the impression that the digital information is actually attached to a place in a way similar to post-its, graffiti and public signs and posters" (Fujimura 2003; Espinoza et al. 2001). Similarly, Thingster, an "open-source weblogging service for locative media," is designed to help users "publish 'virtual post it notes' about any geographic location: a street intersection, a street address, a restaurant, a hiking trail or a geocache" (Hook, Longson, and Degraf 2004). While the metaphor of sticky notes and pencils may not suggest the most substantive notion of writing, they do indicate a strong commitment to human-centered design: these projects aim to be quick and easy to use.

While the "sticky note" metaphor was a way for some early projects to conceptualize locative media applications, the term "geoannotation" (or "spatial annotation") is emerging as a common label for location-aware modes of composition. For example, Urban Tapestries is a software platform that "allows people to author their own virtual annotations of the city, enabling a community's collective memory to grow organically, allowing ordinary citizens to embed social knowledge in the new wireless landscape of the city" (Urban Tapestries 2004) while Andrea Moed's Annotate Space is a project that aims "to develop experiential forms of journalism and nonfiction storytelling for use at specific locations" (Moed 2003). Similarly, the Location Linked Information (LLI) project enables the "annotation of location for communal benefit" (Henkin 2002) and GeoNotes creates "mass-annotations with no or little restrictions on accessing others'[annotations]" (Swedish Institute 2002). The term "geoannotation" suggests that in the future the locations of composition may correspond more literally with compositions about location: the places people write about might also be the places where their writing happens.

Naturally, it may be some time before the full potential of these locative technologies will be realized on a widespread basis; however, compositionists will benefit from paying attention to those already beginning to wrestle with the implications. While some on the bleeding edge of locative technology may be interested in "augmented vision and other sensory-immersive strategies," some locative media theorists are simply interested in finding new ways to tell stories about place, to realize what Andrea Moed calls "the perspective-altering potential of narrative" (Moed 2003). Along these lines, the project Maphub: Urban Storytelling is designed to combine "culture, history, narrative, and caution" to tell "the tales that too often remain untold" (Maphub 2004). The Geographiti project imagines a related scenario: "A community wishes to create a wireless network and also wants to highlight local culture and the hidden history of their neighbourhood" (GPster 2005). What emerges from such an approach is something like the City of Memory project, a "narrative map of New York City that allows visitors to create a collective memory by submitting stories. Visitors link stories together by theme, creating new 'neighborhoods' of narrative that can be explored by others" (Local Projects 2002). All these projects share what the Urban Tapestries project describes as its primary design goal: "to allow its users to embed social knowledge into the fabric of the city via wireless and mobile networks, using a variety of geographic information systems to link memories, stories, histories, images, sounds and movies to specific places" (Urban Tapestries 2004).

In many of these projects, the creation of local knowledge is designed to be a deeply collaborative and grassroots process. MapHub, for example, describes itself as "a peoples' map—a map of an urban geography determined not by traditional methodology but instead by the members who participate and contribute every day in the experience of urban life," and in a broad sense their goal is to "promote alternative and peripheral knowledge of the cultural, historical, and current urban geographical landscape of localized spaces" (MapHub 2005). Such an emphasis is typical, since locative media designers and theorists tend to be acutely aware of the dark side to the technologies they use and are already wrestling with the question, as Howard Rheingold has put it, "whether location-based media will develop as an open system like the Internet, where everybody will be free to associate a review, a photo, a video, a map, a work of art, a political polemic, a database, with specific locations" or whether we will "be passive consumers of pre-packaged content fabricated by a few dozen synthetic superstars" (Rheingold 2004). Many locative media projects have emerged in response to this issue and see it as their primary goal to create what Andrea Moed has described as "more engaging, enlightening digitally mediated interactions with the urban environment" or any other place.

Put simply, locative media projects tend to be concerned with how the use of location-aware media impacts actual places and communities. For example, the designers of Thingster describe the "reward or 'exit strategy'" for the project as being primarily "social and environmental," and their hope is "to enrich neighborhoods such that it becomes easy to discover local services at a lower cost and to create additional environmental awareness." In fact, the authors take as their starting point the reality of a worldwide environmental crisis, and they identify this as the central question the project is trying to wrestle with: "How can we shift our ethical foundations from one of simply protecting human life to one of protecting biodiversity as well?" They base their design rationale on four basic assumptions about the world:

1. Our generation is shifting towards an age of "always-on, always-logged" media where people of all ages are able to publish and share information about themselves, events that are happening, and places and things of interest.
2. Eighty percent of human knowledge is about location. The way we think, the metaphors we use, and our needs and values all come from our fundamental embodiment in the physical world.
3. We are being deluged by a huge volume of digital ephemera. Capturing, organizing, and publishing digital information is hard.
4. As a planetary civilization we are all facing frightening environmental challenges. (Hook, Longson and Degraf 2004)

Such assumptions provide a wise starting point for any reflections on the relationship between place and technology.

WhereProject and 21st Century Neighborhoods

Of course, it is one thing to begin considering the implications of new locative media projects; it is quite another to actually begin using them. Given the demands of academic scholarship and teaching faced by most composition instructors, most of us cannot occupy the position of "early adopters" in relation to new locative media. However, one need not be on the edge of innovation to begin exploring the way new technologies come to bear on place-based pedagogies. With this in mind, we have created two online projects, WhereProject and 21st Century Neighborhoods, both modest implementations of current Web technologies that allow us to begin exploring the implications of technology for place-based teaching in our own scholarship and teaching. We mention these projects simply as works-in-progress that have allowed us to better conceptualize place-based pedagogy and critical technological literacy as sharing a common project.

Both the WhereProject and 21st Century Neighborhoods ultimately seek to foster online communities of interest that in some ways transcend the limits of geography but where the rhetorical goal is to encourage the cultivation of local knowledge. As an individual place blog, the WhereProject is an experiment designed to foster a deeper sense of place through dialogue with others. As an online repository for student writing about place, 21st Century Neighborhoods, at ourmap.org, is a publishing mechanism that allows students to create place-based essays and share them with other students around the country. Both of these projects construct dynamic, collaborative spaces for exploring the complex relationships between writing, place, and technology. What is more, using an open-source application called Drupal to create our sites allows us to use a medium whose design reinforces the spirit of our projects: a free, collaboratively designed application is used to collaboratively create and share knowledge that is open to the public.

I, Tim, created the WhereProject (www.whereproject.org) in January 2004 as an experiment in place blogging and as an academic blog to accompany the dissertation-writing process. Using the open-source content management system Drupal, I began to use my site as a repository for place-related observations, photographs, maps, and links in an effort to more intentionally explore my sense of place in Boston. As the site has evolved, blogging has begun to play a more important role in my academic work, acting as both a heuristic device that fosters regular engagement with places and a collaborative writing tool that encourages me to reimagine my work as graduate student and scholar.

The WhereProject represents a fusion of two interests that I now see as intimately related: place and technology. When I began graduate school as a North Dakotan displaced from Chicago to study in Boston, I was already well on my well way to becoming the "rootless professor" described by Eric Zencey, an academic educated for the road and socialized to believe that the true scholar transcends the limitations of place. When I failed to make a home in ideas alone, my ongoing sense of displacement motivated me to focus on place-based pedagogy in my work in composition. At the same time, I became increasingly involved with online technologies and new media, a development that caused its own form of intellectual and professional disorientation. Though these two interests seemed at first unrelated—even contradictory at times—I soon began to realize they were connected in complex ways and that I needed a space to interrogate their relationship.

Fortunately, place blogging offered such a space, and I was relieved to discover many prolific and thoughtful online writers already inhabiting the genre. The Ecotone circle of bloggers impressed me with the depth and range of their reflections, and I was surprised at how generously and enthusiastically they responded to my interest in place blogging. As I became more comfortable with the public nature of blogging, I began to experience my intellectual work as less solitary and more intertwined with other, like-minded scholars and writers. This experience with Ecotone and the WhereProject suggests that place blogging can function as a heuristic device to help scholars and teachers engage more deeply with place, develop public voices by writing for a diverse online audience, and explore new ways of creating and sharing knowledge in networked settings. If we ultimately teach out of our own experience, we need to find ways not just to theorize writing, place, and technology, but also to practice them. For some of us, blogging about place may be a good place to start.

I, Derek, created a prototype for "21st Century Neighborhoods" in spring 2004. For years I had been teaching composition courses where students created "place portraits" of their home neighborhoods (see Owens 2001), and I had found these studies to be so engaging that I wanted to create a site where they could be shared with others. The site grew out of several specific needs: providing a forum where students could testify about the conditions of their local habitats, enhancing the relevance of student writing by situating it in the public sphere, promoting place-based pedagogy, highlighting the work of other place-based educators, and, eventually, bringing these students' insights to the attention of professionals in the fields of urban studies, planning, and community revitalization. (A full description can be found at ourmap.org.)

Using Dreamweaver and Photoshop software provided through my university, I created a rudimentary Web site featuring a small handful of student essays and photographs. Several attempts at gaining grant funds to promote the project through FIPSE were unsuccessful, as were my attempts at getting my university's IT unit interested in hosting the site on the university server or with providing me with the necessary graduate support to maintain and upgrade the site. And maintaining the site on my own has proved difficult at best, given my range of administrative and teaching responsibilities. (I have dozens of student photo essays in various formats that have yet to be uploaded.) However, as I begin to learn how to use open-source applications such as Drupal—through the generous assistance of my colleague, Tim, who is far more at home in using these technologies than I am!—hopefully by the time this article is in print ourmap.org will have graduated from a static site, where I upload all the material, to one where faculty and students can easily upload their own contributions. This is the intention of the Web site: to evolve into a large online map of local neighborhoods as understood by the students who live in them. If I can make the site easily interactive, it is my goal to eventually have hundreds, if not thousands, of such student essays available at this site.

My own mixed results with ourmap.org—the excitement at initially creating a site, and the difficulties of maintaining it—indicate that we are still in the early stages of promoting this kind of work among writing faculty. If faculty and students are to play a more active role in these interactive technologies, then institutions will have to support their faculty. After all, if, as a tenured member of an English department, I am currently having difficulty finding the time to update and maintain my site, so much the worse for the vast body of severely overworked and undercompensated contingent faculty who teach the majority of the nation's writing courses. As open-source and Web design become increasingly accessible, however, one expects that more of us will be able to shift our pedagogical experiments online, with or without institutional support. And certainly our undergraduate students, who are now the first post-Web generation and are conceptually more at home in online communities, will help show us the way.

Conclusion

New technologies allow opportunities to move beyond the oftentimes reductive binaries of local and global, real and virtual. A place-based pedagogy, for example, ought not be mistaken for a mandatory localism. Taking issue with bioregionalists and deep ecologists for proposing theories of behavior that problematically require constituents to identify themselves according to rigid boundaries of place and with nonhuman entities, respectively, Avner de-Shalit (2000) proposes an environmentally informed sense of community that is conceived around a political but not necessarily local community. Because "organizations such as neighborhood committees, small discussion groups, round tables etc., can function where people actually live in small communities, and where they tend to stay for long periods in the same house," de-Shalit reminds us, many living in cities and in suburban sprawl, and who tend to move frequently, are often unable to maintain the kind of constant local interaction considered essential by the bioregionalist (126). The design of urban and suburban planning, after all, either enhances or works against communitarian impulses—and as new urbanists have observed, the bulk of the post–World War II American landscape has been designed for cars, not pedestrians, thereby severely interrupting opportunities for sustained "village" contact among residents.

In the context of mobility and environmental change, virtual environments may seem "more 'real', insofar as non-virtual environments are vulnerable to endless physical change. When physical environments change so frequently around us, either because of the flow of capital in 'development' of all kinds or because we ourselves are moving through them as travelers, electronic environments may, in fact, offer more stability and familiarity as places to practice" (Holmes 2001, 8). For Stephen Doheny-Farina, such virtual communities of interest function as a compensatory mechanism, suggesting that the "geophysical community is dying. As we invest ourselves in the simulation, the simulated phenomena disappear" (1996, 27).

As the paradigm of "virtual reality" gives way to "augmented reality," we will have to find new categories with which to interrogate the complicated relationship between the Web and place, between the global and the local. Malcolm McCullough argues that pervasive computing will focus attention on place in new ways, making it even more important to think critically about how both places and digital technologies are designed:

> Life takes place. Our accumulated experience of intentional setting means a great deal to us, both as individuals and as societies. Design practices that foster this experience never go out of style. Perception of place may be subjective and fleeting, but grounding life in effective contexts remains absolutely necessary. Resorting to nostalgia hardly helps in doing this, however; there is little to be gained from understanding place mainly as something lost. At least to the more mobile and networked of us, place has become less about our origins on some singular piece of blood soil, and more about forming connections with the many sites of our lives. We belong to several places and communities, partially by degree, and in ways that are mediated. (2004, 171)

Since no place is untouched by globalization, we increasingly need to use the Internet—arguably one of the primary media of globalization—to understand how every experience of the local is now shaped by global forces, often in ways we cannot see or understand very easily. In the context of globalization, does the Web provide us with a certain kind of local knowledge without which we cannot fully understand our local places? In other words, can we now fully know where we are without the Web? (Just consider how essential tools like MapQuest have become.)

In the vision of the Thingster project, geographically oriented social software can play a role in addressing the complex environmental problems we face, helping us overcome the fractiousness and disunity among many like-minded interest groups. "Emerging grass-roots tools for sharing geographic information have a particular value. Such tools provide individuals with a way to share their own view of the world—not a corporate, orthodox or official view with all of the rough edges removed. . . . Grass-roots cartography as it continues to evolve has the potential to let individuals understand their surroundings in depth; to see the web of social, economic and environmental issues that tie their community together" (Hook, Langson, and Degraf 2004). Of course, this does not in any way suggest that online technologies and networked communications could ever become our sole source of local knowledge. However, the invisible threads of online networks and globalized networks of power do affect us, whether or not we are aware of them while hiking in the woods or strolling through our neighborhoods.

Paradoxically, then, the problem might not be that we have too much electronic mediation but that we do not have enough—or more precisely, the mediation we have lacks sufficient depth, interactivity, and collaboration. Place-based pedagogy needs to move both toward less mediation and more. At times, we need to just go out camping or walk around our neighborhoods with a pen and paper. But at other times we need to walk around with a digital camera and a GPS-enabled wireless PDA geoannotating the places that are important to us. The challenge is knowing when and how to do either.

In his book *Bringing the Biosphere Home: Learning to Perceive Global Environmental Change*, Mitchell Thomashow argues that cultivating a complex understanding of place, one that takes into account forces of globalization and the macrolevel environmental issues like global climate change, requires us to modulate our perceptual pace. On one hand, it is challenging to foster a deep sense of place if we only encounter places at the speed of a car or a broadband connection rather than at the pace of walking or biking. On the other hand, he also acknowledges the important knowledge that can be gained both from observing the world from a car window and while surfing the Web. What is important is knowing how to recognize what each observational mode affords, and how to thoughtfully modulate one's perceptual pace. As it becomes more common to travel by foot while simultaneously talking on the phone, being online, or accessing GPS data, it becomes even more important to understand the perceptual advantages of new technologies and how they affect our experience of place.

As McCullough argues, "Humanity naturally adapts to being in the world by using technology. The sustainability of our species depends on the appropriateness of our adaptation. Technologies of world making become dangerous unless they are complemented by technologies of world knowing" (2004, 210). For those us of in composition, the technologies of writing and communication we use are "technologies of world knowing," and for those of us committed to place-based pedagogy, we can no longer ignore the way new technologies shape our sense of place. To revise Cynthia Selfe's famous warning of "the perils of not paying attention" to technology, we think it is equally perilous if our technologies are not encouraging us to pay attention to the places we inhabit.

Works Cited

Bowers, C. A. 2000. *Let Them Eat Data: How Computers Affect Education, Cultural Diversity, and the Prospects of Ecological Sustainability*. Athens: University of Georgia Press.

de Certeau, Michel. 1984. *The Practice of Everyday Life.* Trans. Steven F. Rendall. Berkeley and Los Angeles: University of California Press.

de Rosnay, Joël. 2000. *The Symbiotic Man: A New Understanding of the Organization of Life and a Vision of the Future.* Trans. Phyllis Aronoff et al. New York: McGraw Hill.

de-Shalit, Avner. 2000. *The Environment: Between Theory and Practice.* New York: Oxford University Press.

Doheny-Farina, Stephen. 1996. *The Wired Neighborhood.* New Haven, CT: Yale University Press.

Espinoza, Frederick, et al. 2001. "GeoNotes: Social and Navigational Aspects of Location-Based Information Systems." September. http://www.sics.se/~espinoza/documents/GeoNotes_ubicomp_final.htm (accessed June 26, 2005).

Fagerberg, Petra, Fredrik Espinoza, and Per Persson. 2003. "What Is a Place? Allowing Users to Name and Define Places." *Proceedings of CHI 2003,* April http://www.sics.se/~espinoza/documents/shorttalk232–fagerberg.pdf (accessed June 26, 2005).

First, Fred. 2004. "Sludge: Up Close and Personal." Weblog entry on *Fragments of Floyd.* May 4. http://www.fragmentsfromfloyd.com/archives/002082.html (accessed June 26, 2005).

Fujimura, Noriyuki. 2003. "Geostickies." http://www.andrew.cmu.edu/user/noriyuki/artworks/geostickies/index.html (accessed June 26, 2005).

GPSter. 2005. "Geographiti." http://www.gpster.net/geograffiti.html (accessed June 26, 2005).

Hankin, Matt. 2002. "Geonotes: Virtual notes to real world locations." May 23. Swedish Institute of Computer Science. http://www.sics.se/research/article.php?newsid=105 (accessed June 26, 2005).

———. 2002. Location Linked Information. http://xenia.media.mit.edu/~mankins/lli/ (accessed June 26, 2005).

Haraway, Donna. 1990. *Simians, Cyborgs, and Women: The Reinvention of Nature.* New York: Routledge.

Hayles, N. Katherine. 1999. *How We Became Posthuman: Virtual Bodies in Cybernetics, Literature, and Informatics.* Chicago: University of Chicago Press.

Hemment, Drew. 2004. "The Locative Dystopia." Online Posting. January 9. Nettime. http://www.mail-archive.com/nettime-l@bbs.thing.net/msg01531.html (accessed June 26, 2005).

Holmes, David. 2001. "Virtual Globalization—an Introduction." In *Virtual Globalization: Virtual Spaces/Tourist Spaces,* ed. David Holmes, 1–54. New York: Routledge.

Hook, Anselm, Tom Longson and Brad Degraf. 2004. "Thingster Overview." March 23. http://thingster.org/about (accessed June 26, 2005).

Local Projects. 2002. *City of Memory.* http://www.localprojects.net/cofm/cofm.shtml (accessed June 26, 2005).

Magpienest. 2005. "Ecotone: Writing about Place."http://www.magpienest.org/scgi-bin/wiki.pl?HomePage (accessed June 26, 2005).

Mahala, Daniel, and Jody Swilky. 1997. "Remapping the Geography of Service in English." *College English* 59 (October): 623–46.

Maphub. 2004. "Maphub: Group-based Urban Mapping." http://hactivist.com/maphub/overview.html (accessed June 26, 2005).

———. 2005. "Project Development." http://www.maphub.org/development.html (accessed June 26, 2005).

McCullough, Malcolm. 2004. *Digital Ground: Architecture, Pervasive Computing, and Environmental Knowing.* Cambridge, MA: MIT Press.

Moed, Andrea. 2003. "About." *Annotate Space.* http://www.panix.com/~andrea/annotate/about.html (accessed June 26, 2005).

Owens, Derek. 2001. *Composition and Sustainability: Teaching for a Threatened Generation.* Urbana, IL: NCTE Press.

Reynolds, Nedra. 2004. *Geographies of Writing: Inhabiting Places and Encountering Difference.* Carbondale: Southern Illinois University Press.

Rheingold, Howard. 2003. *Smart Mobs: the Next Social Revolution.* Cambridge: New York: Basic Books.

———. 2004. "Urban Infomatics Breakout." *Feature,* January 13 http://www.thefeature.com/article?articleid=100315 (accessed June 26, 2005).

Ryan, Paul. 1993. *Video Mond, Earth Mind: Art, Communications, and Ecolofy.* New York: Peter Lang.

Urban Tapestries. 2004. "Public Authoring." August 25. http://research.urbantapestries.net (accessed June 26, 2005).

Weisser, Christian R., and Sidney I. Dobrin, eds. 2001. *Ecocomposition: Theoretical and Pedagogical Approaches.* Albany: State University of New York Press.

Part III
Among the Institutions

11

TRANSFERABILITY AND GENRES

AMY DEVITT

"Why don't you teach students how to write a research paper? Students in my advanced biology class don't know how to write their papers." The senior colleague who challenged me at a gathering for women faculty left me speechless at first, not only because of the challenge's inappropriateness in that setting but also because of its ignorance. I thought such a well-respected scholar and teacher would know better than to think that students could be taught writing in their first year and have it suffice for their senior year. I thought such a well-respected scholar and teacher would know better than to think that the research paper could be taught once and for all, and she need not worry about teaching it herself for her own field. Apparently, the myth of general writing skills lives on.

When I was being educated as a scholar and teacher of composition in the 1970s, I learned about the most recent views of writing, views that challenged the current ways of teaching writing but that still included general writing skills. I learned about sentence combining and generative rhetoric, readability, graphemes, errors and expectations, and the paragraph as a discourse unit. I attended to the process of writing (singular at first) and taught my students how to prewrite and revise (ignoring drafting for the most part). The scholars I studied examined the differences between writing and speaking and between "novice" writers and skilled writers. I learned to critique the CBS style of writing (clarity, brevity, sincerity, for the youngsters among my readers) and to concentrate on "the making of meaning." Even as I learned to critique the notion that one style of writing was always better than others, I learned writing and teaching practices that promoted a singular view of writing—the sophistication of the cumulative sentence; the linguistic understanding that could help me lead my error-writing students to Standard English; the syntactic moves that make sentences easier for readers to process cognitively; and the prewriting techniques and revision strategies that could lead my students to a better writing process. What I taught in my perhaps overly rationalized writing classes were strategies and principles of writing that I thought would improve my students' abilities to express themselves in any future writing tasks.

I have learned more since my graduate education, of course, as has the field of composition and rhetoric. Now I know that writing processes are multiple, that there are multidrafters and single drafters, and that no one process works best for every writer. Now I know that every writing event is situated in a specific rhetorical situation, each situation locating writers and readers in particular rhetorical places. Programs in writing in the disciplines instruct students in how writing differs in specific fields. The scholars I read now examine the differences between one writing situation and another and between one writer and another. Even studies of differences based in race, class, or gender are becoming particularized, examining the individual as well as group identities of writers. Our research methods, too, have moved away from empirical studies seeking generalizations to qualitative studies denying generalizability. Writing is so embedded in rhetorical contexts and social structures and institutions that to study one location for writing reveals only that location. Writing is a highly situated act.

What does such a situated view of writing do to the notion of generalized writing skills? It would seem obvious that any skills so generalized as to be transferable from one situation to another would be so generalized as to be virtually meaningless. Perhaps a writer can write sentences, one might argue; hence the writer can write in any situation. But learning to write the cumulative sentence, with its string of descriptive modifiers, in a fiction class does not necessarily transfer to writing effective sentences in a science lab. Learning to write a thesis-support structure does not necessarily prepare a student to write a literary critical analysis. And learning to write a research paper in first-year composition does not necessarily prepare a student to write a research paper in an advanced biology class.

The particularly situated nature of writing is even evident, perhaps counterintuitively, in my current research interest: genres. Contemporary rhetorical theories view genres as social acts stemming from perceived repetitions of situation.[1] Groups of writers construct genres through their actions (social acts) in situations that they perceive to share some similarities of purposes, participants, subjects, and settings (from perceived repetitions of situation).[2] In fact, though, each writing event and each writing situation is unique. Genres capture the ways people categorize those unique writing events as related writing events. The common textual patterns that emerge—and that people may imagine first when thinking of genres—thus develop from common situational expectations. To this extent, genres might seem to represent generalizable writing skills, ones that can move from one unique situation to another within the same genre. Yet genres also differ from one another and in ways that reveal the situatedness of genres and all writing. A research paper differs from a lab report, a letter to the editor from an editorial, a grocery list from a recipe—as the different names for the different genres attest. Each genre represents both perceived similarity of situation across different texts and perceived difference of situation across different genres. In fact, knowing the genre means knowing the different situations. If I am writing a theme, I know that I am probably writing to an English teacher in an English class with the purpose of demonstrating my mastery of specific writing skills. If I am writing a letter to the editor, I know that I am writing to the members of that publication's community to argue my opinion on an issue of general concern. If I am writing a scholarly article, I know that I am writing to colleagues in my general field to enter my research and point of view into the conversation on issues in our field. Each different genre entails a different situation. To know genres is to know both how writing situations are similar and how they differ, to know what genres are and what they are not.[3] Genres, then, reveal the relative similarity of some situations but also the difference of other situations.

Genres further reveal the situatedness of each writing event by revealing how each particular writing event must adapt the expectations of a genre. In other words, there is the similar situation of the genre, and then there is the unique situation of the particular writing task. Writing this scholarly article, I strive to fulfill the expectations of the genre: to explain theoretical ideas to a highly educated set of readers, presenting myself as a rational and well-informed scholar, and expecting the text to appear in a scholarly forum. I write within the purpose, readers, writer, and setting of the scholarly article genre. The details of my particular situation, however, also shape my writing. This work will appear in a collection of articles, in book form, with a length limitation shorter than many scholarly articles, so I work to narrow and condense my argument. The book collection has a common topic of location, so I frame my subject with some nod toward that common topic. Even more particularly, since I have been working in genre theory, not in cultural geography or location theory, I position myself as a writer informed of genre theory and connect the topic to approaches with which I feel sufficiently expert (in my case, treating location as one element of rhetorical situation). I also am experimenting with the genre of the scholarly article in small ways, trying to write a more readable argument with more examples and fewer interrupting citations and unnecessary terminology. That purpose, too, affects the way this particular writing event occurs.

Such variation from the genre's situation does not stem from my being an expert in writing or even from my being an experienced writer. All writers must vary from the genre's situation every time they write, because no two situations are identical. The writer of lab reports has to account for different details of method and results with each report, including the ones that did not turn out as expected. The lawyer writing a motion for summary judgment must make a specific argument to a specific judge. The student writing a freshman theme adapts to the current English teacher's priorities. Even the grocery shopper makes a grocery list suited for the layout of one grocery store and not another. Writers write with purposes, readers, writers, subjects, and settings particular to that instance of writing, and they mesh that particular situation with the situation expected of a genre.

And in meshing the expected genre with the particular situation, location matters, both in its literal sense of physical environment and in its more metaphorical sense of cultural and institutional setting, a component of each rhetorical situation. Different grocery stores make for different grocery lists. Different law courts make for different legal briefs. And different college classes make for different research papers. Location may not be the first, second, and third most important qualities of writing, as it is for real estate, but location is surely among the situational elements that lead to expected genres and to adaptations of those genres in particular situations. The fact that my colleague's students were in a biology class surely did not escape their notice—or at least it should not have escaped their notice if they were to write successfully in that situation. While her assignment may have called for a research paper and hence shared some situational elements with first-year research papers, it was located in an advanced biology class. Because of that location, the situation involved a more complex subject matter, a reader considerably more expert in the subject being written about, and a writer expected to have specific knowledge to offer. That difference of location leads to differences of writing process as well, with different databases to search, different levels of detail to record, and different ideas to generate. The genre may have the same name, but it is in a different game.[4]

Each writing event thus is unique and differs from one location to another. Yet not just my colleague but all readers and writers recognize texts as similar in some ways and call them by a common genre name. Writers create unique texts that nonetheless share generic conventions and expectations with other unique texts. Perhaps a dichotomy between uniqueness and commonality is a false dichotomy. Studying genres suggests that writing is at once unique and common, at once situated particularly in a precise writing event and perceived as similar to other writing situations.[5]

Such perceived similarity of situation might lead to some writing skills being transferable from one writing event to the next, but not, I would argue, outside of a common genre. A writer who skillfully manages the demands of one letter to the editor is likely to be able to write some elements of the next one skillfully as well, though not without adapting to the unique situation of that particular letter. A writer who learns some of the challenges of the literary analysis paper, such as integrating quotations or drawing evidence from literary texts, will likely handle integrating quotations better in the next literary analysis paper. But the uniqueness of each writing event places limits on how far such skills can travel from one location to another. Because genres represent situations, a writer writing one text in a genre will be writing within a situation similar to that of another writing a text in the same genre. Two writers of literary analysis papers will both be writing to educated audiences of one sort or another, in order to argue for an interpretation of a literary text of one sort or another, and writing as close readers intimate with a literary text. That both those writers share some writing challenges and draw on similar writing abilities makes sense. Two writers writing in different genres, however, are writing within situations so significantly different that they are perceived as being of different genres. For a writer to transfer skills from one genre to another, then, the writer would have to abstract skills far from their situation. For writing skills to stretch across different genres would require stretching too far across unique writing situations.

Yet my biology colleague evidently saw her students' writing situation as similar to my first-year students' writing situation, and she named the same research paper genre for both. Even though, as I argued earlier, the change in location changed the genre, perhaps some writing skills would transfer, since her genre name was the same. The fact that her students were evidently performing badly in her genre argues otherwise, and I think it was because the change of location changed the situation more significantly than she realized. Unlike writing two texts in similar situations and hence a similar genre, the students were writing two texts in markedly different situations. With such a significant change in the situation, what the students had learned in writing the genre could not transfer smoothly. That does not mean that what they had learned did not serve them at all, however, but rather that it served them in a different way.

Looking through the lens of genre, I see another explanation for how some skills learned in one location might serve writers in different locations. The writer moving among locations carries along a set of writing experiences, including the genres acquired in those various locations. That set of acquired genres, that genre repertoire, serves as a resource for the writer when encountering an unfamiliar genre. Just as writers perceive unique situations as somehow similar and so perceive and use the same genre, writers perceive newly encountered situations as sharing some elements with prior situations, and so they use prior genres when writing new ones. It is not the writing skills that are transferring from one situation and genre to another; it is the whole genre.

When writers move from one location into another, then, they may at first try to adapt known genres to fit the new location. An accounting student who becomes an associate in a large accounting firm might be asked to write a research memorandum for a partner. Not yet knowing the genres of the new location, the associate might first adapt the research papers and case studies written in college, genres perceived as having some similarities of situation.[6] To some extent, such adaptations can serve the new associate well. The subject seems similar, the research process seems the same, an informative purpose seems suitable, and the partner seems not so different from the professor as a reader. The full consequences of changing location may not be visible until after writing that first research memorandum and getting the response from the partner. The new genre is not the same as the known ones, but knowing some genres gives the associate a place to start, a location, however different, from which to begin writing.

Of course, drawing from known genres in new locations results in mismatches as well. I have worked several years with first-year associates in large corporate law firms. The genre in which they are most commonly asked to write for law partners is the analytical memorandum, a memorandum to answer a question about how the law applies to a specific client's case. When they begin writing for the firm, they typically begin with what they have learned to write in law school, especially blue book exams but also open and closed memoranda and law review articles. As was true for accountants' genres, the subjects seem similar, the research process seems the same, an informative purpose seems suitable, and the partner seems not so different from a law professor. Drawing on these known genres with their known situations from their law school experiences helps the writers conduct research, frame questions, state answers, and cite the law. The change in location from law school to law firm, however, has major consequences for the writer's purpose, subject, and reader. While the law professor wanted to see if the law student could find the relevant case law and accurately analyze the issue, the partner wants to see what the case law says about his or her particular client's case. The primary subject is less the case law than the nexus between the case law and a unique client's case. To change matters further, instead of having a given set of case facts to begin with, the associate in the law firm must sometimes discover the facts of the case, which are often unclear or missing important pieces. The purpose of writing has changed with the location as well. Whereas the student must explain both sides of the law evenly, the partner typically wants the associate to argue the law for the side of the client the firm is representing and to counter the other side. Often, the partner wants not just an analysis of the law but a recommendation: What should the firm do with this specific issue in this client's case?

New associates often have difficulty learning these significant differences of situation that stem from their having changed locations, in part perhaps because the genres appear so similar. The most successful new associates learn, among other things, how their new situation differs from the old. Ones who struggle with writing in the firm often cling to writing strategies learned from old law school genres, unwilling, for example, to make the client's facts paramount or unable to gain enough confidence to recommend a course of action. That fact would seem to be an argument against the use of one genre in a different location. Yet, in my experience, the few who struggle with writing in a law firm the most, the ones who may receive individualized assistance and still not keep their jobs, are the ones who never mastered the genres of law school. They struggle with analyzing the case law to draw any conclusions; they struggle with conducting adequate research or finding relevant cases; they struggle with organizing multiple cases under larger issues. Rather than failing because the genres they know serve them poorly in a new location, these writers fail because they do not adequately know their old genres; they do not control the genres upon which they might draw.

The genres that writers know constitute their genre repertoires,[7] and writers draw from their repertoires to write in a new situation. The known genres that writers use in new situations have been called antecedent genres.[8] Writers may choose antecedent genres wisely or poorly, with obviously different results. Even well-chosen antecedent genres result in mismatches of genre to situation, as happens to associates writing blue book exams in response to the situations of analytical memoranda. Yet, I am arguing, writers are better served by having some genres in their repertoire with somewhat similar situations than by having only genres farther removed from the new situation.

If no two situations are identical and writers still perceive enough similarities to recognize a genre, then perhaps the comparison can work one more step removed: Faced with two *genres* that are not identical yet share some perceived similarities, writers perceive enough similarities to use the known genre while acquiring the unknown genre. The associate knows she must write an analytical memorandum, but that she has not yet acquired that genre. Seeking a similar situation, she draws on the genre she perceives as closest to her current situation, perhaps the blue book exam. The process seems not so different from a writer seeking a genre that suits a particular situation, deciding whether this is a situation for a letter to the editor, a presentation to the city commission, or a protest march. In the example of the associate in a law firm, even though the writer knows that the genre needed is not the same as the known ones, the writer finds enough similarity to decide which genre to use as an antecedent. Or less deliberately, the writer begins writing something familiar because that is what she knows, and she hopes it will work well enough.

If the only genres the writer feels familiar with differ considerably from the needed genre, the antecedent genres will not likely serve the writer well. The associate who never adequately controlled the blue book exam beyond recitation of case law will be unable to use that genre effectively while acquiring the analytical memorandum. Each genre a writer acquires well increases the likelihood of having a genre to use with a situation more similar to the new genre. Writers with fuller genre repertoires may have more baggage to carry, but they can move among different locations—with their different genres—more easily.[9]

I am not arguing that skills learned in one genre are transferable to another genre. To do so would be to abstract writing skills from their situatedness in specific genres, which are themselves embedded in specific situations, including locations. I am arguing that writers use the genres they know when faced with a genre they do not know. These genres are not in fact transferable; they do not meet the needs of the situation fully. But, as antecedent genres, they help writers move into a new genre; they help writers adjust their old situations to new locations.

What then of my colleague in biology who protested that her students did not know how to write a research paper? I suspect her protest may have echoed the protest of the law partner who complains that his new associate cannot write. I suspect her students were using the genres they knew, including in some cases the first-year research paper, in this new location of the biology course. Yet the genre assigned by the professor was enmeshed in this location new to many of her students, and they had not yet acquired the biology paper. What they had to draw from were their previously acquired genre repertoires, including the genres they may have learned in the location of first-year composition.

There, I think, may lie the accountability of composition teachers to their students (and to other teachers). Have the teachers of first-year composition—or writing across the curriculum or writing in the disciplines—given students the opportunity to learn, if not acquire, genres that will serve helpfully as antecedent genres in future writing situations? The first-year research paper may not, in fact, be the most effective antecedent genre for the biology major's paper. Its necessarily often superficial research, overly broad thesis, literary citation system, and usual dependence on nonspecialist secondary sources may serve as poor guides, because it stems from a situation so different from the advanced major course. The analytic paper may be a better antecedent for advanced research papers, with its analytical purpose and narrower subject, even though the first-year reader and writer remain the same. Perhaps even the literary critical paper would serve as a more effective antecedent than the research paper, with its purpose of closely examining text to make an original claim and a reader who is more typically expert in the subject.

My point is that composition courses and programs provide students with additional genres for their repertoires, ones that can serve as antecedent genres for later writing situations. When deciding what genres to assign in writing courses, in addition to the usual curriculum concerns, teachers should consider carefully what purposes, subjects, settings, reader and writer roles—in other words, what situations—might seem most similar to situations students are likely to encounter in the future. What genres might prove the most helpful antecedent genres as students move among other locations, either in school or elsewhere in their lives? Note that I am not arguing for teaching more genres but for choosing carefully the genres we teach. In fact, depth probably matters more than breadth, though that is a researchable question. If students have not acquired a genre well, if they do not control the genre, they will struggle when trying to use the genre as an antecedent in a new location, just as the law associates struggle if they have not adequately mastered the blue book exam when they try to use it as an antecedent genre for their analytic memoranda. If students don't know the genre adequately, in fact, they might not even try it as an antecedent in a new location.[10] Better to acquire one or two genres that may help in the future than to skip among six genres, none of which is acquired fully enough to serve as an effective antecedent genre in new locations. But all genres are not created equal as potential antecedents. When we design writing projects to meet our multiple curricular needs, we should also consider carefully the potential of the genres we assign to help students move into their different locations in the future.

Further, I would argue, composition teachers should be teaching students *about* genres, including how to analyze new genres they encounter, so that they can select their antecedent genres mindfully and deliberately.[11] Students can study how genres work rhetorically, how they interact with their situations, including their cultural and physical locations, and how genres can be changed to adapt to changes in situations. The list of questions below, condensed from a composition textbook, illustrate the kinds of thinking such a genre awareness might encourage.

Questioning Genres

Analyzing Situation

1. Location: Where does the genre appear?
2. Subject: What topics, issues, ideas, questions does the genre address?
3. Participants: Who writes texts in this genre? Who reads texts in this genre?
4. Purposes: Why do writers write this genre and why do readers read it?

Recognizing Patterns

1. What content is included, and how is it treated?
2. What rhetorical appeals (logos, pathos, ethos) are used, and how?
3. How are texts in this genre structured?
4. In what format are texts of this genre presented?
5. What types of sentences do texts in this genre typically use?
6. What diction (types of words) are most common? What voices do you hear?

Using Patterns to Understand Situation

1. Who is invited into the genre, who excluded?

2. What roles for writers and readers does the genre encourage or discourage?
3. What attitude toward readers is implied in the genre? What attitude toward the world?
4. What content is considered most important? What content is ignored?
5. What values, beliefs, goals, and assumptions are revealed through the genre's patterns?
6. What actions does this genre help make possible? What actions does this genre make difficult?[12]

Teaching a critical awareness of genres would enable students not only to understand how genres and situations shape the ways they write but also to become conscious of the ways they are using the genres in their repertoires when they encounter unfamiliar situations.[13] Knowing that they can only write from what they have written before, students with a critical awareness of genres can watch for the ways that their new situations and locations differ from the ones with which they are familiar, can assess how their known genres might fail in the new location, and can anticipate some of the adjustments they would otherwise acquire more slowly and perhaps painfully. With such conscious understanding of the research paper, students in an advanced biology course might even recognize the differences in that location and more successfully adapt to that professor's different expectations, whether the professor has recognized the change in location or not.

Perhaps general writing skills do not exist, but knowledge and experience do. Carrying with them knowledge of genre and experience with antecedent genres, writers carry baggage that can help them go far.

Notes

1. Readers wishing to review recent reconceptions of genre as social acts rather than static forms have any number of sources they might explore, including Miller 1984; Freadman 1987; Bazerman 1988; Freedman and Medway 1994; Russell 1997; Bawarshi 2000; and Devitt 2004, just to name a few. My thinking about all the issues in this piece is, as always, informed by all that I have read in genre theory. For a fuller bibliography, readers may wish to consult the reference list in Devitt 2004.
2. See Miller 1994 for an explicit discussion of how recurrence of situation is perceived recurrence. No two situations in fact can be

identical, so choosing a genre to write within requires recognizing enough commonalities to make one genre seem appropriate.

3. See Freadman 1987 for the idea of genres being known by NOT-statements as well as by what they are,
4. See Freadman (1987), who compares writing within genres to playing a game of tennis.
5. This distinction reminds me of Ferdinand Saussure's linguistic distinction between *langue* and *parole,* a distinction similarly susceptible to criticism as a false dichotomy.
6. For more on the writing tax accountants do, see Devitt 1991.
7. I am adapting the term "repertoire" from Bakhtin 1986 and from Yates and Orlikowski 2002, but here placing the ownership of the repertoire with the individual rather than the social group. Brooks (2002) has previously suggested that his students use familiar genres when learning new hypertext genres.
8. Jamieson (1975) uses the term "antecedent genres" to describe the genres used in two historical cases of writers confronting new situation, including the case of the U.S. president's state of the union address drawn from poorly chosen antecedents.
9. Of course, having a larger genre repertoire might also permit choosing inappropriate antecedent genres more often or might make choosing an antecedent more difficult. I suspect writers rely more heavily on a more limited set of genres with which they feel most comfortable, but that is a matter for research.
10. As I write this scholarly article, I am in the process of examining which genres from high school my students in first-year composition use when moving to the new location of college.
11. For my fuller argument for teaching genre awareness and antecedent genres, please see chapter 7 of Devitt 2004. Readers might also wish to see whether I can carry out such grand schemes by looking at Devitt, Reiff, and Bewershi 2004.
12. Adapted and condensed from Devitt, Reiff, and Bawarshi 2004, 93–94.
13. Such a critical awareness could also form the grounding for programs in writing across the curriculum, but that connection merits its own scholarly piece.

Works Cited

Bakhtin, Mikhail M. 1986. "The Problem of Speech Genres." In *Speech Genres and Other Late Essays,* ed. Caryl Emerson and Michael

Holquist, 60–102. Trans. Vern W. McGee. Austin: University of Texas Press.

Bawarshi, Anis. 2000. "The Genre Function." *College English* 62: 335–60.

Bazerman, Charles. 1988. *Shaping Written Knowledge: The Genre and Activity of the Experimental Article in Science.* Madison: University of Wisconsin Press.

Brooks, Kevin. 2002. "Reading, Writing, and Teaching Creative Hypertext: A Genre-Based Pedagogy." *Pedagogy* 2: 337–56.

Devitt, Amy J. 1991. "Intertextuality in Tax Accounting: Generic, Referential, and Functional." In *Textual Dynamics of the Professions: Historical and Contemporary Studies of Writing in Professional Communities,* ed. Charles Bazerman and James Paradis, 336–57. Madison: University of Wisconsin Press.

———. 2004. *Writing Genres.* Carbondale: Southern Illinois University Press.

Devitt, Amy, Mary Jo Reiff, and Anis Bawarshi. 2004. *Scenes of Writing: Strategies for Composing with Genres.* New York: Longman.

Freadman, Anne. 1987. "Anyone for Tennis?" In *The Place of Genre in Learning: Current Debates,* ed. Ian Reid, 91–124. Melbourne: Deakin University Centre for Studies in Literary Education.

Freedman, Aviva, and Peter Medway, eds. 1994. *Genre and the New Rhetoric.* London: Taylor.

Jamieson, Kathleen M. 1975. "Antecedent Genre as Rhetorical Constraint." *Quarterly Journal of Speech* 61 (December): 406–15.

Miller, Carolyn. 1984. "Genre as Social Action." *Quarterly Journal of Speech* 70 (May): 151–67.

———. 1994. "Rhetorical Community: The Cultural Basis of Genre." In *Genre and the New Rhetoric,* ed. Aviva Freedman and Peter Medway, 67–78. London: Taylor.

Russell, David R. 1997. "Rethinking Genre in School and Society: An Activity Theory Analysis." *Written Communication* 14: 504–54.

Yates, JoAnne, and Wanda Orlikowski. 2002. "Genre Systems: Structuring Interaction through Communicative Norms." *Journal of Business Communication* 39: 13–35.

12

Relocating Knowledge

The Textual Authority of *Classical Rhetoric for the Modern Student*

NANCY MYERS

> Thirty-three years after the initial publication of this book, there is ample evidence that some of the principles and practices of classical rhetoric are still operative in our society as we head into the twenty-first century.
>
> —*Classical Rhetoric for the Modern Student,* 4th ed.

I first encountered *Classical Rhetoric for the Modern Student* (*CRMS*) in a teaching composition seminar for new graduate students in the early 1980s. It was not used as the rhetoric for the first-year composition courses, but as required reading for the seminar. New to the discipline of rhetoric and composition studies, I learned about rhetoric's histories, theories, and strategies through Edward P. J. Corbett's textbook. As a new teacher, I embraced the text's definitions, explanations, and applications as they bridged past and present, theory and practice, and reading and writing by appropriating and adapting classical rhetoric, particularly Aristotle's *Rhetoric*, for composition courses. My experience was not unique. As Robert Connors points out, the textbook's "place in the development of composition-rhetoric is absolutely central because of the dialogic relation between textbooks and teacher training" (1997, 69–70). Because Connors's history examines textbooks from 1776 to 1980, this relationship between textbooks and pedagogy highlights the discipline's consistent focus on praxis. However, this potentially fertile relationship is continually overshadowed by the academic attitudes and traditions that stigmatize all textbooks as rudimentary and derivative. Richard Young reveals his ambivalence toward the role of textbooks in higher education: Textbooks, he says, should be examined and critiqued on "their clarity and pedagogical ingenuity [rather] than on their conceptual originality" because they represent "established paradigms" of a discipline (1978, 31).[1] Gerald Alred and Erik Thelen suggest that this disparaging attitude carries across most departments and disciplines: "[T]extbook authorship has long been viewed as trivial at best and, at worst, as a form of faculty moonlighting" (1993, 466). This stigma quickly puts all textbooks into a biased category of simplified knowledge for the academic masses, or it causes tension in promotion and tenure meetings as faculty try to decide the scholarly quality and originality of a textbook. What is lost because of these attitudes are the nuances and complexity of original knowledge as both theory and practice.[2] By examining how a textbook acquires institutional and disciplinary authority, I demonstrate in this essay the way a textbook can transcend its categorization and stigmatization, while still teaching undergraduate college students. As Connors argues, "The textbook of writing is a witness to the perpetual conflict between old and new, theory and practice, experiment and convention, that define our discipline in unique ways" (1997, 110). Corbett's *CRMS* promotes traditional academic conventions and social decorum, while it simultaneously complicates and champions a praxis model for knowledge formation.

First published in 1965, *CRMS* has been updated, revised, and republished three times in 1971 and 1990 and in 1999, the latter edition with Connors as coauthor. While intended for first-year composition students, the text has found audiences beyond undergraduate college students. As was my experience, composition teachers and graduate students have used *CRMS* not necessarily for first-year composition courses, although it is used there and in other writing courses, but as an introduction for themselves into the world of classical rhetoric and the discipline. With its various editions and audiences, *CRMS* constitutes a multifaceted location—a site situated in time and space. It is a nexus point where academic contexts and cultures, systems of texts, and ways of reading intersect to produce textual authority. Thus, a text—an agreed-upon location of authority—promotes that authority. As a location *CRMS* provides a means to analyze the gains and losses of textual authority in both postsecondary institutions and disciplines. I use the phrase "textual authority" to represent the process and effect of a text within academic contexts and cultures, with systems of texts, and in ways of reading. For example, one means by which textual authority in postsecondary institutions is promoted is within the site of the classroom, including the authority of the teacher, an assigned textbook, and a student-reader. Each element is a part of this multilayered location and integral to textual authority. The teacher by assigning the reading implies that this text has authority in the course, in the institution, in the degree, and in the field. Thus, the text, as a location of authority, provides knowledge necessary to the stability and reproduction of the institution, discipline, and society. I argue that the textual authority of Corbett's *CRMS*, as textbook, operates as a relocation of knowledge from school to society and as a relocation of knowledge from pure to applied. While the first relocation is an expected reproduction of knowledge, the second is an inversion of the postsecondary traditions that privilege specific types of knowledge.

The Textual Authority of *CRMS*

> I must say that I'm a little surprised that it [*CRMS*] continues to have an appeal.
>
> —Edward P. J. Corbett in 1989

Mikhail Bakhtin's concept of "authoritative discourse" provides a systematic understanding of how textual authority occurs. He defines this authority as "the word of the fathers" (1981, 342). This metaphor, invoking both historical and religious connotations, underscores the importance of canonicity and legacy for academe and in rhetoric and composition studies. Textual authority arises from a text's location through its ranking in a larger textual body, its longevity in garnering esteem from disciplinary professionals, and its ability to appear to represent the values of a disciplinary culture, to build on them, and to reinscribe them. As a location *CRMS* promotes the textual authority of "the word of the fathers" in two ways: through its appropriation of past theories and practices of the rhetorical and canonical father, Aristotle, and through its timeliness and continued presence across the discipline's development, suggesting Corbett as father of the relatively new American discipline. In all four editions of *CRMS*, Corbett identifies his indebtedness to Aristotle's *Rhetoric* by stating that his textbook "can be regarded as a mere restatement, with some modifications and extensions."[3] If the best that can be done is a "mere restatement," the *Rhetoric* is still the authoritative word 2400 years later. As the authoritative word of an emerging discipline, *CRMS* garners textual authority through its timeliness and its longevity. The popularity of the 1965 publication surprised even Corbett. According to the second edition's preface, "The first edition of *Classical Rhetoric for the Modern Student* had a more favorable reception and wider classroom use than I had dared hope for" (1971a, vii). Both in that preface and in "Teaching Composition: Where We've Been and Where We're Going," he suggests that the coupling of rhetorical theory with the teaching of composition during the 1960s partly explains the success of his textbook (vii; 1971b, 445). Although not the only textbook from the mid-1960s to embrace historical rhetoric, *CRMS* is the only one of that type that has remained in print for forty years.[4] As both process and topical site, textual authority overlaps with the term "canon" in academe, as it accounts for a text's acquiring of prestige and for the ability of text to embody, extend, and reinforce the values of a disciplinary culture. At the same time, the phrase works against common notions of a stable canon, which carries connotations of specific texts that transcend time and space. Always contingent and never static nor neutral, textual authority is situated in relation to the location that generated it.

As location, *CRMS* establishes and builds its textual authority through its interactions with academic contexts, other texts, and ways of reading. These three spheres of interaction strengthen the association of *CRMS* with the early years and subsequent development of the discipline so much so that "the word of the fathers" becomes the words of the father (Bakhtin 1981, 342). Textual authority like authoritative discourse, according to Bakhtin, may surround itself with "great masses of other types of discourses (which interpret it, praise it, apply it in various ways), but the authoritative discourse itself does not merge with these (by means of, say, gradual transitions); it remains sharply demarcated, compact and inert" (343). Textual authority intensifies in academic contexts; it may happen in any institutional or disciplinary environment where power dynamics are at play, but particularly when inexperienced readers are working to blend in with the community. For instance, Andrea Lunsford has related her initial reading of Corbett's textbook to introductions and invitations into the field of rhetoric and composition studies. In "The Nature of Composition Studies" and again in "Rhetoric and Composition," Lunsford claims that Corbett's textbook was her introduction to the discipline (1991, 4; 1992, 77). The academic context of the two articles reinforces the textbook as the primary authority within the field. "The Nature of Composition Studies" was written for and is the first essay in Erika Lindemann and Gary Tate's anthology *An Introduction to Composition,* a book that "introduces readers to the relatively new academic discipline" (Lindemann and Tate 1991, v). In the MLA tome *Introduction to Scholarship in Modern Languages and Literatures,* "Rhetoric and Composition" is the only essay that deals with the discipline. As the first essay and the only essay on rhetoric in two introductory texts for graduate study, the message is clear: novitiate, read *CRMS*. This layering of introductions upon introductions stated in text and reinforced through assigned readings in graduate courses builds an ethos of scholarly tradition and wisdom for a specific text. In this academic context, Corbett's textbook not only becomes authoritative but verges toward the father's words for a new discipline.

Textual authority arises due to its interaction with other texts. From *CRMS*'s first appearance in 1965, the text's and author's names have become widely recognized and cited, compounding the effect of authority for both the past (Aristotle) and present (Corbett) fathers' texts. Besides those introductory texts by Lunsford, Corbett's *CRMS* also appears in nonintroductory texts within the discipline. In "Revival of Rhetoric in America," Connors, Ede, and Lunsford generalize beyond their personal beliefs about the textbook to all of us working in rhetoric and composition studies: "[E]very scholar working in composition since owes a debt" to Corbett's textbook (1984, 11). This indebtedness evokes an authority of text that through implication extends across *CRMS*'s forty years in print and all aspects of composition, even to those fields of study within the discipline that have little to nothing in common with the content of the textbook. Though narrowing the influence and authority of Corbett's text to historical rhetoric, Gerald Nelms and Maureen Daly Goggin's study of the origins and influence of classical rhetoric on the discipline contributes to the textual authority of the textbook. While the study complicates the influence of classical rhetoric—respondents dated the revival anywhere from the 1940s to the early 1970s—it cites Corbett's *CRMS* four times, more than any other text, and states, "For S. Michael Halloran, as for many of us, the publication of Edward P. J. Corbett's *Classical Rhetoric for the Modern Student* in 1965 marks a watershed in the revival of classical rhetoric" (1993, 15). Nelms and Goggin further valorize the textbook by declaring that it "finally, unambiguously documents the interest in classical rhetoric of composition scholars" (22). This enthymetic phrase "as for many of us" plays on assumptions about the reading audience that scholars in rhetoric and composition studies agree on the discipline's canon, and the word "unambiguously" relies on the assumption that most to all composition scholars have an interest in classical rhetoric. Moreover, "revival," a term which has been used by many and contested by many more, implies that classical rhetoric is the foundation for the discipline.[5] Corbett's text, which once carried this authority with only a few readers, now has become the authority for many, and *CRMS* has become the founding father's words in the new American discipline of rhetoric and composition studies.

Textual authority evolves from ways of reading. For experienced scholars in the discipline, a text's status relies on its ranking within a multivocal, hierarchical, and ongoing textual debate about specific knowledge. This way of critical reading often carries the goal of a textual rejoinder that adds new and corrective knowledge, one aiming to build symbolic capital for the reader. For inexperienced readers new to the disciplinary knowledge, there is little to no textual negotiation or critique; they have limited strategies and knowledge for agreeing with some aspects of a text yet disagreeing with others. The text is the authority. According to Bakhtin, authoritative discourse "is indissolubly fused with its authority—with political power, an institution, a person—and it stands and falls together with that authority" (1981, 343). Just as in Bakhtin's authoritative discourse, textual authority reinforced through academic contexts influences the novice readers' "ideological becoming[s]," and it works to govern how that reader not only understands the world but also interacts with it (342). A study on conceptions of knowing and believing in adult audiences, conducted by Patricia A. Alexander and Filip J. R. C. Dochy, supports textual authority's relationship to beginning readings with findings on the distinctions between belief and knowledge: knowledge is public, objective, and necessarily verifiable, is acquired through educational institutions, and is less valuable for future actions and decisions; belief is private, value-based, and subjective, is passed from one generation to another through particular cultures, and is more powerful than knowledge in influencing "actions or behavior" (1994, 232–33). These definitions imply that knowledge is external to the self, while belief is internalized, of the self. Through its content, higher education reinforces this view of public knowledge as empirical and rational while simultaneously through its cultural contexts instilling a private desire to carry on its tradition by building on or challenging the existing knowledge, adding to the legacy. Textual authority starts as external knowledge and transforms into internalized belief, yet in this beginning process the content of the discourse is not altered. The inexperienced reader, whether a graduate or undergraduate student, takes the knowledge of the text on as his or her own belief. These various and constant invokings of Corbett's *CRMS* have established the text as a site of authority within the discipline. With the reading, knowledge and belief operate simultaneously to support the development of a legacy.

Across this illustration of Corbett's textbook acquiring textual authority—through its intersections with academic contexts, other texts, and ways of reading—knowledge and belief fuse on at least three levels. Novice readers read *CRMS*, and in their desire to succeed in their disciplinary community internalize the text and take it on as their own. Corbett's view of Aristotle's theories is now theirs. On another level, voices of praise within the discipline who associate themselves with the text and its author do not suggest that their readings and/or interpretations of the text vary one from another or that they have moments of conflict or objection to Corbett's presentation of Aristotle's theories. They agree on the text's power, influence, and value for all in the discipline. In their praise of it, they mark it as a static entity, as if its meaning did not change with subsequent readings or multiple readers. Underlying both of these interminglings is the third level: the forgetfulness of interpretation, or what Lawrence Venuti (1986) refers to in translation as the "invisibility" of the translator. The easier the text is to comprehend and apply, the more likely the reader is to forget the translator or interpreter. The more flowing and eloquent the writing style, the more invisible the shaper of Aristotle's theories. Although Corbett is not translating Aristotle's *Rhetoric*, he is re-presenting Aristotle's theories. With the forgetfulness of interpretation, Corbett's Aristotle becomes Aristotle. Corbett's voice, even if intended as guide, becomes Aristotle's voice. As the words of the father, the textual authority of *CRMS* is established within the discipline. Along with its location in the discipline, *CRMS*'s location in both graduate courses and writing courses across forty years marks its textual authority in postsecondary institutions.

CRMS as Relocating Knowledge from School to Society

> One of the most salutary lessons to come down to us from the Greek and Latin rhetoricians and philosophers is that unless we regard human beings as complexes of intellect, will, passions, and physicality, we will not produce well-integrated citizens for any society.
>
> —Preface to *CRMS*, 3rd and 4th eds.

Within postsecondary educational institutions, the textual authority of *CRMS*'s location as a composition textbook in a writing course operates as stable and reproductive means for relocating knowledge from school to society. Pierre Bourdieu and Jean-Claude Passeron state that one objective of an educational system for a stable society is to provide cultural reproduction, enacting both socialization and knowledge agendas (1990, 177–219). Compliance with academic and disciplinary aims earns textual authority for a textbook, marking it as credible and foundational, and necessary as well. *CRMS* promotes stable reproduction through its adaptation and application of classical rhetorical theories and practices, fulfilling a traditional academic knowledge agenda, and through its assumption and argument that the goal of rhetoric and the liberal arts is to prepare students to be ethical human beings in their private and public lives, meeting the socialization agenda. In "Corbett's Hand," Richard Marback refers to Corbett's appropriation of a specific rhetorical system as a reinscription of the dominant power discourses. According to Marback, students are urged to accept and practice that system of interpreting and composing as the "responsible use of such expression within a specific societal structure, being responsible, that is, to maintaining the symbolic order" (1996, 189). In other words, *CRMS*'s location in a writing course promotes an accepted and expected relationship between school and society. However, presentation of and advocacy for this dual agenda are not enough for relocation. To ensure a stable cultural reproduction, *CRMS* must demonstrate that this dual agenda has relevance for students' lives. To enact this process of relocation from school to society, *CRMS* must demonstrate the relevance of past theory and practice for current use and the relevance of the ethical individual in his or her private and public life as instrumental to social well-being. *CRMS* operates as the location—that nexus point—where school and society meet in two ways. First, to make the past relevant to the present, the textbook promotes a technical rhetoric and includes contemporary rhetorical models and adapted rhetorical strategies for reading and writing. Second, the textbook as part of Corbett's corpus provides a code of conduct based in the liberal arts.

CRMS offers a technical rhetoric, based on Aristotle's theories, that readily depicts the relationship between the liberal arts and a stable social order. Corbett's presentation of a technical rhetoric in *CRMS* is supported across all of his scholarship. According to George Kennedy, a technical rhetoric's purpose is civic, its approach pragmatic. A technical rhetoric emphasizes the speech over the speaker or listener and operates amorally (Kennedy 1999, 13–14). Underlying a technical rhetoric is the assumption that rhetoric operates as the link between the humanities as manifested in formal education and a society's members, because that connection is vital for civilization to continue. This link requires Corbett and *CRMS* to appropriate and adapt concepts within Aristotle's three canons—invention, arrangement, and style—and to apply them to current civic, academic, and popular discourses. In "Rhetoric in Search of a Past, Present, and Future," Corbett clearly articulates that he views rhetoric as a link between the humanities and social good: "But I am inspirited by the prospect of rhetoric becoming once again a liberal art which can prepare men to live purposively and harmoniously as social and political beings" (1971b, 176). His textbook illustrates this connection through its inclusion of treatises by politicians and statesmen across the history of the United States, such as texts by Thomas Jefferson in the first edition and by John F. Kennedy in all four editions.

Obviously an attempt on Corbett's part, and Connors' for the fourth edition, to include current and relevant rhetorical models, the readings—as applications for civic, academic, and popular discourses—have shifted over the four editions and forty years. For example, in the third edition, several women authors are included instead of just one, and a Smith Corona typewriter ad and Corbett's analysis of it replace lengthier readings and analyses across the first two editions, one on history by Adlai Stevenson in the first edition and one on civil disobedience by Ronald Dworkin in the second. Again, in the fourth edition textual models are updated with the typewriter advertisement being replaced by one for a Hewlett-Packard color photocopier; moreover, the dominance of image over word in this ad suggests Aristotle's rhetoric as adaptable to visual rhetorical forms.

While Corbett's analyses of the rhetorical models demonstrate reading strategies, his discussions on audience reinforce composing strategies. In the discussions of emotional and ethical appeals, the textbook examines various audience reactions; moreover, later in the text ten pages deal with strategies for analyzing, understanding, and evoking a reaction in the audience (Corbett and Connors 1999, 260–70). In citing Corbett's textbook in connection to rhetoric and advertising, William Grimaldi disparages this use of Aristotle's theories: "[A]s an academic discipline rhetoric has long been identified exclusively with the facile manipulation of language" (1972, 1). This, of course, is not what the textbook promotes, but Grimaldi insinuates that the textbook and advertising employ rhetoric in irresponsible and unthinking ways. When discussing the relevance of rhetoric, Corbett states that it is an "inescapable activity in our lives," so the individual needs to understand how it operates as both a "synthetic art" and an "analytical art" in order to defend against propaganda, demagoguery, and brainwashing and in order to employ it to settle "tensions by the use of the powerful weapon of words" (Corbett and Connors 1999, 24, 25). As educated thinkers and communicators, contemporary users of classical rhetoric are anything but irresponsible and unthinking.

As a conduct book, *CRMS* looks to the future, and in that gaze the relocation of school to society is achieved through the students' knowledge and decision-making abilities. School is the training ground for social life. As Lester Faigley argues in *Fragments of Rationality*, textbooks "both conduct students and offer them a conduct to follow" (1992, 151). *CRMS* asserts Corbett's philosophy that an educated person, able to use rhetoric to analyze and generate arguments, will be aware of his or her choices and act on them for the good of all. In "The Rhetoric of the Open Hand and the Rhetoric of the Closed Fist," Corbett claims all discourses based on persuasion "seek to change attitudes and affect action," but it is the means by which rhetors do this that counts; they allow individual audience members to make decisions and act on them, rather than attempt to coerce them collectively (1989c, 105). What Corbett considers valuable about the discourse of the "open hand," based on Aristotle's *Rhetoric* and developed across the centuries, is its fundamental attempt to gain the good will of the listeners/readers (100–5). So one of the most important contributions of Aristotle's *Rhetoric* for today is its attention to audience: "Training students to know, to realize, people other than themselves is what prepares them for membership in society" (Corbett 1989b, 200). "Other than themselves" acknowledges the multiplicity of those members of society while trying to find commonalities across their unique and unrepeatable experiences. This emphasis on the audience requires that Corbett negotiate the tensions between two concepts of Aristotle's rhetorical theory—its "morally indifferent" stance and its explanation of ethos. Acknowledging the seeming ambivalence within the *Rhetoric*, he argues that the system's potential can be applied for the good of society or to its detriment: "To be able to manipulate words with consummate skill is to be able to manipulate other people for better or for worse" (207). But neither the *Rhetoric* nor Aristotle is accountable for abuses of discourse, since "the hypocrisy in the older rhetoric" is a matter of "human frailty, not of an inherent weakness in that ancient art" (1989c, 112). The rhetor is ultimately responsible for his or her use of the art.

This rhetorical code of conduct encompasses more than just an ability to think, speak/write, and act in individual situations. It is a habit of being, one that is socially based. Because of *ethos* in all of its practical and positive aspects, Corbett argues for rhetoric as the "keystone of liberal arts," and, learned within educational environments, these liberal arts prepare people "to live purposively and harmoniously as social and political beings" (1987a, 251; 1971b, 176). His explanation of rhetoric's role centers on the lack of subject matter for the art. Because the same strategies can be applied by either rhetor or reader/listener and applied across the subjects, rhetoric operates as a synthesizer and analyzer; therefore, it is an "instrumental kind of art" that shapes and determines the disciplines; it generates knowledge both moral and intellectual: "Since good sense and good moral character were, in Aristotle's view, indispensable ingredients in an *ethos* that would favorably dispose an audience . . . texts presented the study of rhetoric not as just a skills course but as the keystone discipline in a liberal-arts program" (Corbett 1987a, 251; 1989b, 206).

As one of the liberal arts, rhetoric is the foundation for the well-being of both the society and the individual. An educated person employs rhetoric to provide freedom and choices for others; Corbett sees these choices as fundamental to a rhetoric used ethically: "Accordingly, where the choices are arbitrarily pared down or eliminated, rhetoric begins to disappear" (1989c, 108). By providing those options, human beings have the opportunity to make "judicious choices," thus becoming "effective citizens" (1989b, 207). Corbett's concern for choices for the individual mirrors Martha Nussbaum's analysis of Aristotle's assumption in the *Politics* "that most men can become really autonomous planners if we give them access to political rights and some kind of good initial moral training" (1980, 426). She states that these choices must come from a private and individual realm rather than a public one: "[T]he *choice* of the good must come from within and not by dictation from without" (423; italics in original). For Corbett, the individual's decisions in both his or her public and private life are affected by the liberal education that she interacts with. As he says at the end of his interview with Victor Vitanza, "We elder statesmen can fade away now, knowing that the fortunes of rhetoric are in good hands" (Corbett 1987a, 264). Because Corbett's ideology claims that social well being depends on the ethical individual who has developed an understanding of rhetoric's power through its interconnectedness to the liberal arts, *CRMS* is a technical rhetoric that fosters strategies for ethical thought, discourse, and action for its readers; thus, it promotes the relocation of knowledge learned in school into the realm of society.

CRMS as Relocating Original Knowledge from Pure to Applied

> [I] wonder if there is an intellectual rigor in this book that is not with some other books. Or has it opened up a world to these people that has not been talked about or one that they're aware of but never had handles on? It's hard for me to know what the appeal has been.
>
> —Edward P. J. Corbett, in 1989

While the textual authority of *CRMS*'s location in the classroom conforms to institutional expectations of relocating knowledge from school to society, the textual authority of *CRMS*'s location within the discipline functions as a relocation of knowledge through its inverting of and challenge to the American academic traditions of knowledge formation. Inversion, as a means for interchanging positions or upending rankings, explains the textual authority of textbooks that represent original knowledge. Academic traditions and attitudes rank scholarship published by highly valued university presses and specialized peer-reviewed journals as more valuable than textbooks. This practice assumes that new and original knowledge in a field is disseminated only through these more elite venues. The textual authority of *CRMS* inverts these traditions in two ways: by privileging an ethically based applied knowledge over an amoral theoretical one and by offering an original praxis model.

In postsecondary American education, textual authority is contingent upon attitudes about the supremacy of scientific inquiry and about disciplinary ranking of publication types. This began during the last quarter of the nineteenth century, when intellectual inquiry in postsecondary academic institutions shifted from the domain of teaching to the realm of publication: "Publication, indeed, had become a guiding interest of the new academician. Each book, each article, was a notch pegged on the way to promotion" (Rudolph 1962, 403). As Sheldon Rothblatt explains about those early attitudes and definitions, new knowledge entailed "the kind of open-ended or 'pure' investigations linked to an ethic of value-free knowledge, as understood at the end of the last century" (2001, 252). Scientific inquiry housed within the walls of an academic institution implicated no political or ideological attachments to the marketplace—it was knowledge for the sake of knowledge. Out of that tradition an entire publishing hierarchy has resulted, tied both to institutional interest and disciplinary growth.

In *Academic Tribes and Territories,* Tony Becher outlines the intersections of institutional interest in new knowledge and the development of disciplinary knowledge. Describing the evolution of academic knowledge and its ranking, he suggests that institutionally scientific research is still considered the elite form and labels it hard and pure knowledge, against the soft and pure approach of the humanities.[6] Noting that these categories are not stable, since many sciences fall into other categories, Becher points out that the natural sciences center on knowledge as impersonal, growth-oriented, linear, and concentrated on new territories and new discoveries, while the soft and pure approaches of the humanities focus on the personal reinvestigating and reinventing of the same territory, "resulting in an enhanced insight into, or an understanding of, familiar objects of knowledge" (1989, 13). Whether hard or soft, the quality is gauged by knowledge's purity; thus, theory reigns as the most prestigious within the discipline and the institution: "[G]ood standing accrues on each scale at the end which emphasizes the theoretical, the quantitative and the sharply defined" (160). Applied knowledge, whether hard or soft, fares even worse than the soft and pure knowledge of the humanities. As application, whether science-based or humanities-based, this form of knowledge is seen as less because its practical use of theory is something "less easy to pin down and analyse" (15). Accordingly, a textbook, seen as practical rudimentary knowledge for undergraduate students, embodies this lesser status.

Although Becher acknowledges the relativeness of these knowledge hierarchies in his study, he points out that "[h]igher education is suffused with considerations of value and almost obsessively taken up with the identification of excellence; grading of a more or less rarified kind is endemic" (160). As an aspect of both institutions and disciplines, policies and practices concerning the quality of knowledge formation are reflected in publication types. Theory appears in scholarly journals and monographs, applied knowledge in textbooks. As Young states, textbooks represent "established paradigms," so the knowledge they present is either foundational or old news (1978, 31). However, I argue that the applied knowledge in textbooks may be original. Appropriation, adaptation, and application are all processes employed in translating theory into practice. These processes extend and interpret theory: they are praxis. But praxis is not just the relationship between theory and practice; it also embraces reflection and action. Citing Paulo Freire, Louise Wetherbee Phelps in *Composition as a Human Science* argues for praxis as "an inseparable relation between reflection and action" (1988, 211). Because *CRMS* provides discourse models and strategies for application to real-world environments, it operates as praxis, one that is ethically grounded, and it relocates original knowledge from the expected pure scholarly venues to the applied. As such, it promotes and advocates a methodology as well as an ideology; it embodies principles of rhetoric and offers ways to generate more rhetoric. As praxis, it inverts and challenges the primacy of theoretical authority over knowledge formation. With its dual roles as methodology and ideology and with its implicit influence on pedagogy as well as instruction on the generation and analysis of literate acts, *CRMS* implicates the classroom and the purposes of teaching and learning in post-secondary education as a reflection of society. In *CRMS* rhetoric is "an inescapable activity in our lives"; rhetoric is praxis: "One of the chief values of rhetoric, conceived as a system of gathering, selecting, arranging, and expressing our material, is that it represents a *positive* approach to the problems of writing" (Corbett and Connors 1999, 24, 25; italics in original). This inescapable activity can be either a "building up" through composition or a "breaking down" through analysis (25). With slight modifications, these same points are made in all four editions.

When the reader opens any of the four editions of *CRMS*, he or she interacts with and reacts to the discipline's historical and ethical relationships with praxis, linking *CRMS*'s original praxis model with the past. Assigning the *Rhetoric* to practical knowledge, Corbett establishes rhetoric's praxis connection back to Aristotle's taxonomy of knowledge: "Since rhetoric was regarded by the ancients as a practical art, an art that citizens had frequently to exercise in the courts and public forums, speakers were constantly aware of a definite audience" (1963, 162). This practical art incorporated a specific relationship between thought and human conduct as represented in political action. As a way of life, as ethical actions and discourses that stemmed from the virtue of the citizen, practical knowledge was valued.[7] In "The Ethical Dimensions of Rhetoric," Corbett states that Aristotle "maintained that an audience's trust is elicited when they perceive that the author is a person of 'intelligence, character, and good will'"; then Corbett explains the implications of the related Greek terms *eunoia*, *arete*, and *phronesis* (1989a, 258, 260–64). Corbett's emphasis on *phronesis* as it relates to moral action extends his argument of praxis beyond the solely political realm to the broader social one.

In her argument about praxis as the foundation of the discipline, Phelps connects praxis to ethics in her interpretation of Hans-Georg Gadamer (1988, 215–18).[8] She contends that praxis reveals the limits of theory and that theory relies on praxis to make it material, through enactment; otherwise it would remain solely "virtual" (239). Bakhtin warns what happens when theory becomes completely separate from the immediacy of the event: "Since theory has broken away from the actually performed act and develops according to its own immanent law, the performed act itself, having released theory from itself, begins to deteriorate. . . . Theory consigns the performed act or deed to the realm of brute Being, drains it of all the moments of ideality in it and draws them into its own autonomous self-contained domain, that is, totally impoverishes the actually performed act" (1993, 55). Theory needs practice as one means of validation and critique. With the immediacy of praxis, theories are transformed. A textbook that offers strategies for writing, reading, and thinking informs theory through the interactions of its readers and through the readers' enactment of and reflection on those strategies. It is the relocation of original knowledge from theory to application.

As it inverts the accepted traditions of original knowledge formation, the praxis model of *CRMS* is not confined to the application of the theories and strategies by the student but reaches into the discipline. Phelps argues that the discipline of rhetoric and composition studies teaches, practices, and studies the "acts of writing, reading, speaking, listening, and inner speech along with nonverbal images and other kinds of symbolism that are interdependent in literate behavior" (1988, 67). As both appropriations and transformations of concepts into practical strategies, *CRMS* involves all three acts of the discipline—methods of teaching, procedures to practice, and methods of inquiry. The textual authority of Corbett's textbook responds to and challenges other textbooks and theoretical treatises that incorporate interpretations of Aristotle's rhetorical theories and methods. As such, *CRMS* operates as cultural capital that supports the discipline through its mediation of institutional reproduction and intellectual challenge, balancing both. Bourdieu explains how change happens in the structures of an institution: "[E]very new position, in asserting itself as such, determines a displacement of the whole structure and that, by logic of action and reaction, leads to all sorts of changes in the position-takings of the occupants of the other positions" (1993, 58). Corbett's *CRMS* has gone through four editions and been continuously in print since 1965. As an instrument of change, its longevity and authority in the discipline is based partly on its mediating ability.

As text in a discipline, a classroom, and an institution, the textual authority of *CRMS*'s location inverts the accepted academic traditions of knowledge formation. In this relocation of knowledge, it allows for the privileging of applied knowledge over the theoretical, and it underscores the praxis roots of the discipline. As relocated knowledge on Aristotle's *Rhetoric*, the textbook maintains a dialogic conversation with Corbett's other texts and statements about Aristotle, rhetoric, and the discipline. Simultaneously, *CRMS*'s location reinscribes accepted academic traditions of knowledge dissemination by relaying the significance of past rhetorical theories to current composing and interpreting practices and by arguing for the importance of a liberal arts education for the well-being of societies. In this way, it relocates the past into the present and advocates for/demonstrates the relocation of the academic into the social.

The textual authority of *CRMS* implicates two aspects of the discipline and academe for future exploration. First, *CRMS*'s location reinforces alternative sites for new knowledge: it relocates new and original knowledge for universities as applied, reflective, and so on. As Alred and Thelen contend, "[T]extbooks on writing can be sites where knowledge is made, tested, and modified" (1993, 472). By valorizing *CRMS* as an integral contribution to scholarship and by acknowledging the textual authority of textbooks within rhetoric and composition studies, the discipline continues to challenge and complicate the established and more traditional forms that represent new knowledge in institutions of higher education. Second, by blurring the distinctions between expert and novice, specialist and generalist, *CRMS* relocates audience lines. For teachers new to the history of rhetoric and the teaching of composition, Corbett's interpretation becomes the basis by which other interpretations of classical rhetoric are judged, and his applications become models for classroom use. For undergraduate students, his praxis argument attempts to move students from the rhetoric of the classroom to the rhetoric of private and public discourse. For the discipline, his textbook links rhetoricians with rhetors. Richard Fulkerson offers an example of audience blurring across disciplines and institutional lines. In his preface to *Teaching the Argument in Writing*, when talking about his graduate study in Victorian literature at Ohio State University during the mid-1960s, Fulkerson invokes Corbett: "I learned much about argument from Dickens, Carlyle, Mill, Arnold, and even Hardy. At the same time, I also worked with Edward P. J. Corbett and read *Classical Rhetoric for the Modern Student*—on my own, since, at the time, no English classes were devoted to rhetoric or composition" (1996, x). As an aspiring Victorian scholar, Fulkerson learned from an undergraduate text on classical rhetoric.

Since 1965, Corbett's *CRMS* has been authorized within the discipline as a privileged text. It has gained its textual authority, first, by invoking Aristotle's *Rhetoric,* which already had a long history across Western education, and, second, by adapting and applying those theories and practices to contemporary composition situations, an argument for social relevance and an archetype for original applied knowledge. Janice Lauer's justification for the value of rhetorical history applies to

Corbett's use of classical rhetoric, particularly Aristotle's theories, in contemporary discourse within the confines of academe: it "discloses promising discursive and teaching practices that have been lost, alerts them to past blind alleys, and positions them among an impressive cohort of predecessors engaged in the important enterprise of literacy development to which they have dedicated their lives" (1995, 4). Corbett's technical rhetoric, based on Aristotle's theories, in *CRMS* illustrates the interplay across textual, institutional, and disciplinary spheres. These interdependent relationships make visible the environments of teaching, relocate new knowledge via praxis, and blur the distinctions between teachers and students and between rhetoricians and rhetors.

Notes

I wish to thank the SUNY reviewers, the editors Christopher Keller and Christian Weisser, and Kristie S. Fleckenstein for their responses to drafts of this text.

1. Ironically, a textbook Young coauthored, *Rhetoric: Discovery and Change*, is widely and regularly cited for its contributions to new knowledge in the discipline.
2. For other recent examinations of the conflicts that exist between textbooks and the discipline, see Gale and Gale 1999.
3. For example, at Corbett and Connors 1999, 494.
4. By 1965 when Corbett's *CRMS* was published, Aristotle's theories of rhetoric had already appeared in three other composition textbooks: Weaver 1957, Hughes and Duhamel 1962, and Winterowd 1965.
5. The disciplinary territory of rhetoric and composition studies, never an easy grouping, is once again being contested and possibly redefined. Recently, debate has appeared as to the compatibility of the fields, modes of inquiry, and theoretical perspectives. For various approaches to this issue, see Olson 2002 and Williams 2002.
6. Actually, Becher divides intellectual inquiry into two realms, the cognitive and the social. Each of those realms has two matrices: the cognitive being hard/soft and pure/applied, and the social being convergent/divergent and urban/rural. In this article, I deal with only the cognitive realm of knowledge.
7. In "On the History and Theory of Praxis," Nicholas Lobkowicz traces the primacy of theoretical knowledge over practical to early Christianity (1967, 20).

8. According to Phelps, for Gadamer *phronesis* represents knowledge employed situationally which keeps both theory and action from becoming nonreflective. While Corbett links praxis with *phronesis* to argue for a rhetoric ethically used, Gadamer opposes "the inappropriately technical application of scientific knowledge to praxis" (Phelps 1988, 216). Both Gadamer and Corbett are trying to balance theory and practice but in distinctly different ways.

Works Cited

Alexander, Patricia A., and Filip J. R. C. Dochy. 1994. "Adults' Views about Knowing and Believing." In *Beliefs About Text and Instruction with Text*, ed. Ruth Garner and Patricia A. Alexander, 223–44. Hillsdale: Lawrence Erlbaum.

Alred, Gerald J., and Erik A. Thelen. 1993. "Are Textbooks Contributions to Scholarship?" *College Composition and Communication* 44: 466–77.

Aristotle. 1984. *Rhetorica*. In *The Rhetoric and the Poetics of Aristotle*, ed. Friedrich Solmsen. Trans. W[illiam] Rhys Roberts. (Translation originally published in 1924.) New York: Modern Library.

Bakhtin, Mikhail. 1981. "Discourse in the Novel." In *The Dialogic Imagination: Four Essays by M. M. Bakhtin*, ed. Michael Holquist, 259–422. Trans. Caryl Emerson and Michael Holquist. Austin: University of Texas Press.

———. 1993. *Toward a Philosophy of the Act*. Ed. Vadim Liapunov and Michael Holquist. Trans. Vadim Liapunov. Austin: University of Texas Press.

Becher, Tony. 1989. *Academic Tribes and Territories: Intellectual Enquiry and the Cultures of Disciplines*. Bristol: Open University Press.

Bourdieu, Pierre. 1993. *The Field of Cultural Production: Essays on Art and Literature*. Ed. Randal Johnson. New York: Columbia University Press.

Bourdieu, Pierre, and Jean-Claude Passeron. 1990. *Reproduction in Education, Society and Culture*. Trans. Richard Nice. London: Sage. (Orig. published in 1977.)

Connors, Robert J., ed. 1989. *The Selected Essays of Edward P. J. Corbett*. Dallas: Southern Methodist University Press.

———. 1997. "Shaping Tools: Textbooks and the Development of Composition-Rhetoric." In *Composition-Rhetoric: Backgrounds, Theory, and Pedagogy*, 69–111. Pittsburgh: University of Pittsburgh Press.

Connors, Robert J., Lisa S. Ede, and Andrea A. Lunsford. 1984. "The Revival of Rhetoric in America." In *Essays on Classical Rhetoric and Modern Discourse,* ed. Connors, Ede, and Lunsford, 1–15. Carbondale: Southern Illinois University Press.

Corbett, Edward P. J. 1963. "The Usefulness of Classical Rhetoric." *College Composition and Communication* 14: 162–64.

———. 1971a. *Classical Rhetoric for the Modern Student.* 2nd ed. New York: Oxford University Press.

———. 1971b. "Rhetoric in Search of a Past, Present, and Future." In *The Prospect of Rhetoric,* ed. Lloyd F. Bitzer and Edwin Black, 166–78. Report of the National Development Project. Englewood Cliffs, NJ: Prentice-Hall.

———. 1987a. "Rhetoric's Past and Future: A Conversation with Edward P. J. Corbett." *PRE/TEXT* 8: 247–64.

——— 1987b. "Teaching Composition: Where We've Been and Where We're Going." *College Composition and Communication* 38: 444–52.

———. 1989a. "The Ethical Dimensions of Rhetoric." In Connors 1989, 255–66.

———. 1989b. "Rhetoric, the Enabling Discipline." In *Selected Essays of Edward P. J. Corbett,* ed. Robert J. Connors, 194–208. Dallas: Southern Methodist University Press.

———. 1989c. "The Rhetoric of the Open Hand and the Rhetoric of the Closed Fist." In *Selected Essays of Edward P. J. Corbett,* ed. Robert J. Connors, 99–113. Dallas: Southern Methodist University Press.

Corbett, Edward P. J., and Robert J. Connors. 1999. *Classical Rhetoric for the Modern Student.* 4th ed. New York: Oxford University Press.

Faigley, Lester. 1992. *Fragments of Rationality: Postmodernity and the Subject of Composition.* Pittsburgh: University of Pittsburgh Press.

Fulkerson, Richard P. 1996. *Teaching the Argument in Writing.* Urbana: NCTE.

Gale, Xin Liu, and Fredric G. Gale, eds. 1999. *(Re)Visioning Composition Textbooks: Conflicts of Culture, Ideology, and Pedagogy.* Albany: State University of New York Press.

Grimaldi, William M. A. 1972. *Studies in the Philosophy of Aristotle's "Rhetoric."* Hermes: Zeitschrift für Klassische Philologie 25. Wiesbaden: Franz Steiner.

Hughes, Richard, and P. Albert Duhamel. 1962. *Rhetoric: Principles and Usage.* Englewood Cliffs, NJ: Prentice Hall.

Kennedy, George A. 1999. *Classical Rhetoric and Its Christian and Secular Tradition from Ancient to Modern Times.* Rev. ed. Chapel Hill: University of North Carolina Press.

Lauer, Janice M. 1995. "Historical Study within Rhetoric and Composition." Paper delivered at the Conference on College Composition and Communication, Washington, DC, March 24.

Lindemann, Erika, and Gorg tate, eds. 1991. In *An Introduction to Composition Studies.* New York: Oxford University Press.

Lobkowicz, Nicholas. 1967. *Theory and Practice: History of a Concept from Aristotle to Marx.* Notre Dame, IN: University of Notre Dame Press.

Lunsford, Andrea A. 1991. "The Nature of Composition Studies." In Lindemann and Tate 1991, 3–13.

———. 1992. "Rhetoric and Composition." In *Introduction to Scholarship in Modern Languages and Literatures*, ed. Joseph Gibaldi, 77–100. 2nd ed. New York: MLA.

Marback, Richard. 1996. "Corbett's Hand: A Rhetorical Figure for Composition Studies." *College Composition and Communication* 47: 180–98.

Nelms, Gerald, and Maureen Daly Goggin. 1993. "The Revival of Classical Rhetoric for Modern Composition Studies: A Survey." *Rhetoric Society Quarterly* 23: 11–26.

Nussbaum, Martha Craven. 1980. "Shame, Separateness, and Political Unity: Aristotle's Criticism of Plato." In *Essays on Aristotle's "Ethics,"* ed. Amelie Oksenberg Rorty, 395–435. Berkeley and Los Angeles: University of California Press.

Olson, Gary A., ed. 2002. *Rhetoric and Composition as Intellectual Work.* Carbondale: Southern Illinois University Press.

Phelps, Louise Wetherbee. 1988. *Composition as a Human Science: Contributions to the Self-Understanding of a Discipline.* New York: Oxford University Press.

Rothblatt, Sheldon. 2001. "The 'Place' of Knowledge in the American Academic Profession." In *The American Academic Profession*, ed. Stephen R. Graubard, 245–64. New Brunswick, NJ: Transaction.

Rudolph, Frederick. 1962. *The American College and University.* New York: Knopf.

Venuti, Lawrence. 1986. "The Translator's Invisibility." *Criticism* 28: 179–212.

Weaver, Richard. 1957. *Composition: A Course in Composition and Rhetoric.* New York: Holt.

Williams, James D., ed. 2002. *Visions and Revisions: Continuity and Change in Rhetoric and Composition.* Carbondale: Southern Illinois University Press.

Winterowd, W. Ross. 1965. *Rhetoric and Writing.* Boston: Allyn and Bacon.

Young, Richard E. 1978. "Paradigms and Problems: Needed Research in Rhetorical Invention." In *Research on Composing: Points of Departure,* ed. Charles R. Cooper and Lee Odell, 29–47. Urbana, IL: NCTE.

Young, Richard E., Alton L. Becker, and Kenneth L. Pike. 1970. *Rhetoric: Discovery and Change.* New York: Harcourt.

13

Cultural Geography and Images of Place

NEDRA REYNOLDS

Although composition's location is still predominantly on college or university campuses, in the last several years an increasing number of composition scholars have moved away from campuses in order to understand reasons for composing that have little to do with academic discourse (Cushman 1996; Gere 1994). Within the academic environment, too, composition's locations are changing. Emboldened by Kathleen Yancey's keynote address at the 2004 CCCC, the stepchildren of English departments are packing up and moving out to go it alone, taking with them plans to build a major that might incorporate visual and multimedia rhetorics. As a result, *where* composition should be located is, quite literally, a crucial question for many writing programs, with political, economic, and intellectual repercussions. In addition, how to situate writing instruction within nonacademic communities becomes a matter of understanding place-based concerns. Informing these discussions, this chapter argues, should be a keen awareness of how places—real and imagined—matter to the construction of knowledge. As composition programs across the country consider new directions or purposes—a writing major, for example—and other environments for the teaching of writing, this essay argues that close attention to place and location, informed by cultural geography, will help to inform those considerations.

Cultural geography is the study of how places come to have meaning through acts of the everyday, how encounters with place are shaped by a number of conditions or reproduced images, or how places reproduce the identities and power structures of those who occupy them. How do social groups or individuals develop senses of place? How are geographies of exclusion mapped onto the landscape, and why should we be aware of them? Cultural geography examines the ways in which places are contested spatially and how identity and power are reproduced in the everyday, in mundane or ordinary landscapes. According to Linda McDowell, cultural geographers examine "how the increasingly global scale of cultural production and consumption affects relationships between identity, meaning, and place. Attention is focused on the ways in which symbols, rituals, behaviors and everyday social practices result in a shared set or sets of meaning that are, to greater or lesser degrees, place-specific" (1994, 147).

This emphasis on place, the influence of postmodernism notwithstanding, makes geography very much a *seeing* discipline, whose premises and proofs, methodologies and conclusions, stem from visual evidence. The importance of seeing is a fundamental element, of course, of mapping or cartography—that is, the representation of space in 2–D or in digital forms, using lines and measurements and colors and textures. For contemporary research in geography, a reliance on visual evidence is particularly difficult to avoid or resist because of the wide availability of images, cameras, surveillance systems, and the like. Maps and photographs provide the most obvious cases of geography's investment in the visual, but new technologies are also expanding the visual terrain. Geographic information systems (GIS) and Global positioning systems (GPS), for example, combine to create a large toolbox of spatial processing functions, widely used in research projects where geographic information from a number of different sources must be integrated. Both GIS and GPS rely on digital map data that can be stored and manipulated on-screen, and digital map data is then brought to life on-screen through a GIS.

Visual data is crucial to our understandings of place and space in part because images, like public spaces, can be commodified, a process that intensified with the expanse of modern cities and the singular images with which they became associated: New York = the Statue of Liberty, or San Francisco = the Golden Gate Bridge. As geographers know, certain images, reproduced and consumed, create our conceptions of particular places, to the point that we assume we "know" Paris if we recognize a picture of the Eiffel Tower. Visual images are often tangible, physical, and reproducible; they can be bought and sold, copied and distributed, enlarged or reduced or sharpened—all of which has a huge influence on people's experiences with or responses to place. The ease with which images can be produced and consumed is one of the reasons theorists react against the dominance of the visual—because a reproduced image can come to stand in for reality, erasing the consequences of space and time.

The visual is dominant as a way of knowing in a number of contexts. Gunther Kress writes about the "spatial-simultaneous logic of the visual" (1999, 68) and argues that written language "is being displaced from its hitherto unchallenged central position in the semiotic landscape, and that the visual is taking over many of the functions of written language" (68). The visual, according to Kress, is a spatially and simultaneously organized mode, using the medium of light and the materiality of certain kinds of substances. The logic of writing draws upon both the logic of the visual and the logic of speech (81); however, while writing depends more on narrative, the visual depends more on display (82). Display and arrangement are the fundamental features of the logic of the visual (as opposed to speech, which is sequential and temporally organized), demanding more attention to the product. As images do the work formerly performed by language, the logic of sequence is diminished. Written passages, then, become blocks of text, visual elements in a visual unit (81).

Visual Rhetoric and the Harvard Video

As our profession increasingly communicates through visual rhetorics and multimedia, it is particularly urgent to understand how these media function with different audiences or in different environments. In a recent issue of the *WPA Journal*, Rebecca Moore Howard makes a case for using multimedia rhetoric to promote shared premises for writing instruction. In other words, a video is a good medium for promotional purposes particularly when the fundamental assertions are not in dispute. She contends that "multimedia rhetoric has an emotional effect on its audience and thus has a heightened potential for effecting change in . . . the assumptions, that people hold about the nature of writing and writing instruction" (2003, 10). Relating the experience of producing and sharing a multimedia production at her own university, Howard's article proposes multimedia rhetoric as "an effective means of grounding a dialectic about writing at one's institution" (20). Multimedia rhetoric, in Howard's view, does not serve to advance an argument already underway but is most useful in a diffuse, nondirect way, when the nature of the argument is being formed (20). I want to explore Howard's assertion in the context of one example of visual rhetoric, the video *Shaped by Writing: The Undergraduate Experience*, produced and distributed as part of the longitudinal study of writing at Harvard University. I'm interested in this film both for what it says about writing and also for what it communicates about *locations* for writing instruction. As I'll argue, *Shaped by Writing* assumes a *placelessness* to writing instruction, or the idea that teaching writing in colleges and universities is part of a universal effort with shared premises. In tension with its assumptions, however, is the film's own geography, one dominated by large buildings, fine furnishings, and oversized books. The film illustrates at least three key principles of cultural geography: that places reproduce the exclusionary practices of the culture; that the built environment, in kind, reproduces elements of identity and power; and that spaces are often designed to keep difference out. Research in cultural geography establishes that people take great pains to avoid areas that are unfamiliar, intimidating, or frightening. People's perceptions of places are strongly influenced not only by gender, race, class, sexualities, and disabilities but also by stories, anecdotes, lore, and legend. Understanding how places communicate—through their inhabitants, architecture, or history—can then lead to an inquiry into why some bodies feel excluded from certain places or how the social production of space operates to allow some bodies in and to keep others out. Rhetorics and teaching practices informed by cultural geography keep us mindful of the power of image and anecdote in the construction of place.

The Harvard Study of Undergraduate Writing began in 1997, funded by the Andrew W. Mellon Foundation and the then president of Harvard, Neil Rudenstine. In the largest study of its kind, Harvard researchers tracked 25 percent of the class of 2001 through surveys, interviews, and analysis of individual essays. After collecting "more than 600 pounds of student writing, 520 hours of transcribed interviews, and countless megabytes of survey data," the researchers "wanted to bring the eloquent, passionate voices of the students themselves into a larger pedagogical discussion" (Harvard College 2002). The aim of the study was to "gain a better understanding of the role writing plays in college education and to compose as complete a portrait as possible of the college writing experience." The aim of the film was to share those findings with viewers and to "serve as a starting point for discussions about undergraduate writing, both among faculty and between faculty and students" (Sommers n.d.).

At the 2003 CCCCs in the Trianon Ballroom of the New York Hilton, approximately four hundred to five hundred people attended Nancy Sommers's presentation on the Harvard study, where copies of the video were distributed to all those in attendance. Following the conference, I received, and I assume others on professional mailing lists also received, another copy of *Shaped by Writing*, with a photocopied letter from Nancy Sommers inviting viewers to "let me know how the film plays at your school."

The fourteen-minute film features eight recent graduates of Harvard's class of 2001, along with a few professors, who were invited *to speak on camera.* A year after graduation, these students of chemistry, comparative religion, cognitive neuroscience, government, and other fields *speak on camera* about their writing experiences in college. "A Brief Guide to the Film" shares the origins of the film and summarizes the following topics, which run in one- to two-minute segments: first encounters, challenge of academic writing, process, feedback, working with sources, disciplines, and ownership.

One Discussion of the Video

Were these eight students shaped by writing, as the title suggests? Or shaped by Harvard? In this view, it is impossible to separate the two.[1] My analysis begins by sharing one local conversation about the film and then examines the shared premises on which the film builds, including images of place that formulate the message. As Johnathon Mauk writes, "[P]articular college spaces create, and are created by, particular forms of socialization. . . . college spaces are designed to create particular effects. . . . The geography of a campus and the architecture of its buildings . . . are projections or products of a prevailing imagination . . . the materiality of a campus . . . is inextricable from its sociality" (2003, 383). Images from *Shaped by Writing* support Mauk's claim, and those students who do walk through Harvard's gates and across the grounds as an act of the everyday, even though they may come from vastly different backgrounds, begin to embody the stature of the built environment as well as the discourses of power and privilege produced there. My goal is to explore how Harvard is constructed as a place through this film—and why the wide circulation of this film matters to composition's other locations.

As the film's promotion invites, twelve teaching colleagues met to view and discuss *Shaped by Writing* in the spring semester of 2004.[2] After viewing the film once, the discussion began, but the film kept running in the background, muted, while we continued to talk about it. Participants began by identifying lines from the film that struck or pleased them; for example, one said, "I love what they said about students working harder when they are writing for each other." Others were amused by students' shock in discovering that their writing needed work. There were satisfied nods when one writer in the film said, "Criticism is not about fixing; it's about making choices," and when another said, "Once I had realized that someone else was actually reading my papers, then [a number of] concepts became open to me." Many approved of a professor's comment that students must learn "not to *distrust* sources but to interrogate" them.

What struck viewers first, then, were lines from the film that resonated with their own practices, or those concepts that many writing instructors try to convey to their own students; the graduates express what most writing teachers hope their own students would say. Fairly rapidly, however, our discussion moved from points of recognition to misrecognition—most pointedly, "These are not *my* students" and "My students are not going to be this excited," or this articulate, or this reflective. These state university writing instructors seemed particularly suspicious of one graduate's claim that to get a C+ is motivating, or another's that getting a paper returned slashed with red ink has been somehow *good* for them. One of the earliest comments, in fact, was about how enthusiastic the speakers are, making others wonder aloud about how the film's featured participants were selected.

Once questions were raised about how the film was produced, they merged quickly into questions about the local context: "How do they teach writing at Harvard?" It struck many of us that nowhere in the video do viewers get an overview of the Harvard writing program or *any* explicit references to Harvard. Our group of viewers wondered out loud, however, "Who teaches writing at Harvard? What size are the writing classes? What are the requirements or expectations?"

We decided not to pursue the questions about Harvard's class size or use of contingent faculty, but to address instead the many other issues the video raises, including why it was made. Some of our group speculated that it was really a promotional film for Harvard's expository writing program, perhaps best viewed by parents, alumni, donors, or prospective students. But the film might also be trying to reassure writing instructors that their hard work matters, that students do appreciate their writing classes, if not until after graduation. Perhaps the film was mass distributed as a sort of public service to all of those institutions where writing faculty (for good reasons) feel beleaguered. If so, as one of our group pointed out, that is a depressingly condescending reason for what was obviously a very expensive production. Still, it is hard to tell what the raison d'etre for *Shaped by Writing* is, at least outside of the Harvard gates. If it were modeling response group workshops or coaching writing instructors through responding to student writing, or following students closely through a writing project, then it would fit solidly in the genre of instructional videos. But it does not seem to be this kind of animal.

Viewers were in agreement, however, that the film is "very pro-writing" and shows little conflict, dissension, or contradiction—a result, perhaps, of not showing writers in the throes of wrangling with a subject or an argument. From these retrospective accounts, we noted the difficulty of gauging if students really do value the work of writing when the film features college graduates—not students currently engaged in writing projects—and graduates of Harvard, who, for all of their diversity, are nevertheless products of one of the world's finest institutions of higher learning. While one member of our discussion group wondered if we were reacting to the film *because it was Harvard*, others thought that reaction perfectly appropriate, since the film was sent to our writing program specifically for the purpose of stimulating discussions about writing. While we did not agree about everything, our discussion group did agree that the film seems to be trying hard to represent a universal experience for writing, to convey the values of a liberal arts education, and to celebrate undergraduate writing. This point is made first by the opening line of the film: "My writing course my freshman year changed my life." Also in the opening sequence one says, "I couldn't imagine college without writing now," and another concludes, "I loved it."

As Howard suggests about multimedia rhetoric, *Shaped by Writing* does work through pathos (e.g., the graduates' enthusiasm) rather than logos, and it probably plays very well indeed at institutions where the shared premises for writing instruction are not in contention or where the location for composition is clearly at the center of a liberal arts curriculum.

For institutions where that is not necessarily the case, why does it matter that this film was produced at Harvard? Isn't it more important that it asks undergraduates to talk about their experiences with writing—and cannot some of those experiences be generalized to any institution? Not if we take into consideration the ways in which other parts of the film—beyond the dialogue—contribute to communicating a message about places, campuses, and educational values. In particular, shots of gates, steps, polished wood furnishings and interiors, large buildings, and dozens of books serve to establish a geography that excludes viewers who do not recognize or are not comfortable around such artifacts or surroundings. Through their size, accessibility, occupants, and atmosphere, places communicate who belongs and who does not. In the film, messages about place include shots of imposing entry gates along with iron railings, Victorian-style streetlights, and, in particular, a man rowing on the Charles River. The Harvard graduates are featured in a variety of settings: on the steps of Widener Library, in richly paneled rooms with large reference books (one set that looks something like the OED) in the background, in chemistry labs, in front of computer desks, and in various office settings, with shelves of books and personal photographs as backdrops. There are numerous shots of books on shelves or students pulling books off shelves, leafing through books, or bending over open books. While these may have been intended mostly as "filler," these repeated images fit with one professor's comment that Harvard's program is asking students to enter another world. Books symbolize the world of ideas; opening a book is to open a passport into another world, and books hold the promise of reaching, to quote one graduate, "what feels like core." While viewers could argue that the (bucolic) settings, backdrops, and segues are random or insignificant and serve only to highlight the narration—that, in other words, the Harvard scenery is beside the point—cultural geographers would counter that the surroundings and the material conditions have everything to do with the knowledge being produced.

Examples of visual rhetoric, like *Shaped by Writing*, present an opportunity to demonstrate how geographies of exclusion work—how spaces are constructed, intentionally or not, to keep difference out. The film keeps difference out by, first, relying only on "talking heads" who speak in isolation or individually on camera. Participants in our discussion identified tensions between current social theories of writing and the number of individual voices in the film. Noting very few shots of what looks like writers working together on writing,[3] these viewers were concerned that the video does not do much to represent writing going on—and offers little sense of the labor involved.

Traditionally in composition and other fields, successful pieces of writing are considered to be those that "overcome" place and time, those that universalize an experience. *Shaped by Writing* operates firmly within this expectation. Because of its assumptions about a universal experience for writers and a placelessness to writing instruction, the film does not acknowledge that first encounters, working with sources, or feedback might differ by institution or curriculum. For example, one professor says, "We're asking them to conduct themselves like academics." While that may be appropriate at Harvard, other writing programs have been convinced by Joseph Harris's argument that students might be asked to become intellectuals (1997, 89). When students at Harvard are faced with writing tasks, for example, the answers lie in books. For at least two graduates who mention "close reading" explicitly, composing is a matter of reading and responding to that reading. The images of books on shelves might be fitting for an elite liberal arts institution; however, at institutions where the emphasis is more on professional writing or electronic writing than on writing "papers" or theses, the books seem anachronistic or even quaint.[4]

Even more striking is the emphasis on "originality." More than one graduate addresses originality as a dominant criterion for a worthy writing project or as a reward for good writing—especially the exhilarating feeling that the writer may be the first one to ever think of something. Originality is valued highly, but so is precision. As one professor says, it is "the most difficult skill" to communicate "precisely" on paper, because it is about "getting exactly the right words in exactly the right order." The values of writing put forth by the film, therefore, have to do with originality and precision, which may or may not support the goals of liberal arts education but that certainly communicate a transformative message about the role of writing in an undergraduate's experience in college.

Locating Writers' Identities

Undergraduates writing in community colleges, small private colleges, metropolitan universities, large state universities, or online universities do not share the same experiences with space or realize the same emerging identities as writers. To resist the idea of a "universal" or placeless experience with first-year or required composition, some composition scholars make the argument that first we must situate writing in time and place or at least examine the influence of place; second, and more importantly, however, we must also explore "how the writer's sense of that time and place is the source of meanings, motivations, and identities" (Flower 2003, ix). We need to understand, Flower writes, "the ways writers must negotiate . . . [ideologies, intentions, and values] as they interpret the world around them in their own literate acts" (ix). Students at every college, no matter what the conditions, must negotiate the ideologies and values of their institution, a task no easier or harder at Harvard than at Rio Grande College or West Chester University or Northeast Iowa Community College. One of the ways students begin that negotiation is by drawing on visual evidence: who can park where, and where on campus are students welcomed (or not)? Where is the writing center, the commuter lounge, the multicultural center?

How are the differently-abled accommodated? Do the classrooms for general education courses have broken windows, smart boards, Internet access, air conditioning? The values of an institution (not to mention the endowment) are communicated loudly and clearly through the conditions for teaching and learning and through the ways in which space is used or assigned. When *place* becomes the source of "meanings, motivations, and identities," then acts of writing should be as diverse as the places from which they are generated.

In *Shaped by Writing: The Undergraduate Experience*, Harvard is constructed as a place characterized by shared sets of meaning and place-specific privilege. What does the film suggest, however, about other locations for writing and writers? The production of this film occurred simultaneously with a number of projects and publications that would contradict its universalist assumptions. For several years now, many composition scholars have been engaged in connecting writing and teaching practices to place and time, situating the rhetorician's role in social change (Cushman [1996]) or in environments for writing other than academic (Gere [1994]). Recent work in rhetoric and composition has begun to recognize the intersections of pedagogy and place (Weisser and Dobrin 2001; Owens 2001; McComiskey and Ryan 2003) and asserts a responsibility to the communities in which their institutions function. Influenced by Deweyan goals and movements in service learning, ecocomposition, and material rhetorics, composition is experiencing a decided shift towards place-based pedagogies, along with a corresponding increase in client-based or case-based projects that connect writing students with their environments, with surrounding organizations, or with businesses. A number of technical, professional, and academic writing faculty are acknowledging the ways in which student writers are shaped by the place, institutions, and communities, as much as they are by acts of writing—that these two cannot, in fact, be separated. The recent collection *City Comp: Identities, Spaces, Practices*, for example, illustrates a number of ways in which composing practices emerge from local environments (McComiskey and Ryan 2003). In it Barbara Gleason introduces readers to the Center for Worker Education in Brooklyn (194–99); Krista Hiser features a GED program in San Francisco's Tenderloin district (57–70); Paula Mathieu writes about her experiences working with the working poor and the homeless of Chicago on the publication *StreetWise* (71–84); and Ann M. Feldman discusses the Great Cities Initiative at UIC (204–7). Many of these chapters support Feldman's and her colleagues' assumption "that writing is a way of acting in the world, rather than just a way of demonstrating basic skills or achieved knowledge" (212).

Unlike in the Harvard video, there is little in the recent volume *City Comp* that suggests the universality or "exportability" of projects, approaches, or pedagogies. Here, composition grows directly from the local context, and the opening essay, about teaching writing in Birmingham, Alabama, provides a historically situated example of places where the composition classroom embraces the city as both material and rhetorical space (21–37). Focused on the urban myths that have constructed Birmingham, the course invites students to discover and respond to competing myths of the city as presented in media productions and recruitment materials. Much of this volume gives writing instructors ideas not for teaching students to compose paragraphs but for helping them to compose *knowledge* (162)—knowledge of and from their local environments, wherever they may be. *City Comp,* in all of its versions, offers possibilities for changing the ways we imagine students, places, and practices and insists that theories and practices should be developed directly from and enacted through the lives of people, their homes and neighborhoods and daily pathways.

The representation of Harvard's geography in *Shaped by Writing* sends a quite deliberate message that college campuses *own* writing, and that writing means traditional essay or academic writing. The function of *Shaped by Writing* is to reassert the role of academic writing instruction at a time when new technologies and diverse (student) bodies continue to make college campuses and disciplinary fields unsettled places to be. In the midst of a shift—as writing programs come to mean professional writing, community writing, public writing, and/or technical writing—this film tries to reassure viewers about the traditional roles and locations for writing instruction. As the argument emerges in the midst of postprocess theories of writing, which value difference and contradictions and leave so much about writing instruction unresolved, it is easy to see how *Shaped by Writing* offers a comforting sameness and predictability; it seems remarkably like a cinematic five-paragraph theme, where the initial shock of students' need for "remediation" is replaced by the rewards of revision. Rather than being inoculated (Paine 1999), Harvard students are transformed.

Visual Representations of the Work of Writing

According to Howard, multimedia rhetoric is especially useful when an argument is still being formed. This video may demonstrate, therefore, a nascent argument in composition about "where" writing should be located or take place. By keeping writing and writing instruction confined to colleges and universities and keeping the work of writing confined to academic essays, the video enforces the status quo in the institutional and intellectual positionality of composition studies—that, for example, writing instruction means college students, not participants in a community literacy program or a nonprofit organization. If only college students are shaped by writing, and if the writing is limited only to lab reports or thesis-driven arguments, then composition's locations are clear. However, if writers are found "everywhere"—wandering city streets or in local businesses and organizations—then where do writing instructors locate themselves and their work?

Cultural geography can help us understand the ways in which campuses, city blocks, neighborhoods, and other spaces are designed to exclude, and how their representations reproduce those exclusions. By their mission and their architecture—through the built environment—college campuses, even the open admissions kind, do not welcome everyone. These types of exclusions are well illustrated in *Shaped by Writing*, in both the Harvard images and the way that it situates writing as an academically centered act. The geography of the Harvard video—*where* it was produced, as well as where it was promoted and circulated—demonstrates how theoretical and physical locations are interconnected. According to the video, Harvard's theoretical allegiances (originality, style, and precision) are as traditional as the entrance gates, the wood paneling, and the large reference books.

Questions raised by this video—for example, is process writing necessarily "placeless"?—might be considered by members of academic writing programs who are trying to become freestanding departments; to offer majors in rhetoric, professional or technical writing, or creative nonfiction; or to connect to cities and communities. Ideally, composition programs should be located wherever the intellectual and spatial can come together.

Recognizing those conjunctions begins by understanding local conditions and local geographies, including how others will respond to the visual evidence of a particular physical location and what message a room or building sends to those who encounter it. Physical locations—not always in our control—should represent a program's philosophical approach to writing, as happens so eloquently in the Harvard video. At Harvard, the intellectual approach to writing (writing courses designed to bring "naked" students into another world) does fit with the campus geography: at least as represented in the film, there is no disagreement that academic discourse is the goal and that Harvard's commitment to writing as a core element to a liberal arts education is being met by academic writing, process, feedback, working with sources, and ownership.

A different writing program, however, may want to put its emphasis on public writing by teaching courses at a local community center, online, and/or at a large local business. Other writing programs may want to match up their emphasis on outreach with a prominent writing center. Programs rich in technical or professional writing may want a strong online presence.

Local conditions will, of course, determine the best alternatives for where writing should be, theoretically and philosophically, in the curriculum, and where writing departments should be located *physically*. Such decision processes should consider—quite literally—where the work of writing takes place and what the location says about the value of the work. Writing faculty might ask themselves what message their location sends about whom writing instruction is for—is it only for first-year college students? Only for those who are technology-savvy? Only for those intending to teach? At URI, when the College Writing Program had the opportunity to relocate, we were concerned that the building be central to the campus, that it get a lot of student traffic, and that it *not* be relegated to a basement. While we were successful in having those requirements met, we had to compromise by moving into a building that is more characterized by "service" than by academics—and had to realize that most academic units on campus see us in a service role. Such information is useful, however, in strategizing how to change the perception of writing on campus. When offered visual evidence of our change in status—the Writing Center now has a bigger, lighter space, and our faculty offices are three times the size they were—visitors know that our profile has changed. As they move through the world of the everyday, people rely on visual evidence to decide if they are safe or welcome or invited to participate. Understanding more about this process might help writing programs—of all shapes and sizes and theoretical allegiances—to define their identities, decide whom they serve, and where they might best fulfill their mission.

Composition's forays into visual rhetoric—or visual representations of the work of writing—might be guided by cultural geography, which forces us to analyze the relationship between spaces and identities. *Shaped by Writing* certainly illustrates the challenges of making an argument with images rather than with prose. Watching the video "geographically" indicates that inclusion cannot simply be added on but must be built in. The field of composition needs more longitudinal studies and more videos featuring student writers; in fact, the best response to the film is for campuses to make their own videos about writing: 100 such videos, each from a different place, might give composition teachers alternative representations of the work of writing, of the messiness and the confusion and the ways in which student writers are shaped by the place, the institution, as much as they are by acts of writing.

Notes

1. Let me emphasize that I am talking only about the video, not about the Harvard longitudinal study or its findings.
2. The discussion would have been very different, of course, had students attended (as the film's promotion also invites), or had a different group of instructors been able to join us that day. This discussion is not shared here as a particularly representative one, but as a local one.
3. Nancy Sommers has shared with me that there is a second video in production that *will* feature writers at work.
4. The references in the film to forms of writing include papers, essays, lab reports, and master's theses.

Works Cited

Cushman, Ellen. 1996. "The Rhetorician as an Agent of Social Change." *College Composition and Communication* 47: 7–28.

Flower, Linda. 2003. Foreword to *City Comp: Identities, Spaces, Practices*, ed. Bruce McComiskey and Cynthia Ryan. Albany: State University of New York Press.

Gere, Anne Ruggles. 1994. "Kitchen Tables and Rented Rooms: The Extracurriculum of Composition." *College Composition and Communication* 45, no. 1: 75–92.

Harris, Joseph. 1997. *A Teaching Subject: Composition Since 1966.* Upper Saddle River, NJ: Prentice Hall.

Harvard College. 2002. *Harvard Study of Undergraduate Writing.* Copyright by the President and Fellows of Harvard College. http://www.fas.harvard.edu/~expos/index.cgi?section=study (accessed August 30, 2004).

Howard, Rebecca Moore. 2003. "WPAs and/versus Administrators: Using Multimedia Rhetoric to Promote Shared Premises for Writing Instruction." *Writing Program Administration* 27, nos. 1–2 (Fall/Winter): 9–22.

Kress, Gunther. 1999. "'English' at the Crossroads: Rethinking Curricula of Communication in the Context of the Turn to the Visual." In *Passions, Pedagogies, and 21st Century Technologies*, ed. Gail E.

Hawisher and Cynthia L. Selfe, 66–88. Logan: Utah State University Press.

Mauk, Johnathon. 2003. "Location, Location, Location: The 'Real' Estates of Being, Writing, and Thinking in Composition." *College English* 65, no. 4: 368–88.

McComiskey, Bruce and Cynthia Ryan, eds. 2003. *City Comp: Identities, Spaces, Practices.* Albany: State University of New York Press.

McDowell, Linda. 1994. "The Transformation of Cultural Geography." In *Human Geography: Society, Space, and Social Science,* ed. Derek Gregory, Don Martin, and Graham Smith, 146–73. Minneapolis: University of Minnesota Press.

Owens, Derek. 2001. *Composition and Sustainability: Teaching for a Threatened Generation.* Urbana, IL: NCTE.

Paine, Charles. 1999. *The Resistant Writer: Rhetoric as Immunity, 1850 to the Present.* Albany: State University of New York Press.

Shaped by Writing: The Undergraduate Experience. Copyright 2002 by the President and Fellows of Harvard College.

Sommers, Nancy. n.d. Undated letter included with the video *Shaped by Writing: The Undergraduate Experience.* .

Weisser, Christian R., and Sidney I. Dobrin, eds. 2001. *Ecocomposition: Theoretical and Pedagogical Approaches.* Albany: State University of New York Press.

Yancey, Kathleen Blake. "Made Not Only in Words: Composition in a New Key." Chair's Address. Conference on College Composition and Communication. San Antonio, Texas, March 25, 2004.

14

NOTES TOWARD A DYNAMIC THEORY OF LITERACY

CHRISTOPHER SCHROEDER

The cafeteria buzzed with usual lunchtime chatter, but the mostly Hispanic students, grabbing hamburger patties and fistfuls of fries, seemed young. With overflowing plastic plates, they streamed to tables separated by white plastic chains and black standards. My escort ushered me through the chains and toward a table where I was told to wait. He made the rounds from table to table, stopping to talk to handfuls of people. Others arrived, and then later, he returned. Two were teachers at Roberto Clemente High School in Humboldt Park, the same school and neighborhood featured in Reymundo Sanchez's cult hit *My Bloody Life* about his experiences as a member of the Latin Kings. (My wife grew up in Humboldt Park.) Others were college students in the education program or local high school students. Together, they and my escort comprised the staff of the 2004 Summer Transition Program, an academic support program designed to facilitate the transition of the students from high school to the university. Starting in June, this program runs from 8 a.m. to 4 p.m. Mondays through Thursdays for eight weeks, and it is offered on three different sites—the main campus of Northeastern Illinois University and at satellite campuses of the Center for Inner City Studies and El Centro—within the city of Chicago. Upon completing this program, students can receive up to six credit hours toward a college degree.

Recently, I have become interested in the experiences of these Hispanic students and others like them, particularly in terms of intellectual work both inside and outside of the university. To be sure, Hispanic experiences in the United States are different, as Juan Gonzalez elaborately documents in *Harvest of Empire*; they are so different that generalizing about these experiences is difficult at best. Still, some observations about their background suggest significant differences. For example, these students, as Hispanics, are part of the largest ethnic group on campus (37%)—larger than Asian Americans (14%), African Americans (10%), and even European Americans (34%). In this way, conventional roles of minority and majority are altered, in part, within this institutional space, at least in terms of student population, although as expected these conventional roles exist in the relations between students and faculty.

Beyond ethnic orientations, other significant differences between these students and their college peers characterize the spaces occupied by these students and their peers. As compared to other college students across the country, the students at Northeastern differ in terms of diversity, family background, employment, attendance, and academic preparedness. On the whole, the students at Northeastern are much more likely to be minorities, commuters, and living with or caring for family members. For example, over one-half of the students at Northeastern are classified as minority as opposed to less than a third of students at average four-year public colleges, and not surprisingly, a substantial majority of these students are first-generation college students. These and other salient differences are presented in Table 14.1. And if the students in the cafeteria are anything like those who participated in the previous year's Summer Transition Program, 67% will not initiate study groups, 52% will not use office hours, 64% will not avail themselves of tutoring options, and 50% will not visit academic counselors (Hansen 2005).

Beyond these institutional spaces, the students in the Summer Transition Program move within unique urban spaces and political places. For example, Hispanics comprise 26% of the city's entire population, and they live in a city that has the second-largest Mexican and Puerto Rican population in the entire United States (Guzmán 2001, 7). Beyond the urban space, the students in this program move within a more complicated political context of the state of Illinois. In this larger place, these students and other non-English speaking Illinois residents represent what Elliot L. Judd characterizes as "dilemmas for policymakers" (2004, 46). According to Judd, language policies in Illinois, though complicated, clearly designate English as the dominant language of schools and government (46). Moreover, the use of English has been linked to economic conditions of schools and even political identity throughout

Percentages	Average Four-Year Public College	Northeastern Illinois University
• percent of minority students	29	55
• percent of students who speak English as a second language	9	45
• percent of first-generation college students	34	79
• percent from low-income families (under $25,000)	17	34
• percent who live within ten miles of campus	17	64
• percent who live with family or relatives	30	96
• percent who provide more than twenty hours of care for dependents living with them (first-year status/senior-level status)	4/12	20/22

Table 14.1. Student Demographics as Northeastern Illinois University

the state's history. In 1845, Illinois declared that no school would receive public funds unless it used English, and in 1923, the state passed a law designating *American* as the official language of Illinois (35, 41). (Not incidentally, the U.S. Congress allowed a similar measure to die without a vote in the same year.) While the designation was officially changed from *American* to *English* in 1969, the message is nonetheless clear.

In more ways than one, the everyday lives of these students are complicated and confusing. For example, they live in a state where English is the de facto, if not the official, language of government and schools, and yet they live in a city where on the average more than one of every four people they encounter—more than one of every three peers at the university—is Hispanic. Given the conditions outlined previously and others, the lived experiences of these students presumably influence their intellectual work, and especially their efforts to satisfy the literacy requirements of the university, which are fairly typical. For example, all of these students must pass at least one introductory writing course, conducted in English, and a competency exam. In the course, they will be introduced to "a variety of formats" and learn "strategies for invention and revision" and "fundamentals of argument," as well as how to critique writing and secondary sources and to "edit for grammar, spelling, and mechanical errors," likely in a language that is not their mother('s) tongue. In this language, they will be required to produce four or five multidraft essays, three to five pages each, along with one to three in-class essays. In addition, some of them—those who major in education and in business but not in arts and science—will also take a second-semester writing course, which is characterized as a "[c]ontinuation of practice in composition with an emphasis on a variety of forms of writing and longer essays, culminating in the annotated research paper." And some of them will also write in their other courses, although based upon a recent informal survey conducted on my campus, the number of faculty for whom they will write is less than even I, a former (and cynical) WAC coordinator, expected.

In addition to a writing course or courses and writing for other courses, all of the students in the Summer Transition Program, as well as their peers, will also have to pass a competency exam. While all students are encouraged to attempt the exam after they have earned sixty credit hours but before they have earned ninety, they must complete it, according to the official university policy, in order to graduate, although options, such as a portfolio review, are available to those who cannot pass after multiple attempts. Called the English Competency Exam, it is designed, according to the handout, to certify "college-level competency in reading and writing." For the reading portion, these students will be given thirty-five minutes to complete a standardized test divided into a vocabulary section, comprised of eighty words, and a comprehension section, composed of thirty-eight questions about seven different reading passages. To pass this portion, these students must collect 105 of 156 possible points—one for each correct vocabulary bubble they fill in and two for each correct comprehension bubble they darken. For the writing portion, they will have 150 minutes—two and one-half hours—to argue for or against one of three different issues, such as whether all students or only those who engage in extracurricular activities should pay the activity fee or whether both husbands and wives or just husbands should financially support families. While the students will not have seen the prompts in advance, they will know, if they are savvy enough to read the handout from the Writing Lab, that they must produce "a well-organized essay of 500–700 words" in support of their position on the issue, using "logical arguments and specific details," and must "proofread" for grammar, punctuation, and mechanics.

In these expectations, many probably hear echoes of expectations at their own institutions, which is not surprising, judging from my experience at private and public colleges and universities in the South, on the East Coast, and in the Midwest. What is surprising, however, is that within an institution where students use more than fifty different languages, the expectations are surprisingly homogeneous.

❧

On the way to the zoo near our house, my wife asks if we know the Tagalog word for "house." "*Bahay*," she says, "*bahay* is house in Tagalog."

"*Bahay*," our five-year-old says. She will start school in a month.

"*Bahay*," I say. I have long been asking my wife to teach us more Tagalog.

"Butthead," our four-year-old says. In the rearview mirror, he is smiling.

❧

As a way of contextualizing their experiences, I want to make some observations about these students' locations, as the nexus of spaces, or material realities, and places, or ideological existences. These observations are based upon the initial results of a long-term research project designed to better understand the experiences of these students and others like them. In general terms, these observations are an attempt to understand the significance of location upon literacy performances. Among other implications, these observations reveal some limitations of dominant models of literacy. After examining these limitations, I suggest some directions for new models of literacy.

To begin understanding their experiences, I compiled a survey comprised of selected questions asked of all twelfth graders across the country. These questions were culled from the Nation's Report Card (National Assessment of Educational Progress) in Writing from categories designated as "student factors" and "factors beyond schools." This survey asks questions, for example, about students' experiences with and attitudes toward writing and reading, both inside and outside of schools, as well as their exposure to television, newspapers, and magazines, their access to and use of e-mail and computers, and other potential influences upon their expectations about and approaches to literacy events and literacy acts. In this, the survey both situates these students within a national context and focuses on salient contextual features that affect discursive performance, both inside and outside of classrooms. In general terms, the results of the survey suggest a much more complicated location than stereotypical generalizations about linguistic differences or minority experiences will allow.[1] More specifically, the data suggest that, on the one hand, the students in the Summer Transition Program must confront substantial obstacles that their national peers do not, and, on the other hand, the students in this program are perhaps better positioned than their national peers for educational success and intellectual work.

According to their responses to the survey, the students in the Summer Transition Program overwhelmingly identify themselves as Mexican or Mexican-American. As such, they qualify as one of John Ogbu's *involuntary minorities*, or those for whom mainstream languages and cultures are not obstacles to overcome, as they are for *voluntary minorities*, but threats to resist, although I hasten to add that such boundaries are permeable and often dependent upon individual perception and a host of other variables. These obstacles have been well documented in both popular and academic texts (e.g., Richard Rodriguez's *Hunger of Memory* and Marcia Farr's *Latino Language and Literacy in Ethnolinguistic Chicago*). In much the same way, the students in the Summer Transition Program will be forced to confront issues of language much more than their national peers will. For example, 63% of the Summer Transition students (STS) live in homes where a language other than English is mostly or always used, as opposed to only 10% of their national peers (NP), and only 7% of these students live in homes where English is exclusively used, as compared to 68% of their peers.

These and other conditions have numerous social and educational implications. As Rodriguez describes, Hispanic students who are not motivated to use Spanish often become isolated from their families and traditions, yet those who do not need to use English at home experience a motivation that is academic, in both senses (cf. Potowski 2005, 172). The problems for performance are obvious and not so obvious. The most obvious, perhaps, is the fact that the majority of these students will be forced to perform at the university in a language that they never or almost never hear at home, which is a challenge that can only complicate the already complicated process of education. Beyond the obvious problems of writing in English-dominated classrooms, some of these students, particularly those who, as Spanish heritage speakers, acquire Spanish despite being fluent in English, could have even more complicated performances than previously suspected. For example, recent research has suggested that when writing in Spanish, these students perform somewhere between the performances of native Spanish speakers and those who are learning Spanish as a second language (Spicer-Escalante 2005). Although more research is needed, reports to this effect allow us to speculate, at least, that when writing in English, these students would span the range between those who, born in the United States, are native English speakers and those who, born outside the United States or into homes dominated by Spanish, are learning English as a second language.

Beyond language, the surveys completed by the students in the Summer Transition Program identify three other areas that potentially affect their performances—their homes, their experiences with and uses for writing and reading, and their beliefs in and attitudes about literacy. In general, the students in the Summer Transition Program are much more likely than their national peers to live in homes with parents who have had less education yet offer more attention and interaction. According to the students in this program, 28% of their mothers and 32% of their fathers did not finish high school, as opposed to 11% and 12% of their peers' mothers and fathers. By the same token, only 12% of their mothers and 4% of their fathers graduated from college, as contrasted with 35% of their peers' mothers and fathers. At the same time, the parents of students in the Summer Transition Program are more likely than those of their national peers to know when their children finish their homework (58% for STS and 48% for NP) or watch television (60% for STS and 16% for NP). This attention is significant in light of the fact that both the Summer Transition Students and their national peers report that their parents share similar standards for completing homework and watching television. In fact, 79% of the Summer Transition Students and 77% of their national peers report that their parents have strict rules or at least expectations for completing homework, and 49% of these students and 40% of their peers report that their parents have what their children would characterize as strict or moderate rules for watching television.

In addition to less education and more attention, another difference in the homes is the amount of familial interaction and other support of literacy and education. In general, the students in the Summer Transition Program are more likely to discuss with their families what they have learned in school or what they are reading. More specifically, 32% of the students in this program talk every day with their parents about what they have learned in school as opposed to only 18% of their national peers, and 54% of them talk at least once or twice a week about what they are reading, as contrasted with 35% of their peers. In this way, the homes of these students provide the scaffolding for literacy and education that leads to successful experiences and performances. At the same time, their homes tend to have fewer materials of literacy and education. While just over one-half (52%) of the students in this program report having more than twenty-five books in their home, more than three-fourths (77%) of their national peers make the same

Percentages	Summer Transition Program	National Peers
• percent who have an atlas or an encyclopedia in their homes	64%/66%	83%/89%
• percent of students whose homes regularly receive magazines or subscribe to newspapers	50%/41%	75%/55%
• percent of students who report having a computer in their home	84%	90%

Table 14.2. Summer Transition Program

claim. Moreover, fewer of these students have atlases or encyclopedias in their homes, live in homes that regularly receive magazines or that subscribe to newspapers, or have computers in their homes, as the accompanying table shows. In addition to the linguistic differences of their homes and of books printed in Spanish, the presence or absence of print represents another layer of complexity, particularly for second-generation Hispanic students (Del Valle 2005). At the same time, the differences in computers could represent significant issues of expertise or larger cultural orientations, although for some Hispanic students, the computer bridges their lives in the United States and the history of their families beyond its borders (Cohen 2005).

In addition to differences in language and homes, another area surveyed was the experience with or use for writing and reading. In general, the results suggest that the experiences of the students in the Summer Transition Program are fairly consistent with their national peers. For example, 21% of students in the program and 23% of their peers report reading six to ten pages per day in school and for homework, and 10% of each report reading between sixteen to twenty pages per day in school and for homework. In much the same way, 38% of these students and 41% of their peers report reading for fun either once or twice a week, if not almost every day. Though somewhat less than reading, the writing experiences reported by these students are similar to those of their national peers. Specifically, a similar percentage report writing for themselves outside of schools. For instance, 21% of these students and 23% of their peers report writing in a journal or diary between once or twice a week and almost every day, and 13% of them and 19% of their peers write stories or poems for fun between once and twice and almost every day. These similarities seem to hold, too, for electronic writing, even though, as previously indicated, the students in the Summer Transition Program report having fewer computers to use in their homes. For example, 49% of these students and 53% of their national peers report e-mailing their friends and family at least once or twice a week, if not almost every day.

Besides language, home, and experiences with or uses for writing and reading, the other general focus of the survey is belief in and attitudes about literacy. Here the results are particularly interesting. While the students in the Summer Transition Program report similar levels of experience with and uses for reading and writing in their lives, they also report differences in their beliefs in and attitudes about literacy. In general, the STS tend to believe more in the benefits of literacy and to enjoy reading and writing more than their national peers. While both groups report similar beliefs in the benefits of reading, the students in the Summer Transition Program seem to enjoy reading more. For example, 86% of these students and 80% of their peers agree or strongly agree that when they read, they learn much, yet 66% of the STS agree or strongly agree that reading is one of their favorite activities, as opposed to only 39% of their peers. At the same time, the students in this program seem to believe more in the power of writing and to enjoy it more. For instance, 95% of these students agree or strongly agree that writing helps them to share their ideas, as opposed to 67% of their national peers, and 55% of these students agree or strongly agree that writing generally, whether letters or stories, is one of their favorite activities, as contrasted with 35% of their national peers.

In general, the surveys completed by the students in the Summer Transition Program suggest that they occupy complex locations, both within universities and their communities. Already, these spaces and places are characterized by differences, both from college students generally and from their fellow residents in Chicago and Illinois. In addition, their locations represent significant linguistic and familial differences. Within these spaces, the students in the Summer Transition Program have similar experiences with and uses for writing and reading, yet in these places, they tend to believe more in the power of literacy and to engage it more in their daily lives. Surely, these conditions shape their performances and, as such, should be acknowledged within meaning-making exchanges, not merely as conditions that shape their performances but also as resources and opportunities that can be used.

❧

At home, my kids hear mostly English, but when I am on campus, they are spoken to in English but listen to Tagalog, or Visayan or Illocano or one of the other Filipino dialects used by their *lolo* and *lola* at their *tita's* house. Tagalog and English. English and Tagalog. Sometimes Taglish. Our daughter told us that her *lolo* has two names. One is a familial name, an American English morpheme with Tagalog phonemes. The other is a Filipino curse. At least she has stopped saying that her *lola* speaks Spanish.

❧

As these data suggest, standard generalizations about Hispanic students in our classrooms cannot adequately account for the range of locations that these students, and others like them, occupy. In ways suggested previously and in others, the students in the Summer Transition Program will confront different challenges, both in degree and in kind, from those faced by their peers. For example, the complexity of their locations dramatizes the ethics of presuming a uniformity of context and privileges a cultural mind-set of rationality, explicitness, and order that the English Competency Exam rewards (Farr and Nardini 1996; cf. Severino, Guerra, and Butler 1997). Some of these challenges are part of larger social and cultural prejudices, which have been explored by others (e.g., Villanueva 1999). In the remainder of this chapter, I would like to focus on the challenges that these students, and others like them, will face as they engage in intellectual work. Elsewhere, Helen Fox, Patricia Bizzell, and I (2002) have explored the links between the intellectual work and authorized discourses. Here, I want to turn to the dominant models of literacy, using the locations of these students as a way of continuing an emerging critique of disciplinary constructs, such as language, discourse, and identity.

Such critiques first began with the appearance of the *contact zone,* a much used and, more recently, much critiqued theoretical construct that allowed theorists and, later, practitioners to conceive of differences. As is well known, the contact zone formed the basis of Patricia Bizzell's (1994) early reconfiguration of English studies, and it served an organizing principle for a composition textbook coauthored by Bizzell and Bruce Herzberg. Though some, such as Richard Miller (1994), Joseph Harris (1997), R. Mark Hall and Mary Rosner (2004), and others, have explored its limitations, the contact zone has contributed to the efforts to shift conversations about discursive performance away from *deficiency,* first started with Shaughnessy (1977), to *difference,* and other theorists, such as James Slevin (2001), have situated difference at the center of their theoretical speculations. In many ways, others have pushed these critiques to the next level by analyzing embedded constructs within our practices and theories that, in one way or another, presume an *essentialization* that has been called into question by *difference.* Building, for example, upon a critique of the reifications on which U.S. writing instruction is based, Bruce Horner and John Trimbur (2002) argue for acknowledging the ways our discipline supports an English-only policy; for recognizing the limits of disciplinary division of labor; for resisting ways of identifying students in terms of fixed categories of language, ability, and identity; and considering ways our programs can encourage writing in other forms and languages.

In much the same way, my concern is the reification not of language, which is the concern of Horner and Trimbur, but of literacy. Too often, faculty, employers, and the general public operate with the chimera of good writing, as a performance that conforms to some universal standards. In contrast, those with background in composition and literacy often pride themselves on advocating models that, reflecting a larger social turn, recognize the extent to which becoming literate involves being socialized into specific discourses. For the most part, these socialization models theorize a one-way process of socialization into a target discourse. Though David Bartholomae is being ironic, his often quoted description is particularly useful in illustrating this model: students must "appropriate (or be appropriated by) a specialized discourse" and must do so as if they are full-fledged participants within the university (1985, 135). Beyond composition studies, a similar model exists. For instance, James Paul Gee defines literacy as the "mastery of a secondary Discourse" with a Discourse being a particular way of "saying(writing)-doing-being-valuing-believing combination" (1996, 143, 127). These models lead to considerations of the discourse of a historian or of law school, as if these are static entities into which people are socialized either through acquisition, which is the unselfconscious mastery, or through learning, which requires conscious study.

Though seemingly dated, these purportedly enlightened models have been widely institutionalized and advocated by respected theorists in composition studies and writing across the curriculum (WAC) programs. For example, Susan McLeod and Elaine Maimon challenge the "flourishing" myths in order to "set the record straight," which they did in an article entitled "Clearing the Air: WAC Myths and Realities" for *College English*. In this article, they identified four "myths" about WAC, and after addressing each of these, they argue that in contrast, WAC is a "pedagogical reform movement" and a "programmatic entity" with interrelated components, including faculty development, curricular commitment, student support, assessment, and administrative structures and budgets (2000, 574, 579ff.). Near the end of their article, McLeod and Maimon identify, as "models of the kinds of work scholars of WAC should aspire to," John Bean's *Engaging Ideas*, Christopher

Thaiss's *The Harcourt Brace Guide to Writing Across the Curriculum*, and Art Young's *Teaching Writing Across the Curriculum* (McLeod and Maimon 2000, 582). In McLeod and Maimon's words, these models present "a fair and realistic view of WAC" and "draw upon praxis as well as theory," and they enable our profession "to move forward without the promulgation of myths that obscure and distort scholarly exchange" (582). As such, these selections represent, according to McLeod and Maimon, a consensus among specialists across the country.

While each of these contributes something valuable and different to the efforts of writing across the curriculum programs, each of them also attests to the extent to which WAC is invested in institutional agendas and conventional models of literacy. In general, each of them authorizes an autonomous model of literacy, one that has been widely criticized by writing scholars both inside of WAC (e.g., Russell 2001) and outside of it (e.g., Farr 1993; Trimbur 1990; Faigley 1997). In each case, the goal of writing is to socialize students into academic thinking and texts with little, if any, acknowledgment of the impact of context upon texts, and alternatives, if acknowledged, are subordinated to this end. In, for example, a chapter on formal writing assignments, Bean devotes more than twenty-one of twenty-three pages to thesis-driven arguments, to which he appends a discussion of alternatives that spans less than one and one-half pages. Moreover, the socialization of students is often the ostensive goal of writing to learn activities. For example, Thaiss justifies the use of writing to learn by explaining "that initiating students into academic life means giving them the tools to collect, evaluate, and express information as professionals do" (1998, 13). Together, writing to communicate and writing to learn, Young maintains, create "a middle ground of conversational language and learning" that serves as a space "where students gain knowledge, develop scholarly habits of mind, and acquire rhetorical communication competence in a variety of public and academic contexts" (1999, 58). In these and other ways, these models reinforce the expectations of faculty across the campus for whom these guides are directed.

Although these purportedly enlightened models seem to foreground intradiscursive differences, they ultimately dismiss intercultural differences and, with them, the experiences and histories of these students and others. In part, these models do so by positing homogenous notions of discourse, as if all historians or lawyers reproduce the same discourse or, at the very least, can (and should) do so. While acknowledging some discursive differences, these models authorize versions of discourse that still position these students and other presumed novices as outsiders who must learn to control the standard discourse before they can become insiders. One of the problems is that these models still ignore the political contexts for literacy, at least in the sense that performances can occur in a power vacuum. While these models now allow us to assess the performances of these students and others like them as *different*, they are nonetheless *deficiently different*, at least in the sense that they lack the standard discourse and, as a result, insider status. A second, and perhaps larger, problem is that these models are based upon inaccurate assumptions about the nature of discourse as standardized and, consequently, homogeneous. In fact, these assumptions are challenged by the very performances of purported insiders. To cite a recent example, A. Suresh Canagarajah in *A Geopolitics of Academic Writing* documents the discursive and cultural differences between what he calls center scholars and periphery scholars. Even within the United States, such assumptions fail to acknowledge the different experiences of practicing academics, as Christopher Thaiss and Terry Myers Zawacki's (2002) interviews suggest. The irony, here, is that the limits of these assumptions have long been recognized by students. Victor Villanueva explains that as a student, he learned the hard way to practice what he calls professorial discourse analysis, which amounts to analyzing previously published research of specific teachers and then imitating it for their required assignments (1993, 71).

From another perspective, the larger problem is that alternatives perpetuate similar essentialisms, if only at a smaller level. For example, contact zones are theorized as sites where coherent discourses and selves compete, spaces where students and other participants are authorized as (relatively) passive victims of dominant discourses, people who are violated by dominant languages and cultures, people who themselves never violate or even act. One result of this is that existing models of literacy dismiss the lived experiences and elide the complexity of locations and lived experiences. Perhaps more so than others, the students in this program have already assumed any number of selves and values before they arrive at the university, and by their presence, they acknowledge the extent to which they value the legitimacy represented by the university, if only as a means. In the larger picture, few of them will be able to survive, let alone thrive, without engaging in the practices of the university. Moreover, the engagements that they make, or learn to make or even do not make, are temporary, contingent engagements, ones that can be and, I suspect, often are undone as soon as they walk out of the classroom door or leave the campus, just as happens with more mainstream students (e.g., Anna and Nick in Chiseri-Strater 1991). And surely these engagements are not ones that they reproduce away from school without significant social consequences.

All of these positions, as Jacqueline Jones Royster (1996) points out, are part of the larger sense of self and, I would add, place that emerges from cross-boundary performances, which draw upon dynamic contexts, ways of knowing, language abilities, and experiences.

Ignoring, for now, the paternalism of such assumptions, another concern, at least for me, is that these negotiations can be, and quite possibly should be, seen as legitimate forms of intellectual work (see also Fox 1999; Schroeder, Fox, and Bizzell 2002). As a result, we need an alternative model of literacy that can authorize the locations that these students and others must negotiate as they write and read. Such a model would focus less upon approximating a target discourse or upon producing a product and more on the act or performance of negotiating these differences. As such, it would be a dynamic model of literacy, one that would go beyond rejecting deficiency and embracing difference to seeing difference, particularly the negotiation of differences—linguistic, cultural, epistemological, institutional—as a basic practice of intellectual work. Such a model would recognize the complex intellectual work that the students in the Summer Transition Program and others like them perform each time they listen to lectures, write term papers, or submit exams. In these and other acts, a dynamic model of literacy would presume the multiple and overlapping contexts that must be considered in order to understand specific performances. Such a model would allow us to recognize, at the very least, significant gaps in our knowledge, such as the fusion of transnationalism and hybridization that Ralph Cintron believes is necessary to understanding the experiences of Latinos in Chicago (2005, 381). While I believe that similar gaps exist, although perhaps to a lesser degree, for all performances, these and other gaps highlight the particular significance of interpretive politics and social justice for the students in the Summer Transition Program, many of whom are arriving at the university without the advantages, such as levels of parental education, that their peers bring.

Fortunately for them, the basis for such models has begun to appear in current research within linguistics and literacy studies (e.g., Baron 2001; Duranti and Ochs 1996; Barton, Hamilton, and Ivanič 2000; Cope and Kalantzis 2000). One of the most promising developments is the discussion of syncretic performances that integrate competing cultural elements, which has already been used to describe, for example, Samoan-American homes or Mexican Catholicism (Duranti and Ochs 1996; Farr 2005b, 309). Similar developments can even be found within composition studies despite its tendency, as Paul Matsuda

(1999) points out, to ignore research in second-language writing and speaking (see also Camitta 1990 and Dyson 1999). One example is the relatively recent work of Charles Bazerman, David Russell, and others with activity theory and genre systems, which presumes that texts, along with their production and consumption, can only be understood within the activities—the human interactions—that produce and find use for them (Bazerman and Russell 2003, 1). For instance, Linda Flower uses activity theory, as well as what she calls a social cognitive theory, in order to understand the ways that community literacies engage in intercultural rhetoric, which draws upon cultural differences to generate knowledge and action (2003, 239ff.). However, Flower's theorization still invokes relatively coherent discourses, such as "the elite discourses of policy, regional talk, social services and academic analysis," and at least in her earlier treatment, she seems to understand these negotiations as ultimately cognitive and thereby runs the risk of slighting the ways that these negotiations represent complex positionings within confluences of cultural variables (2003, 250; Flower 1994). Another example is recent efforts to bring postcolonial theory into composition studies, as illustrated by *Crossing Borderlands*, a recent collection of essays edited Andrea Lunsford and Lahoucine Ouzgane. Nevertheless, neither of these has begun to consider the challenges of these models for current institutional practices, such as the English Competency Exam for the Summer Transition Program students.

Besides integrating research on second-language literacy and acknowledging the significance of locations, a dynamic model of literacy brings additional benefits. Though space prevents me from exploring these in detail, let me cite two that seem particularly exciting to me. First, a negotiated model of literacy allows us to begin considering the relation of symbolic and materialist dimensions of everyday life. In doing so, a dynamic model of literacy would dramatize the presumption of such a link, running throughout much composition research, between how one performs, or is allowed or encouraged to perform, and his or her experiences. Second, such a model contextualizes intellectual work as contingent upon any number of assumptions, not in the static sense of an authoritative historical or social context but in the fluid, and potentially unique, sense that is represented by these students (and increasingly more and more students), in the locations of their lived experiences and everyday knowledges. In this way, such a model offers potential benefits to the university as well, because it enables us to debate whether other discursive and cultural practices might be as valuable, if not more so, as the ones we privilege today.

And finally, a dynamic model of literacy can begin to fulfill the rhetoric about social justice that, as Steven North (1991) points out, is often left unrealized in our work by acknowledging the multiplicity of locations, as well as their impact upon textual performance. In outlining a theory of justice as fairness, John Rawls maintains that we should structure our locations as if we did not know our location within the world, as if we might be male or female, rich or poor, mainstream or nonmainstream, or anywhere in between. Using this standard for justice, a dynamic theory of literacy permits those of us who are concerned about social justice to come closer to fulfilling the rhetoric that surrounds our work, if only because it affords an opportunity for other practices to be admitted as legitimate means of intellectual work. Or at the very least, it removes the presumption of the *deficient* and even the pejorative *different*, which is always judged against a standard (i.e., that which is not different, or the same). Modifying Rawls's position somewhat, let me suggest that the standards for literacy should be the ones that we would hope are used for our own children and those whom we value, no matter what locations they occupy. For mine and for me, a dynamic theory of literacy will do just fine.

Appendix: Survey Questions (Clustered)

Personal Information

- What is your gender?
- Which race/ethnicity best describes you?
- If you are Hispanic, what is your Hispanic background?

Parental Education

- How far in school did your father go?
- How far in school did your mother go?

Language

- How often do people in your home talk to each other in a language other than English?

Presence/Absence of Literacy Materials

- Is there a world atlas in your home? It could be a book of maps of the world, or it could be on the computer.
- About how many books are there in your home?

- Is there a computer at home that you use?
- Is there an encyclopedia in your home? It could be a set of books, or it could be on the computer.
- Does your family get any magazines regularly?
- Does your family get a newspaper at least four times a week?

Parental Involvement

- On a school day, about how many hours do you usually watch TV or videotapes outside of school?
- Do your parents know whether you finished your homework each day?
- Do your parents know the amount of time you spend watching TV on a school day?
- Which statement best describes the rules that your parents have about getting your homework done?
- Which statement best describes the rules that your parents have about the amount of TV you can watch on school days?

Experiences with and Uses for Writing and Reading

- About how many pages a day did you have to read in school and for homework?
- How often do you read for fun on your own time?
- How often do you talk about things you studied in school with someone in your family?
- How often do you talk with your friends or family about something you have read?
- How often do you write e-mails to your friends or family?
- How often do you write in a private journal or diary on your own time?
- How often do you write stories or poems for fun on your own time?

Belief in and Attitudes about Literacy

- Please indicate how much you disagree or agree with the following statement: When I read books, I learn a lot.
- Please indicate how much you disagree or agree with the following statement: Reading is one of my favorite activities.
- Please indicate how much you disagree or agree with the following statement: Writing helps me share my ideas.
- Please indicate how much you disagree or agree with the following statement: Writing things like stories and letters is one of my favorite activities.

Notes

1. See the appendix for survey questions.

Works Cited

Baron, Naomi S. 2000. *Alphabet to Email: How Written English Evolved and Where It's Heading.* London: Routledge.

Bartholomae, David. 1985. "Inventing the University." In *When a Writer Can't Write: Studies in Writer's Block and Other Composing-Process Problems,* ed. Mike Rose, 134–65. New York: Guilford.

Barton, David, Mary Hamilton, and Roz Ivanič, eds. 2000. *Situated Literacies: Reading and Writing in Context.* London: Routledge.

Bazerman, Charles, and David Russell, eds. 2003. *Writing Selves/Writing Societies: Research From Activities Perspectives.* Fort Collins, CO: WAC Clearinghouse and Mind, Culture, and Activity.

Bean, John. 1996. *Engaging Ideas: The Professor's Guide to Integrating Writing, Critical Thinking, and Active Learning in the Classroom.* San Francisco: Jossey-Bass.

Bizzell, Patricia. 1994. "'Contact Zones' and English Studies." *College English* 56: 163–69.

Bizzell, Patricia and Bruce Herzberg. 1995. *Negotiating Differences: Cultural Case Studies for Composition.* St. Martin's Press.

Camitta, Miriam P. 1990. "Adolescent Vernacular Writing: Literary Reconsidered." In *The Right to Literacy,* ed. Andrea Lunsford, Helene Moglen, and James Slevin, 262–68. New York: Modern Language Association.

Canagarajah, A. Suresh. 2002. *A Geopolitics of Academic Writing.* Pittsburgh: University of Pittsburgh Press.

Chiseri-Strater, Elizabeth. 1991. *Academic Literacies: The Public and Private Discourse of University Students.* Portsmouth, NH: Boynton/Cook Heinemann.

Cintron, Ralph. 2005. Afterword to Far 2005a, 379–87.

Cohen, Jennifer L. 2005. "Global Links from the Postindustrial Heartland: Language, Internet Use, and Identity Development among U.S.-Born Mexican High School Girls." In Farr 2005a, 187–215.

Cope, Bill, and Mary Kalantzis, eds. 2000. *Multiliteracies: Literacy Learning and the Design of Social Futures.* London: Routledge.

Daniels, Harvey A. 1983. *Famous Last Words: The American Language Crisis Reconsidered.* Carbondale: Southern Illinois University Press.

Del Valle, Tony. 2005. "'Successful' and 'Unsuccessful' Literacies of Two Puerto Rican Families in Chicago." In Farr 2005a, 97–131.

Duranti, Alessandro, and Elinor Ochs. 1996. "Syncretic Literacy: Multiculturalism in Samoan American Families." In *Research Report 16*, 1–15. Santa Cruz, CA: National Center for Research on Cultural Diversity and Second Language Acquisition.

Dyson, Anne Haas. 1999. "Coach Bombay's Kids Learn to Write: Children's Appropriation of Media Material for School Literacy." *Research in the Teaching of English* 33: 367–401.

Faigley, Lester. 1997. "Literacy after the Revolution." *College Composition and Communication* 48: 30–43.

Farr, Marcia. 1993. "Essayist Literacy and Other Verbal Performances." *Written Communication* 10: 4–38.

———, ed. 2005a. *Latino Language and Literacy in Ethnolinguistic Chicago.* Mahwah, NJ: Lawrence Erlbaum.

———. 2005b. "Literacy and Religion: Reading, Writing, and Gender among Mexican Women in Chicago." In Farr 2005a, 305–21.

Farr, Marcia, and Gloria Nardini. 1996. "Essayist Literacy and Sociolinguistic Difference." In *Assessment of Writing: Politics, Policies, Practices*, 108–19. New York: Modern Language Association.

Flower, Linda. 1994. *The Construction of Negotiated Meaning: A Social Cognitive Theory of Writing.* Carbondale: Southern Illinois University Press.

———. 2003. "Intercultural Knowledge Building: The Literate Action of a Community Think Tank." In *Writing Selves/Writing Societies: Research From Activities Perspectives*, ed. Charles Bazerman and David Russell, 239–79. Fort Collins, CO: WAC Clearinghouse and Mind, Culture, and Activity.

Fox, Tom. 1999. *Defending Access: A Critique of Standards in Higher Education.* Portsmouth, NH: Boynton/Cook Heinemann.

Gee, James Paul. 1996. *Social Linguistics and Literacies: Ideology in Discourses.* 2nd ed. Bristol: Falmer Press.

Gonzalez, Juan. 2000. *Harvest of Empire: A History of Latinos in America.* New York: Penguin.

Guzmán, Betsy. 2001. "The Hispanic Population." In *U.S. Census Brief.* May. Washington, DC: U.S. Census Bureau.

Hall, R. Mark, and Mary Rosner. 2004. "Pratt and Pratfalls." In Lunsford and Ouzgane 2004, 95–109.

Hansen, Edmund. 2005. Personal Interview. September 22.

Harris, Joseph. 1997. *A Teaching Subject: Composition Since 1966.* Upper Saddle River, NJ: Prentice Hall.

Horner, Bruce, and John Trimbur. 2002. "English Only and U.S. College Composition." *College Composition and Communication* 53: 594–630.

Judd, Elliot L. 2004. "Language Policy in Illinois: Past and Present." In *Ethnolinguistic Chicago: Language and Literacy in the City's Neighborhoods*, ed. Marcia Farr, 33–49. Mahwah, NJ: Lawrence Erlbaum.

Lunsford, Andrea A., and Lahoucine Ouzgane, eds. 2004. *Crossing Borderlands: Composition and Postcolonial Studies.* Pittsburgh: University of Pittsburgh Press.

Matsuda, Paul Kei. 1999. "Composition Studies and ESL Writing: A Disciplinary Division of Labor." *College Composition and Communication* 50: 699–721.

McLeod, Susan, and Elaine Maimon. 2000. "Clearing the Air: WAC Myths and Realities." *College English* 62: 573–83.

Miller, Richard. 1994. "Fault Lines in the Contact Zone." *College English* 56: 398–408.

North, Stephen. 1991. "Rhetoric, Responsibility, and the 'Language of the Left.'" In *Composition & Resistance*, ed. C. Mark Hurlbert and Michael Blitz, 127–36. Portsmouth, NH: Boynton/Cook Heinemann.

Ogbu, John U. 1990. "Minority Education in Comparative Perspective." *Journal of Negro Education* 59: 45–57.

Potowski, Kim. 2005. "Latino Children's Spanish Use in a Chicago Dual-Immersion Classroom." In Farr 2005a, 157–85.

Rodriguez, Richard. 1983. *Hunger of Memory: The Education of Richard Rodriguez.* New York: Bantam.

Royster, Jacqueline Jones. 1996. "When the First Voice You Hear Is Not Your Own." *College Composition and Communication* 47: 29–40.

Russell, David. 2001. "Where Do Naturalistic Studies of WAC/WID Point? A Research Review." In *WAC for the New Millennium*, ed. Susan H. McLeod, Eric Miraglia, Margo Soven, and Christopher Thaiss, 259–98. Urbana, IL: National Council of Teachers of English.

Sanchez, Reymundo. 2000. *My Bloody Life: The Making of a Latin King.* Chicago: Chicago Review Press.

Schroeder, Christopher, Helen Fox, and Patricia Bizzell, eds. 2002. *ALT DIS: Alternative Discourses and the Academy.* Portsmouth, NH: Boynton/Cook Heinemann.

Severino, Carol, Juan C. Guerra, and Johnnella E. Butler, eds. 1997. *Writing in Multicultural Settings.* New York: Modern Language Association.

Slevin, James F. 2001. *Introducing English: Essays in the Intellectual Work of Composition.* Pittsburgh: University of Pittsburgh Press.

Spicer-Escalante, María. 2005. "Writing in Two Languages/Living in Two Worlds: A Rhetorical Analysis of Mexican-American Written Discourse." In Farr 2005a, 217–39.

Thaiss, Christopher. 1998. *The Harcourt Brace Guide to Writing Across the Curriculum.* Fort Worth, TX: Harcourt Brace College Publishers.

Thaiss, Christopher, and Terry Myers Zawacki. 2002. "Questioning Alternative Discourses: Reports from Across the Disciplines." In Schroeder, Fox, and Bizzell 2002, 80–96.

Trimbur, John. 1990. "Essayist Literacy and the Rhetoric of Deproduction." *Rhetoric Review* 9, no. 1: 73–86.

Villanueva, Victor. 1993. *Bootstraps: From an American Academic of Color.* Urbana, IL: National Council of Teachers of English.

———. 1999. "On the Rhetoric and Precedents of Racism." *College Composition and Communication* 50: 645–61

Young, Art. 1999. *Teaching Writing Across the Curriculum.* 3rd ed. Upper Saddle River, NJ: Prentice Hall.

15

Shifting Locations, Genres, and Motives

An Activity Theory Analysis of Service-Learning Writing Pedagogies

TOM DEANS

By extending the site for writing from classroom to local community, service-learning pedagogies change the location of composition: novice writers venture off campus to work with local citizens and organizations. Yet there is no normative model for community-based pedagogy. It comes in various of shapes and sizes and enacts a diverse range of literacies, genres, and objectives. Some service-learning initiatives ask students to undertake client-based projects—Web site content, newsletter articles and profiles, research reports, press releases, and so on—that serve the workplace needs of local nonprofit organizations. Some initiatives invite students to compose personal and critical essays that reflect on their field experiences of tutoring youth, working at homeless shelters, and so on. Some initiatives structure direct partnerships with local citizens to facilitate collaborative writing ventures that provoke awareness, spark creative expression, or broker grassroots problem-solving. Many service-learning programs, even individual courses, mix and match these approaches.

We should note that most iterations of community-based writing instruction do not replace the classroom as a site for learning and doing; instead, they introduce additional sites in the local community.

It is tempting to focus our analysis of service-learning on those locations for writing (college classrooms, local communities, nonprofit organizations) and especially on how each location shapes written discourse. Yet while place can be a promising locus of analysis, location runs up against its limits rather quickly because it is rooted in a spatial metaphor. In this essay I propose that we attend to location less in terms of *place* and more in terms of *activity*.

This leaves us with a guiding question: What happens when we imagine the locations for writing less as places and more as systems of activity? In pursuing it I rely on cultural-historical activity theory, and such an approach to service-learning writing pedagogy steers us away from thinking about how writing is relocated from classroom to community and toward thinking about the interactions and contradictions between two activity systems (the university and the community partner organization) as they overlap in a third activity system: the service-learning classroom itself. I argue that activity theory reveals why some service-learning pedagogies thrive and others falter, suggest some concrete strategies that teachers can employ to help student writers effectively negotiate community-based writing projects, and offer a fruitful way to rethink how we do research on service-learning.

I limit the scope of my inquiry to what I have elsewhere called *writing for the community* and *writing with the community* versions of service-learning, each of which require students (even if as only one part of a course) to enter nonprofit organizations or local communities as novice writers, producing or coproducing documents in nonacademic genres that circulate beyond the classroom (Deans 2000). I set aside *writing about the community*, a popular mode of service-learning in which students perform direct service (such as tutoring youth or participating in an environmental cleanup), reflect upon it, and then fold that outreach experience into their academic writing (journals, personal essays, critical essays, research papers). I focus on *writing for* and *writing with* modes because those kinds of service-learning invite students to use writing itself as a tool to expand their involvement in activity and genre systems beyond college classrooms and academic disciplines.

Discourse Communities and/or Activity Systems

Scholarship on service-learning in composition started to gather momentum in the 1990s, in the wake of the social turn in composition, which so prominently featured the discourse community as a tool for understanding writing. Consequently, much research on service-learning and related phenomena such as school-to-work transitions relied heavily on the discourse community as a conceptual frame for analyzing writing across contexts.

More recently, some writing researchers have been building a case for using the activity system rather than the discourse community as the basic unit of analysis (Bazerman 2004; Bazerman and Russell 2002; Dias 2000; Dias et al. 1999; Prior 1998; Russell 1995; Russell 1997). It can be tempting to use the terms *discourse community* and *activity system* interchangeably. After all, both emphasize the social nature of writing; both help us imagine how individual writing practices are situated within and shaped their institutional and cultural contexts; both upset the notion that writing is a discrete skill that can be readily transferred across contexts; and both help us explain how and why writers behave—even succeed or fail—in various situations. What, then, can approaches based on activity theory offer that those grounded in discourse community theory cannot?

While activity theory may have its roots in the Soviet psychology of L. S. Vygotsky and A. N. Leont'ev, I concentrate on how Yrjo Engeström has interpreted that tradition and on the ways that composition scholars such as Charles Bazerman, David Russell and Paul Prior, among others, have used activity theory to help us understand the dynamics of writing in school and at work. Such proponents of activity theory tend to commend discourse community advocates for the ways that they affirm the social and context-driven nature of writing. Indeed, both movements emerged in large part as rejections of the tendency in Western cognitive psychology to view human behavior (including writing) apart from social context. But activity theorists point out that the discourse community is generally imagined as a static, uniform, ahistorical thing or place (Prior 1998). One *enters* a discourse community, almost as one would enter a building. The spatial metaphor suggests that individuals undergo enculturation into a location or apprenticeship to a community where shared rules and normative conventions prevail. Such a view calcifies the divide between outside and inside, between social context and individual behavior; it also assumes that context largely determines individual behavior. Using the discourse community as the main unit also masks the struggles and contradictions roiling within a community (Harris 1989). It steers our attention away from the dynamic interactions among various communities, it pays little attention to individual agency, and it offers no means for explaining how individuals or collectives change over time (Russell 1997).

In contrast, activity theory—also termed cultural-historical activity theory and sociohistorical theory—discourages us from seeing contexts as specific locations or as containers of behavior and encourages us to explore the dynamic relations between social contexts and the actions of individuals. Activity theory puts more emphasis on doing things than on being someplace (Prior 1998, xii). It also assumes that social systems are goal-driven rather than just there, examines tools as they are used to get things done in systems, and attends to the contradictions that emerge both within and between systems.

Activity theory posits the activity system as the basic unit of analysis. An activity system is any collective, ongoing, historically conditioned, tool-mediated human interaction (Russell 1997, 510). Some examples are a family, a religious organization, a nonprofit agency, a political movement, a college course, a school, an academic discipline, and a profession. An activity system can be large (such as a research university) or small (such as one course within that university) or smaller still (one's immediate family). And obviously we are all involved in several activity systems that overlap, interact, and even conflict. In this essay I consider universities and nonprofit organizations as separate activity systems but devote the bulk of discussion to how the service-learning classroom itself functions as an activity system deeply influenced by the other two.

The minimum elements of an activity system include the object, subject, mediating tools, rules, community, and division of labor (see figure 15.1).

- The *subject* refers to the individual or subgroup that is chosen as the point of view in the analysis. For example, I will focus most on students as subjects, although teachers and community partners will also be considered.
- Activity theory assumes that human behavior is goal driven, something that tends to get washed out in discourse community theory, and *object* refers to the intended purpose of the activity. Object is often conflated with *motive*, that is, the motive or motives that inspire and propel the activity.
- *Tools* are the instruments—physical, linguistic, and otherwise—that help do the work of the system. To meet with sustained success in an activity system, individuals need to appropriate its tools, just as they must also, to some degree, adopt the objectives and motives of the system.
- The *community* comprises the individuals and/or subgroups that share the same general object/motive.

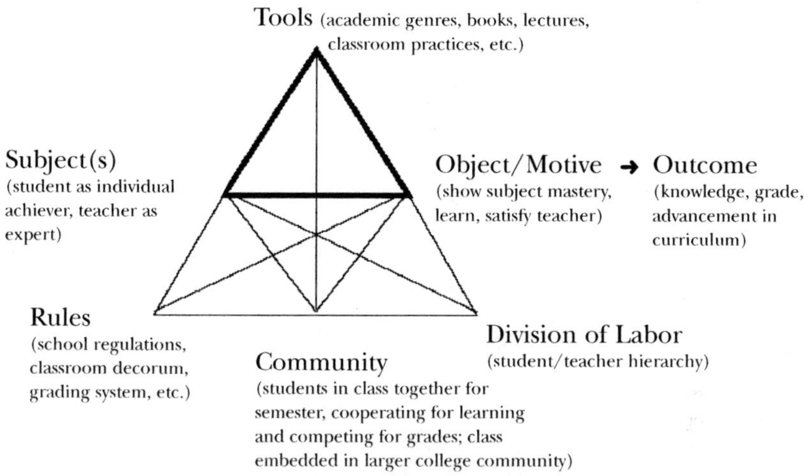

Figure 15.1. The Basic Structure of an Activity System, Featuring the Example of a Typical First-Year Composition Course (Adapted from Engeström 1987 and Engeström 1996).

- The *division of labor* refers to both the horizontal division of tasks between the members of the community and to the vertical division of power and status.
- And *rules* refers to the explicit and implicit regulations and norms that constrain actions within the system. (Engeström 1987; Engeström 1996, 67)

These terms supply a vocabulary for analyzing individual behaviors in relation to social systems, and are represented visually in figure 15.1. The heart of the activity system is the trio at the top: subject, tools, and object/motive. The rules, community, and division of labor form what Engeström calls its "social basis" (1999).

All of the connecting lines run in both directions, and the components of the system interact continually. The system involves what Paul Prior calls the cogenesis of persons, practices, artifacts, tools, institutions, and communities (1998, 32). Moreover, the whole activity system changes over time, often incrementally but sometimes through dramatic crises or upheavals.

By making a case for activity theory, I am not arguing that we abandon discourse community approaches entirely. In fact, in my own advanced service-learning courses I continue to introduce my students to discourse community theory to help them recognize the social and situated nature of composing. One of the weaknesses of the discourse community as a unit of analysis—that it tends to imagine community as static, unified, and ahistorical—can translate into a strength when one is teaching students to write across diverse contexts. Discourse communities sit still. We can pick them up and examine them. We can name discourse communities, define their boundaries, list their conventions, discuss the process of being socialized into them. Still, in this essay I push for an additional mode of analysis because activity theory directs our attention to several factors that are not sufficiently accounted for in discourse community approaches: *tools,* especially written genres as tools writers use; *motives,* both personal and institutional; and *contradictions,* both within systems and between systems. Service-learning, because it is a pressurized situation in which different activity systems are combined to form a new one, proves a revealing laboratory for activity theory.

Locating (and Teaching) Genres, Motives, and Contradictions

An activity theory analysis could begin with any one of the system's key elements—any of the nodes on the triangle in figure 15.1. I begin with tools, especially written genres as tools, and then move on to motive/object. After considering each in brief, we will explore how contradictions are understood in activity theory and consider how these concepts pertain to service-learning writing pedagogies.

Genres

Perhaps no tool is more important to writers than is genre. Whereas discourse community approaches tend to emphasize the shared, seemingly fixed conventions of genres in a particular community—as well as the variation in those conventions across communities—activity theory sees genres as tools that writers use to get things done. They are "forms of life, ways of being, frames for social action" (Bazerman 1994, 1). Experienced writers use such tools routinely; newcomers must appropriate such tools if they have any hope of expanding their involvement with others in an activity system (Russell 1997, 521). But while genre theory—some of it informed by activity theory—has recently emerged as a vital strand of composition theory (see Amy Devitt, this volume), few who study service-learning in composition have taken genre as a locus of analysis, which is curious, given the ways that many service-learning pedagogies invite a mix of academic and nonacademic genres.

David Jolliffe's work marks one exception. He has alerted us to how paying more attention to activity theory and genre theory can enrich our understanding of how community writing relates to school writing. He argues that we should pay more attention to how genres function as tools for writers and how the genres being employed in a classroom or in a service-learning project signal the writer's degree of participation in various activity systems. For example, while all service-learning courses describe themselves as engaged with the community, Jolliffe argues that only by examining whether and how students actually use written genres do we get a sense of their involvement *as writers* in activity systems beyond those of school. Do the students stick to the tools of school (essay, paper, journal)? Or do they pick up the tools—the civic and workplace genres—of community groups and nonprofits? In his call for attending more to genre, Jolliffe follows the lead of David Russell, who claims that by "tracing the relation of a disciplinary or professional genre system to an educational genre system, through the boundary of a classroom genre system, a researcher, reformer, or participant can construct a model of ways classroom writing is linked to writing in wider social practices" (Russell 1997, 546).[1]

More service-learning researchers need to do just that sort of tracing. Likewise, more service-learning teachers need to get students to reflect on how genres serve as active tools (rather than as passive formats), and on how learning particular genres can be a means of participating in new activity systems. When teaching students to write for nonprofits, many instructors approach the differences between academic and nonacademic contexts by inviting students to practice textual and audience analysis. And while those are fruitful strategies, I propose that we should devote just as much attention to genre analysis. Students should investigate not only *what* textual conventions prevail in a given community and *whom* their writing will address but also *how* particular tools (especially genres) are necessary for getting the work of writing done. Teachers should invite students to analyze the social action that genres perform: how they are tools-in-use rather than fixed formats (Miller 1984; Russell 1997, 511); how genres can be both stable and open to variation; and how single genres figure in larger genre sets and genre systems (Bazerman 1994).

In my own writing-for-the-community courses I have recently begun devoting more time to explicit reflection on genre. For example, I lecture on Carolyn Miller's notion of genre as social action and distill some key points from genre theory; I assign Anne Beaufort's *Writing in the Real World*, an ethnography of novice writers in a nonprofit agency, in which Beaufort concludes that writers need genre knowledge just as much as they need discourse community knowledge, rhetorical knowledge, subject matter knowledge, and process knowledge. After a student project team has held initial interviews of key contacts at their community partner organization and examined the texts that circulate within it, I require a genre analysis assignment. Each team must collect several examples of the genre that their project calls for (or the closest approximations of it that they can find), inventory the patterns of sameness and difference across the examples, reflect on how writers and readers use those genres in activity systems, and consider how the genre interacts with related genre sets, as well as if and how it has changed over time.[2]

Motives

Discourse community approaches privilege the *who, what* and *where* of writing over not only the *how* (tools) but also the *why* of the writing (its motive). Most tend to think of motivation as a psychological state located in the individual, but activity theory frames motivation as a social phenomenon. *Motive* is often conflated with *objective* or *goal*, and activity theory assumes that activities, including writing, are goal-directed. The motive signals "the overall direction of the activity" in the system (Russell 1997, 511). Activity systems have social motives, and individuals/subjects within those systems adopt, reject, or adapt those motives. Indeed, how one relates to a variety of social motives constitutes a significant part of one's identity. In this sense we move closer to Kenneth Burke's use of motive and can refine the term further by naming institutional or systemic objectives as *social motives* (Miller 1984; Dias et al. 1999, 20–21).

Some motives of activity systems, such as schools, are obvious (promoting learning, socializing youth) and some less so (reproducing cultural stratification, ranking students and sorting them into different fields). Likewise, a nonprofit agency may have obvious social motives (raising awareness on a particular issue, addressing a community need) and more opaque ones (perpetuating its own survival). Moreover, students arrive at college already deeply invested in other activity systems—those of family, friends, neighborhood, work, religion, and so on—and those life-world activity systems come with their own social motives (which often align powerfully with the "real world" or "doing good" traits associated with service-learning).[3] When the motives of all three activity systems (school, nonprofit, and life-world) complement one another, we find a powerful amalgam, one celebrated in the success stories of service-learning. When the social motives conflict too radically, we get trouble.

A key question for analysis then becomes *Which social motives are afoot in the service-learning writing classroom, and how do students navigate them?* Furthermore, *How do students align themselves with the social motives of the various activity systems in play (especially school and community organization), and how do they deal with the contradictions among them?* While I defer the discussion of contradictions to the next section, here I want to suggest that just as we can track if and how novices adopt, adapt, or reject the tools (genres) of disciplines and community organizations, we should attend to how they respond to the social motives of activity systems.

One pragmatic thing that teachers can do, as with genre, is to draw more deliberate attention to the social motives of all the stakeholders in a service-learning experience. For example, in anticipation of service-learning projects in my own classrooms I pose the most simple of questions: Why do we write in school? As students look at me with expressions that seem to say, "Come on, don't be an idiot," I nudge them to volunteer answers: "Because we have to." "To get a good grade." "Because teachers need a way to test whether we know the material." "To explore and share our ideas." We then push from these local responses to the deeper social motives, and I suggest those posited by Dias et al. in *Worlds Apart: Acting and Writing in Academic and Workplace Contexts*: students write to show what they know because schools use writing to promote and document learning (the epistemic motive); but writing also enables students to be "graded and slotted," which is another social motive of schools and universities: to sort and rank students (1999, 44).

And then I ask, Why do people write in workplaces such as nonprofit agencies? "To get their message out." "To get grant money." And so on. We find that in the workplace writers compose documents that contribute in pragmatic ways to shared organizational goals. Here people do not usually write to show what they know. (In fact, the carryover of that motive—usually manifest in showy overwriting—is one of the main frustrations that managers have with recruits fresh out of academia.) In class we put the social motives on the table and discuss how they might cooperate and conflict, and in these discussions the *why/social motive* of writing trumps the *where/location* of writing.[4]

Provoking in our students a meta-awareness of different social motives for writing can prove valuable in dispelling misunderstandings that surface as novices take on complex rhetorical projects in community settings. But awareness of social motives is not enough. To make service-learning projects work well, educators and community partners must to some degree *adopt* each other's social motives.

Teachers and community partners who opt into service-learning already share some common motives, such as a broad commitment to addressing social problems through service. But as an educator my priority is promoting individual student learning, while a manager in a nonprofit must be concerned with getting the work of the organization done, and done well. While I may be an educator, in a service-learning context I need to adopt some motives and practices of a manager, even when that seems to cut against my teaching instincts. And while my community partner may be a manager, he or she needs to adopt some of the motives and practices of a teacher, even when that puts a drag on efficiency. For example, in service-learning courses I implement several workplace-like practices that are absent from my other courses: I cancel classes to give students time for agency meetings; I replace whole classes with team work sessions; I cede much of my authority to judge what counts for quality writing—and even a fair amount of the authority to determine grades—to my community partner; I comment more assertively on drafts, giving up some of the let-students-muck-around-and-discover-their-own-mistakes learning motive for the get-it-done-right-for-the-organization motive. Likewise, my more effective community partners open spaces for learning and mentoring, even when doing so might prove time-consuming and inefficient. As experienced service-learning teachers know, some community partners work out much better than others, and the most helpful are the ones who see students as learners-in-development rather than as miniature professionals. Such community partners see themselves as not just project managers but also as educators, thereby adopting the epistemic motive of schooling. They stretch to appropriate some unfamiliar motives; I do the same.

Students, too, must to some degree adopt the motives of their community partner activity systems. When the teacher and community partner motives are reasonably well aligned (or at least understood), service-learning tends to go well. But trouble sets in when, for example, a student who holds fast to school motives, which keep the student focused on what he or she thinks the teacher wants rather than on what the community partner needs, on getting a good grade rather than on getting the job done well, and on individual learning rather than on the collective contribution to the community partner. More interesting and typical, though, are the cases where students genuinely struggle, as writers, with competing social motives. For example, when community partners ask my students to compose profiles of volunteers, clients, or events for use in their public relations materials, students usually embrace the project and do it well. However, often students feel caught in a double bind: they are under pressure to write public relations stories that celebrate the people and events, and from their genre analyses of similar profiles, they have learned that profiles put a positive spin on their subjects. But students often wince at having to portray people or events with too rosy a glow about them; rather they feel the pull of objectivity associated with academic and journalistic activity systems. By analyzing the social motives in play, students can negotiate the situation with more dexterity.

I have largely set aside consideration of the motives of the life-world activity systems that students bring to our courses, but ideally we should also account for those too, especially in service-learning. Career-minded students often find their motives reflected in the "real world" character of much community-based writing, but more powerful tend to be ways that the religious, ethical and political sensibilities of our students converge with the social motives of organizations committed to social justice. One only need imagine what unfolds as a young man whose mother died of breast cancer takes on a writing project with a women's health advocacy organization. Likewise, one need only imagine the prickliness of projects that require students to work as writers in community organizations whose values and motives they reject.

Service-learning projects are at their most powerful when they create generative, complementary relationships among the school activity system, the community partner activity system, and the students' more personal identities as reflected in their life-world activity systems. In at least one of those systems—and more often in all three—students can discover compelling motives to write well. But they usually need to negotiate some tricky contradictions along the way, and activity theory can help us see those more clearly.

Contradictions

Those who adopt the discourse community model nearly always acknowledge that writers belong to several different communities at once, a phenomenon often represented visually by the overlapping circles of a Venn diagram. While such an approach affirms the complexity of a writer's context, it also tends to freeze time and divert our attention from the tensions and conflicts. In contrast, activity theory demands that we examine contradictions both within and between systems. In fact, contradictions are perhaps the most important locus of analysis—both the contradictions themselves and the ways that systems work through contradictions. Here I focus on the most salient contradictions that emerge as school and workplace/community systems intersect in the activity system of the community-based writing course.

Contradictions are natural to activity systems and should not necessarily be tagged as negative. As David Russell remarks, "An activity system constantly works through contradictions" (1997, 531). They surface within individual systems and when one activity system interacts with another. They present subjects (or indeed any node of the activity system triangle) with "double binds" that can sometimes be accommodated, sometimes prove disruptive or debilitating, and sometimes spark collective transformation or the creation of whole new activity systems (Engeström 1987).

Contradictions in the writing classroom are nothing new, of course. For example, teachers find themselves in the often contradictory roles of both advocate and judge (Elbow 1983), or trying to negotiate the double bind of both honoring process-oriented classroom practices and responding to institutional pressures to sort and rank students through grading systems (Agnew 1997). Nora Bacon has already recognized how service-learning occasions reflect one of the central contradictions of our profession: that composition theory affirms that acts of writing are tightly bound to their rhetorical contexts, the first-year composition requirement, and yet most teachers of writing, even as they make nods to rhetoric, still rely on assumptions about writing as a generalizable skill (2000, 1). As my discussion of motives suggest, writing-for-the-community and writing-with-the-community pedagogies stir up even more contradictions that tend to remain dormant in more typical composition classrooms.

Linda Flower and Virginia Chappell have been among the first to recognize how conceptualizing contradictions from an activity theory perspective can illuminate what happens with community-based writing initiatives. Yet they do so in different ways: Flower (2000) cites contradictions between academic and community cultural logics as a starting place for inquiry into local problems; Chappell (2005) argues that when teaching writing-for-the-community courses we should provoke student awareness of academic/nonprofit agency contradictions as part of a process of helping them navigate professional writing proj-

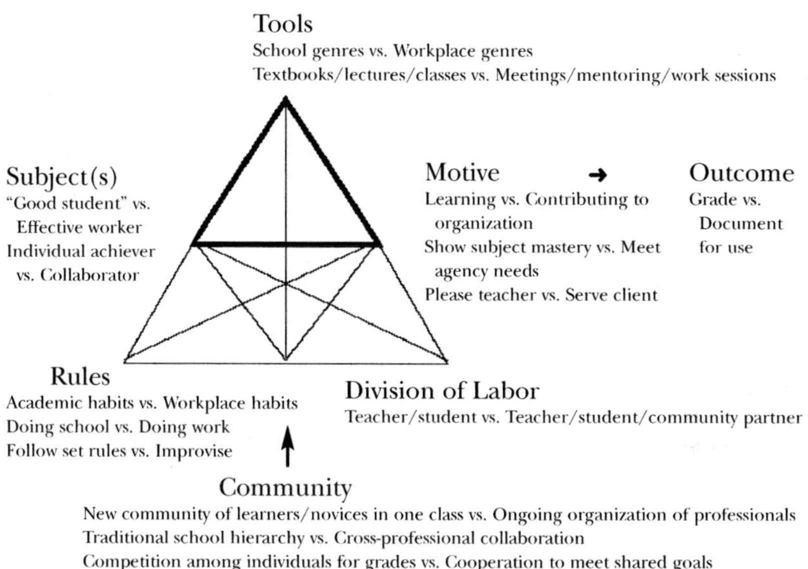

Figure 15.2. Contradictions in the Service-Learning Classroom Activity System from the *Student* Point of View (adapted from Engeström 1996, 88).

ects more critically and effectively. While my purposes run parallel with Chappell's, I rely more heavily on Engeström's detailed models of activity systems to reveal contradictions that emerge in the service-learning course activity system. Figures 15.2 and 15.3 —one from a student point of view and the other from a teacher point of view—illustrate several of those contradictions.

These diagrams illustrate a variety of contradictions that are organic to service-learning, and as with my discussions of genre and motive, I suggest that researchers look to contradictions as points for launching analyses and that teachers make contradictions more visible to students. As we help students identify the double binds, we open contradictions to reflection.

I have already suggested how the social motives of schools and nonprofits can both contradict and cooperate. But I dodged some of the trickier aspects of contradictions raised by university/community partnerships. What happens, for example, if students and teachers eagerly adopt the social motives of their community partners? They

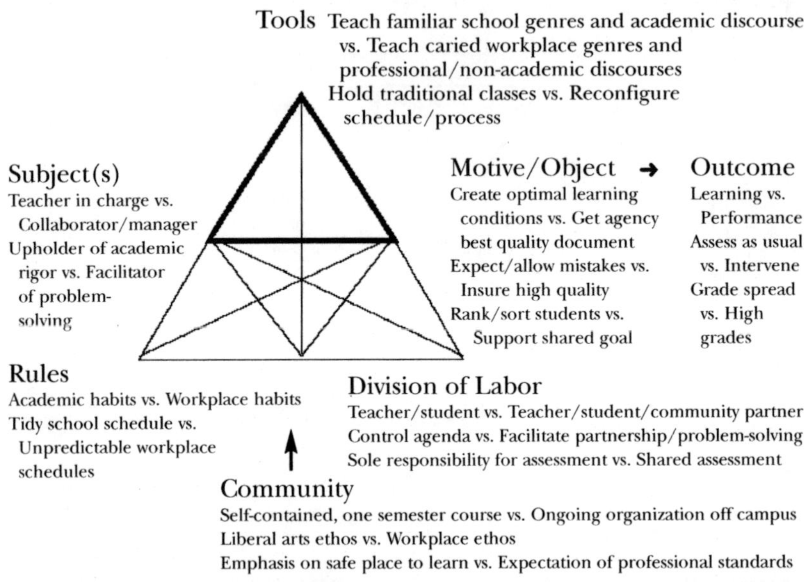

Figure 15.3. Contradictions in the Service-Learning Classroom Activity System from the *Teacher and Institutional* Points of View (adapted from Engeström 1996, 88).

focus all their energies on doing the highest-quality collaborative writing in workplace and civic genres; they put aside thoughts of grades; collaborative work—students with each other, student team with community partner, teacher with students—trumps creating opportunities for individual learning. And the projects get done, and done brilliantly, but no one person can claim ownership of the text, and individual contributions are tough to decipher. When the school activity system makes its demand for individual assessment, do all the students then get A's? If so, at semester's end the teacher will no doubt encounter a double bind as a department chair or dean raises an eyebrow at the sight of such consistently high marks and the implied lack of rigor. The sorting/ranking/gatekeeping social motive of schooling presses for stratification; the workplace motive presses for effective documents that serve the collective needs of the organization, even if at the expense of individual learning and assessment.[5] What kind of change, if any, this double bind will provoke is uncertain, but activity theory at least offers a way to put it on the table and analyze it. And as figures 15.2 and 15.3

illustrate, service-learning invites a wide range of such contradictions, all potentially vexing and all potentially generative.

Notes

1. Service-learning researchers should account for both the *breadth* of the genres evident in a given activity system (that is, inventory how many different genres surface in a particular community-based writing course) and the *depth* of genre use (that is, assess how well students understand and practice the more specialized genres of particular academic disciplines and/or community groups). As David Russell remarks, "Genres embody expectations for the future, as well as linking us to past human activities. And learning to read or write a new genre can be—if one sees genre in its breadth and depth—a way of imaging different ways of being in the world, actually seeing one's self or one's student as potential participants [sic] in different worlds of human activity (activity systems) within the universe of discourse" (Russell 2002, 228).
2. For details on the assignment see Deans n.d.; for similar approaches, see Bazerman 2004 and Kain and Wardle 2005.
3. The term "life-world activity system" is borrowed from Russell 1997. Powerful personal motives can also emerge *during* college, as when students develop a new political awareness and align themselves with new (to them) social and ideological causes; personal motives can also emerge during service-learning projects themselves, usually as a result of interaction with community partners. Out of admiration for the work of the nonprofit organization and affection for its employees ("I don't want to let them down") students often discover the motivation to persist through multiple drafts.
4. One case that illustrates motive trumping location occurred several years ago when I taught a first-year writing course on a disability theme and as part of that course arranged service-learning projects (a research report on student attitudes toward disability, the revision of print materials to distribute to incoming students, and so on) with the disabilities services office on campus. Even though students never stepped off campus, they experienced whiplash as they shuttled between the social motives of school and workplace.
5. For an intriguing discussion of how this contradiction plays out in a client-based professional writing course, see Freedman and Adam 2000. Two other telling studies of students negotiating

contradictions in activity systems are Ketter and Hunter 2002, and Lundell, Britt, and Beach 2002.

Works Cited

Agnew, Eleanor. 1997. "Cross Purposes: Grade Deflation, Classroom Practices." In *Grading in the Post-Process Classroom: From Theory to Practice,* ed. Libby Alison, Lizbeth Bryant, and Maureen Hourigan, 36–50. Portsmouth, NH: Boynton/Cook.

Bacon, Nora. 2000. "Building a Swan's Nest for Instruction in Rhetoric." *College Composition and Communication* 51, no. 4 (June): 589–609.

Bazerman, Charles. 1994. "Systems of Genres and the Enactment of Social Intentions." In *Genre and the New Rhetoric,* ed. Aviva Freedman and Peter Medway, 79–101. London: Taylor and Francis.

———. 2004. "Speech Acts, Genres and Activity Systems: How Texts Organize Activity and People." In *What Writing Does and How It Does It: An Introduction to Analyzing Texts and Textual Practices,* ed. Charles Bazerman and Paul Prior. Mahwah, NJ: Lawrence Erlbaum.

Bazerman, Charles, and David Russell, eds. 2002. *Writing Selves/Writing Societies: Research from Activity Perspectives.* Fort Collins, CO: WAC Clearinghouse and Mind, Culture, and Activity. Available at http://wac.colostate.edu/books/selves_societies/.

Beaufort, Anne. 1999. *Writing in the Real World: Making the Transition from School to Work.* New York: Teachers College Press.

Chappell, Virginia. 2005. "Good Intentions Aren't Enough: Insights from Activity Theory for Linking Service and Learning." *Reflections* 4, no. 2 (winter): 34–53.

Deans, Thomas. 2000. *Writing Partnerships: Service-Learning in Composition.* Urbana, IL: NCTE.

———. 2006. "Genre Analysis and the Community Writing Course." *Reflections: A Journal of Writing, Service Learning, and Community Literacy* 5, no. 1 and no. 2: 7–25.

Dias, Patrick. 2000. "Writing Classrooms as Activity Systems." In *Transitions: Writing in Academic and Workplace Settings,* 11–29. Cresskill, NJ: Hampton.

Dias, Patrick, Aviva Freedman, Peter Medway, and Anthony Pare. *1999. Worlds Apart: Acting and Writing in Academic and Workplace Contexts.* Mahwah, NJ: Lawrence Erlbaum.

Elbow, Peter. 1083. "Embracing Contraries in the Teaching Process. *College English* 45 (April): 327–39.

Engeström, Yrjo. 1987. *Learning by Expanding: An Activity Theoretical Approach to Developmental Research.* Helsinki: Orienta-Konsultit Oy.

———. 1996. "Work as a Testbench for Activity Theory: The Case of Primary Care Medical Practice." In *Understanding Practice: Perspectives on Activity and Context,* ed. Seth Chailkin and Jean Lave, 64–101. Cambridge: Cambridge University Press.

———. 1999. "Activity Theory and Individual and Social Transformation." In *Perspectives on Activity Theory,* ed. Yrjo Engeström, Reijo Mietinen, and Raija-Leena Punamaki, 19–38. Cambridge: Cambridge University Press.

Engeström, Yrjo and Reijo Mietinen. 1999. Introduction to *Perspectives on Activity Theory,* ed. Yrjo Engeström, Reijo Mietinen, and Raija-Leena Punamaki, 1–18. Cambridge: Cambridge University Press.

Flower, Linda. 2002. "Intercultural Inquiry and the Transformation of Service." *College English* 65, no. 2 (November): 181–201.

Freedman, Aviva, and Christine Adam. 2000. "Write Where You Are: Situation Learning to Write in University and Workplace Settings." In *Transitions: Writing in Academic and Workplace Settings,* 31–60. Cresskill, NJ: Hampton.

Harris, Joseph. 1989. "The Idea of Community in the Study of Writing." *College Composition and Communication* 40 (February): 11–22.

Jolliffe, David A. 2001. "Writing Across the Curriculum and Service Learning: *Kairos,* Genre and Collaboration." In *WAC for the New Millennium,* ed. Susan McLeod, Eric Miraglia, Margot Soven, and Christopher Thaiss, 86–108. Urbana, IL: NCTE.

Kain, Donna, and Elizabeth Wardle. 2005. "Building Context: Using Activity Theory to Teach About Genre in Multi-Major Professional Communication Courses." *Technical Communication Quarterly* 14, no. 2: 113–39.

Ketter, Jean, and Judy Hunter. 2002. "Creating a Writer's Identity on the Boundaries of Two Communities of Practice." In Bazerman and Russell 2002, 307–29. Available at http://wac.colostate.edu/books/selves_societies/

Lundell, Dana Britt, and Richard Beach. 2002. "Dissertation Writers' Negotiations with Competing Activity Systems." In Bazerman and Russell 2002, 483–515. Available at http://wac.colostate.edu/books/selves_societies/

Miller, Carolyn. 1984. "Genre as Social Action." *Quarterly Journal of Speech* 70:151–67.

Prior, Paul. 1998. *Writing/Disciplinarity: A Sociohistoric Account of Literate Activity in the Academy*. Mahwah, NJ: Lawrence Erlbaum.

Russell, David. 1995. "Activity Theory and Its Implications for Writing Instruction." In *Reconceiving Writing, Rethinking Writing Instruction*, ed. Joseph Petraglia, 51–77. Mahwah, NJ: Lawrence Erlbaum.

———. 1997. "Rethinking Genre in School and Society: An Activity Theory Analysis." *Written Communication* 14, no. 4: 504–54.

———. 2002. "The Kind-ness of Genre: An Activity Theory Analysis of High School Teachers' Perception of Genre in Portfolio Assessment Across the Curriculum." In *The Rhetoric and Ideology of Genre: Strategies for Stability and Change*, ed. Richard Coe, Lorelei Lingard, and Tatiana Teslenko, 225–242. Cresskill, NJ: Hampton.

Contributors

John Ackerman is an associate professor in the Department of English at Kent State University.

Robert Brooke is professor of English at the University of Nebraska-Lincoln, where he directs the Nebraska Writing Project and edits the Studies in Writing and Rhetoric series. His most recent book is *Rural Voices: Place-Conscious Education and the Teaching of Writing* (2003).

Jennifer Clary-Lemon is assistant professor of writing at the University of Winnipeg. Her most recent project is *Relations, Locations, Positions: Composition Theory for Writing Teachers* (2006), which she coedited with Peter Vandenberg and Sue Hum. Her scholarly interests include writing and positionality, theories of identity, rhetorical activism, and disciplinarity.

Thomas Deans is director of the University Writing Center and associate professor of English at the University of Connecticut. He is the author of *Writing Partnerships: Service-Learning in Composition* (2000) and *Writing and Community Action: A Service-Learning Rhetoric and Reader* (2003). Other teaching and research interests include rhetoric, writing in the disciplines, pragmatism, and Shakespeare.

Amy Devitt is professor of English at the University of Kansas, where she teaches courses in rhetoric, writing, and English language. Her research specialties have included standardization and genre theory. Her most recent book is *Writing Genres.* Along with Mary Jo Reiff and Anis Bawarshi, she has also written a textbook for composition entitled *Scenes of Writing: Strategies for Composing with Genres.*

SIDNEY I. DOBRIN is associate professor of English and director of writing programs at the University of Florida. He is the author and editor of numerous articles and books, including *Saving Place: An Ecocomposition Reader, Constructing Knowledges: The Politics of Theory-Building in Composition, Natural Discourse: Toward Ecocomposition* (with Christian Weisser), and *Don't Stop Believing,* a history of the band Journey which Sid has been following for over 25 years.

ELIZABETH ERVIN is an associate professor of English at the University of North Carolina–Wilmington, where she teaches a variety of classes in writing, rhetoric, and women's studies. She is author of the textbook *Public Literacy* as well as of various articles and chapters that have appeared elsewhere.

KRISTIE FLECKENSTEIN is associate professor of English at Florida State University. She is the author of *Embodied Literacies: Imageword and a Poetics of Teaching,* recipient of the Conference on College Composition and Communications 2005 Outstanding Book of the Year Award. She has published in a variety of venues, including *College English, Rhetoric Review, JAC,* and *College Composition and Communication.* Her current project explores the intersections of visual practices, social action, and composition pedagogy.

CYNTHIA HAYNES is director of first-year writing and associate professor of English at Clemson University. Her research interests include rhetorical theory, composition theory and pedagogy, digital rhetorics, "serious design," computer game studies, and the deconstruction of multimediation. Haynes spent 2005/2006 on leave as visiting associate professor at the IT University of Copenhagen, Denmark, in the Research in Innovative Communication group.

JOHNDAN JOHNSON-EILOLA is a professor of communication and media at Clarkson University, where he teaches and writes about information architecture, mass media, new media, and rhetoric. His recent books include *Datacloud, Central Works in Technical Communication* (with Stuart A. Selber) and *Writing New Media* (with Anne Wysocki, Cynthia Self, and Geoff Sirc).

CHRISTOPHER KELLER is associate professor of English and director of the writing program at the University of Texas–Pan American. He coedited *Writing Environments* with Sid Dobrin (2005) and is currently finishing up a monograph, *Topographies of Composition Studies: Power, Place, Disciplinarity.* He teaches undergraduate and graduate courses in composition, technical communication, and American nature writing.

TIM LINDGREN is an instructional designer and doctoral candidate at Boston College, where his dissertation research focuses on the genre of place blogging and examines how people use new media to foster a deeper sense of place. His essay "Blogging Places: Locating Pedagogy in the Whereness of Weblogs" appeared in the fall 2005 issue of *Kairos: A Journal of Rhetoric, Technology, and Pedagogy.*

JASON MCINTOSH is a doctoral candidate in composition/rhetoric at the University of Nebraska-Lincoln. His focus areas are computers and writing and place-based pedagogies.

NANCY MYERS is an associate professor of English at the University of North Carolina at Greensboro where she teaches composition, linguistics, and the history of rhetoric. She received the UNCG Alumni Teaching Excellence Award in 2002. Along with Gary Tate and Edward P. J. Corbett, she is an editor of the third and fourth editions of *The Writing Teacher's Sourcebook.* In addition to her other articles, she most recently published "Genre as Janus in the Teaching of Writing" in *Relations, Locations, Positions: Composition Theory for Writing Teachers* (2006).

DEREK OWENS is associate professor of English and director of the Institute for Writing Studies at St. John's University. He lives on Long Island with his wife, Teresa, and son, Ryan.

NEDRA REYNOLDS is professor of writing and rhetoric at the University of Rhode Island, where she directs the College Writing Program. She is the author of *Geographies of Writing: Inhabiting Places and Encountering Difference* (2004), and she coedits *The Bedford Bibliography for Teachers of Writing* (6th edition, 2004). Her articles have appeared in *Rhetoric Review, Journal of Advanced Composition, College Composition and Communication, Writing Program Administration,* and a number of edited collections.

THOMAS RICKERT is an associate professor in the English department at Purdue University. He is interested in classical and postmodern rhetorical theory and cultural studies, especially of the psychoanalytic variety. His most recent work is on complexity theory, spatiality, and ambience.

STUART A. SELBER is an associate professor of English and an affiliate associate professor of information sciences and technology at Penn State. He is the author of *Multiliteracies for a Digital Age*, which has won two book awards: the 2005 Distinguished Book Award from Computers and Composition, and the 2005 Best Book in Technical or Scientific Communication from the National Council of Teachers of English.

CHRISTOPHER SCHROEDER is an associate professor of English at Northeastern Illinois University, where he teaches undergraduate and graduate courses in composition and literature. He is the author of *ReInventing the University* and coeditor of *ALT DIS* (with Helen Fox and Patricia Bizzell). At the present, he is working on a long-term research project involving Latinos and institutionalized literacies.

PETER VANDENBERG is professor of English at DePaul University in Chicago, where he teaches undergraduate courses in writing and graduate courses in composition theory, contemporary rhetorics, and new media. He has published in numerous journals and edited collections, and with Sue Hum and Jennifer Clary-Lemon he has coedited *Relations, Locations, Positions: Composition Theory for Writing Teachers* (2006).

CHRISTIAN WEISSER is an associate professor of rhetoric and composition at the Harriet L. Wilkes Honors College of Florida Atlantic University. His recent books include *Moving Beyond Academic Discourse: Composition Studies and the Public Sphere* as well as *Ecocomposition* and *Natural Discourse* (both with Sid Dobrin). Christian currently serves as editor of the journal *Composition Forum.*

Index